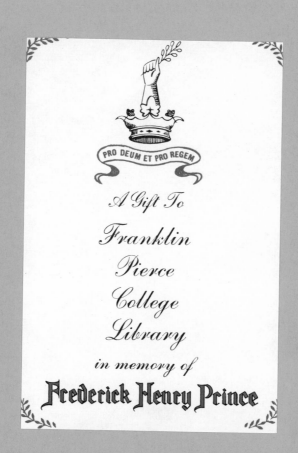

THE *ROMAN DE LA ROSE*

A Study in Allegory and Iconography

THE
ROMAN DE LA ROSE

A Study in
Allegory and Iconography

BY JOHN V. FLEMING

PRINCETON UNIVERSITY PRESS

PRINCETON, NEW JERSEY

1969

Printed in the United States of America
by Princeton University Press, Princeton, New Jersey

This book has been composed in Linotype Caslon Old Face

Preface

ECENT years have witnessed a quickening interest in the *Roman de la Rose*, if the appearance of increasing numbers of scholarly studies is a reliable indication.[1] Yet as any scholar who has blenched before the annually expanding girth of the *PMLA* bibliography knows, recent years have by this standard witnessed a quickening interest in *everything*, so that it may be premature to applaud what is possibly a mere incidental statistic in the publications explosion as the end of the sad eclipse which has for several centuries almost totally obscured this great medieval poem from the sympathetic attention of literary scholars. Perhaps the most promising sign is the publication now in progress of a new and welcome edition of the poem. In any case, it has seemed to me that there is still a marked need for a book which defines the subject of the *Roman*—to explain in general terms what the *Roman* is about—and such is my modest ambition in the present work. The principles which have guided my inquiry are explained in the first chapter, so that there is probably little required by way of prefatory material.

The neglect of the *Roman de la Rose* by romance philologists is curious but massive, and the most important work on the poem done in recent years comes from the hands of various "English" scholars—C. S. Lewis, Alan Gunn, Charles Muscatine, D. W. Robertson, Rosemond Tuve. Most "English" scholars, I suppose, first encounter the *Roman* in the fragmentary translation ascribed to Chaucer. My pleasure in the old poem began there, at any rate, even as my serious scholarly interest in it was born of incredulity at the brief account of the poem introducing the *Romaunt* in the Robinson edition. Soon thereafter I had the opportunity to hear a quite different interpretation of the poem advanced by Professor D. W. Robertson, Jr., which excited not merely incredulity but outrage; and the fruitful argument which began then has become fiercer over the years during which I have been forced to retreat from a broad front to the obsessive defense

[1] For an annotated bibliography of recent work on the *Roman* see Marc-René Jung, "Der Rosenroman in der Kritik seit dem 18. Jahrhundert," *Romanische Forschungen*, LXXVIII (1966), 203-57.

of a few iconographic minutiae. The *Roman* is the most important (in the sense of being the most widely-read and most influential) vernacular poem of the Middle Ages. Robertson's achievement in offering the first convincing interpretation of it in five and a half centuries is a particularly impressive one, and I have been extremely fortunate in enjoying his guidance as a student and, in recent years, his counsel as a colleague.

There may be said to be a polemical tradition connected with the *Roman*. Jean de Meun himself freely used such sources as William of Saint-Amour's *De periculis novissimorum temporum*, a work which perhaps exceeds the restraining limits set down for polite academic debate, and the first sustained critical discussion of the *Roman* itself is aptly called the "Querelle du Roman de la Rose." In this debate extreme positions were articulated: Gerson said he would gladly burn the last copy of the poem in existence, and Jean de Montreuil accused Christine de Pisan of acting like a Greek whore. Hardly less violent has been the quarrel about the Quarrel, as anyone who has read André Combes' arraignment of Alfred Coville must agree. My own opinion is that the vast bulk of recent scholarship dealing with Jean de Meun's poem, much of it from the pens of learned and distinguished scholars, is fundamentally wrong-headed, and that the critical judgments which emerge from it frequently do not stop short of absurdity. While I have seen no purpose in a systematic review of other people's ideas about the *Roman*, it has seemed wrong to me to avoid altogether confrontation with published opinions with which I disagree. There is, accordingly, a certain amount of sharp comment in this book, directed at specific scholarly assessments of the *Roman* and at general critical principles which are, in my view, stumbling-blocks not only to the understanding of Jean's poem but to much else in medieval literary and pictorial art besides. Since my book presents what is at the moment very much a minority view of the *Roman*, it has been necessary at times to argue especially vigorously, but I hope it is always apparent that my arguments are advanced in a spirit of critical inquiry and scholarly debate. I have small doubt that those with whom I here take issue will be less open in the expression of their judgment of my work. Jean de Meun, of course, was able to offer up his book for the correction of *Sainte Iglise*; it is a further testimony to the general decline in human felicity since the thirteenth century that I can turn only to the Modern Languages Association of America.

My most pressing scholarly debts I have acknowledged in my footnotes. Anyone working with the text of the *Roman* leans heavily on the monumental edition of Ernest Langlois (Société des anciens textes français, 5 vols., Paris, 1914-1924), from which citations in the present work are taken; and anyone working with the manuscripts must begin with his serviceable catalogue.[2] So far as the iconography is concerned, the path is stonier. It is greatly to be regretted that Müntz never brought to publication the study of the iconography of the *Roman* which he had undertaken;[3] he was one of the great art historians of his day, and enormously learned. One suspects that his study would have been altogether more satisfactory than that of Alfred Kuhn.[4] Kuhn's work was a great pioneering effort, completed under difficult conditions, and it has the great virtue of presenting a substantial *corpus* of illustrations of the *Roman*, including the complete sequence from a fine fourteenth-century exemplar in Vienna. But the narrow focus of Kuhn's stylistic study, his apparently total lack of interest in the *Roman* as a poem, and the very substantial number of errors in his descriptions and discussions of the manuscripts all weaken his work and limit its usefulness.

The greatest influence on my own approach to the *Roman*, as will be obvious, is the fundamental iconographic analysis of the poem in Robertson's *Preface to Chaucer* (Princeton, 1963). The appearance of Rosemond Tuve's *Allegorical Imagery* (Princeton, 1966) with its extended and often brilliant analysis of the *Roman*, which independently concurs with the main lines of Robertson's argument, suggests that perhaps at last criticism of the poem is being redirected along tenable lines. The iconographic materials which Miss Tuve adduced for her particular purpose of documenting the "posterity" of medieval poems in the Renaissance are necessarily late in date, and her use of them is frequently cavalier; yet the conviction of her general approach argues per-

---

[2] *Les manuscrits du Roman de la Rose* (Lille, 1910).

[3] "Iconographie du Roman de la Rose," *Académie des Inscriptions et Belles-Lettres: Comptes Rendus*, 4e série, XXVII (1899), 15-16.

[4] *Die Illustration des Rosenromans* (Freiburg-im-B. diss., 1911), republished in expanded form under the same title in the *Jahrbuch der kunsthistorischen Sammlungen des allerhöchsten Kaiserhauses*, XXXI (1913), 1-66.

suasively for the possibilities of its method. It would be wrong to neglect C. S. Lewis' beautiful book *The Allegory of Love*; the main lines of its account of the *Roman* are brilliantly wrong, but scattered about its pages lie some stunning *obiter dicta* without which students of the poem would be much the poorer. I have also found the specialized articles of Lionel Friedman particularly enlightening and stimulating.

As the subtitle of my book indicates, one of my principal concerns has been iconographic analysis—the study of the illustrations in a very large number of manuscripts of the *Roman*. The rationale for this investigation is explained in the first chapter, but it is probably necessary to anticipate in a formal way one specific objection. It has recently been maintained that the study of emblematic iconography in the manuscripts of the *Roman* can have "no relevance" since, it is claimed, "the context is secular":[5] in a religious work the reader would feel what is called a "push" towards understanding traditional emblems, but in a "secular" work there would be no "push" and hence no iconographic understanding. This strikes me as a peculiarly ignorant and unhappy misconception. What may be regarded as the most typical copies of the *Roman* produced in northern France in the second half of the fourteenth century were made up with the *Testament de maistre Jehan de Meun*, at the same time and as part of the same manuscript, written by the same scribes and illustrated by the same illuminators. Are we really to believe that the readers of these manuscripts, while "pushed" by the context to comprehend the Gothic icon of the Trinity which decorates the *incipit* folio of the *Testament*, would find "no relevance" in the fact that Oiseuse appears as a Gothic icon of *luxuria* in the *Roman*? What of such a copy of the poem as MS français 25526 in the Bibliothèque nationale in Paris, the 163 folios of which are lavishly decorated, recto and verso, with the most wide-ranging exemplary marginalia? Would the readers be unable to understand the lengthy sequences illustrating the life of Christ, His childhood and His Passion, just as they would regard the "secular" horse who nervously attends the copulating "pilgrims" at folio 111^v as merely a decorative detail without conceptual relevance?

The medieval readers of the *Roman* were not, I think, pushed

[5] F. Parmisano in *Medium Ævum*, xxv (1966), 279.

and pulled and jerked about as they went from one folio of their manuscript to the next because they had no rigorously discrete categories of the "secular" and the "sacred." R. G. Collingwood has written with his wonted aptness to this very point. "The Gothic style of the churches was the Gothic style of the house and the castle"; he says, "it was simply everyday architecture turned to the construction of one building instead of another. So in the book painting what we should call sacred and secular subjects are inextricably blended; the fact being that the artist never contemplated the existence of the distinction which to us is so real. All art was religious art, or, what comes to the same thing, all art was secular art; there was no special kind of art used for religious purposes, because there was no feeling that these purposes stood by themselves."[6]

So far as the *Roman de la Rose* is concerned, the relevance of iconographic study seems indisputable, and the first chapter of my book attempts to explain some specific ways in which such study can aid literary history. The uniquely abundant and diverse iconography of the *Roman* offers an unusual perspective on a major medieval poem, and the critical judgments which iconographic analysis yield both complement and confirm judgments which emerge from rhetorical analysis and the study of relevant intellectual background. But the iconographic "method" is merely one of many tools at the scholar's disposal, and an imperfect one at that. Except in the rare instance of holographic illustration (as in the Barberino codex of the *Documenti d'Amore*), the iconographic schedule of a medieval text is a gloss at one remove at least from the author's own hand. Furthermore, we know far too little about the actual ways in which copies of the *Roman* were commissioned and executed; the degree to which illustrators followed formal instructions, existing exemplars, and iconographic clichés from sources outside the *Roman* rather than simply their own reading of the text; and, in many cases, the kinds of people for whom illustrated copies were made. So while it seems to me absurd to argue that the analysis of pictorial iconography can have "no relevance" for the study of the *Roman*, it would be equally wrong to look upon the "method" as a safe and sufficient one in itself. The present book makes no such assumption; its discussion of pictorial

[6] *Speculum Mentis* (Oxford, 1924), pp. 27-28.

iconography in manuscripts of the *Roman* is both elementary and partial, and part of an approach to the poem which has as its specific aim literary explication. That the recent appearance of a "Christian interpretation" of the *Roman* should be suspiciously regarded as some exotic new thing has struck me as extremely curious, since I cannot conceive of a convincing interpretation of the most popular poetic work of late medieval Christendom which will not be "Christian." My book is neither a *catalogue raisonné* of the poem's iconography, nor a synoptic stylistic history of its illustrations, but an attempt to explain, guided by iconographic indications among others, what the *Roman de la Rose* is about.

It would be entirely inadequate to reduce to a conventional formula the substantial debts of gratitude I have incurred over several years and in many countries while I have been working on this book. The manuscripts of the *Roman* lie delightfully scattered throughout the capitals and most pleasant provinces of Europe, and to search them out would have been a great delight even without the unvarying assistance, cooperation, and learned guidance I have found at the libraries, great and small, which I have visited; such kindnesses have no doubt been but imperfectly repaid by this book, but without them I could not have brought it to completion. I am of course extremely grateful to the many libraries which have given me permission to publish illustrations from manuscripts in their keeping, acknowledgement for which appears formally in the illustration matter, and whose photographic services have supplied me with pictures. In particular I am grateful to the Bibliothèque nationale in Paris, whose holdings of *Roman* manuscripts are so extensive; the Bibliothèque royale in Brussels; the British Museum; the Bodleian Library at Oxford where as an undergraduate I first came under the spell of the men and books of the Middle Ages; and the Pierpont Morgan Library in New York. Conversation and debate with friends and colleagues in Madison and Princeton have given my thinking about the *Roman* some direction, and my researches were further aided by access to the unique photographic archives of the Warburg Institute in London and the Index of Christian Art here at home.

Princeton   JOHN V. FLEMING
1968

Contents

Illustrations
Following Index

THE *ROMAN DE LA ROSE*

A Study in Allegory and Iconography

CHAPTER ONE

Text and Glose

I

THE GREAT *Roman de la Rose* of Guillaume de Lorris and Jean de Meun is now chiefly celebrated, it would seem, for its celebrity—known by name and reputation to even the most casual student of late medieval culture but read *in toto* by only the most indefatigable. We hear of its enormous vogue as evidenced by the remarkable number of manuscripts surviving from the two centuries following its completion, its widespread influence on its own and other vernacular literatures, its prose redactions, foreign translations, imitations, moralizations. Its place in literary history is entirely secure: that of a catalyst for a dozen other poems; the dunghill of Ennius from which Chaucer and perhaps Dante gathered gold; a happy hunting ground in which to stalk sources. To literary historians it is a famous poem and, by common consent, a naughty one. A recent English translation renders what Jean was pleased to call his *jolis Romanz* as "the rollicking *Romance of the Rose.*"

The *Roman* was famous in the Middle Ages, too, especially in the fourteenth century, though there is no historical evidence to suggest that its great reputation then rested on any "rollicking" qualities. It rested, rather, upon what a knowledgeable French rhetorician and literary historian at the beginning of the fifteenth century called Jean de Meun's "moult noble doctrine," a doctrine rooted also in his translation of Boethius and in his beautiful *Testament*.[1] The present book is an attempt to discover what that doctrine was and, by focusing attention upon the poem as illuminated by a wealth of neglected manuscript materials, to advance a "medieval reading" of it which can perhaps explain its medieval as opposed to its modern reputation. My book attempts, in short, to outline that interpretation of the *Roman de la Rose* enjoyed by its urbane readers at the apex of its popularity in the fourteenth century.

[1] *Recueil d'arts de seconde rhétorique*, ed. E. Langlois (Paris, 1902), p. 12.

Such an undertaking is not without obstacles, since the very possibility of the "historical" criticism of literature is doubted by many literary theoreticians. "The total meaning of a work of art cannot be defined merely in the terms of its meaning for the author and his contemporaries," says one book widely read and respected by literary students. "It is rather the result of a process of accretion, i.e., the history of its criticism by its many readers in many ages."[2] With the first half of this pronouncement even the would-be "historical" critic must be sympathetic, for he knows that he can never, however hard he may try, recapture the significantly mutable cultural milieux of Homer or Chapman's *Homer* or Keats' "Chapman's Homer." He can only make what he hopes are intelligent attempts to do so. He can only, in Boccaccio's words, "read, persevere, sit up nights, inquire, and exert the utmost power of his mind." The accretion theory, on the other hand, is rather more difficult to accept, for it is painful to think of works of genius as so many of Rorschach's ink blots, accreting "meaning" with each new patient who views them. With specific reference to the *Roman* such a suggestion is particularly depressing. The "total meaning" of some works presumably mellows nicely, like a Stilton cheese at Christmas, with age and nibbling; but the "meaning" of the *Roman* in this sense has curdled, soured. Indeed, the *Roman* can hardly survive its modern interpretation.

One of the great canards of Western aesthetics maintains that "Ars longa, vita brevis est." The life of a work of art is seldom much longer than that of its maker. It merely has a much more durable corpse. In truth, a work of art is captured forever within its capsule of stylistic history, and when the style of the times changes it faces three possible fates. It may disappear from view, unsympathetic and unadaptable to a new stylistic moment, as did the once "great" pilgrimage poems of Guillaume de Deguilleville. Or, by overt adaptation or "renovation" it may be made acceptable to the prevailing style: witness Molinet's recension of the *Roman*, or Dryden's *All for Love*. Finally—and this is by far the most common case—it can, by critical accommodation, survive, indeed thrive, in a stylistic moment far different from its

[2] René Wellek and Austin Warren, *Theory of Literature* (New York, 1949), p. 34.

4

own. Milton becomes a Satanist, Langland a Marxist, and both sell in paperback editions.

What seemed at first with Wellek and Warren the modest beginnings of another attack on *Geistesgeschichte* thus reveals an audacious yet valid claim: that of the literary critic as creator, a modern resurrection man, who deals in old bones but rather miraculously makes all things new. Quite rightly did Alan Gunn subtitle his ambitious and exacting modernist reconstruction of the *Roman* a "Reinterpretation of the *Romance of the Rose.*" A "reinterpretation" can give the poem "value for our age."[3]

The present work does not aspire to the creation of meaning nor to the discovery of any but medieval meanings in the poem. Yet even such a narrowly historical, indeed archeological, undertaking as my own can make some claims to creativity if not to art, for it involves new formulations of historical materials. Such creativity, however, will not involve any ingenious explications of the allegory of the *Roman*, though it must begin with the claim that the poem is indeed an allegory. So far as I know this premise has never been denied. The poem is either a tedious account of a young man with horticultural interests or it is *alieniloquium*, "saying something else," as Isidore's standard definition of *allegoria* puts it. Furthermore, everybody knows just what else it is that the story is all about.

The allegory of the *Roman* (unlike that, say, of *The Pearl*) is hardly recherché; its few tricky aspects are carefully glossed within the text of the poem itself. Jean de Meun's thousands of lines of verse add very little to the allegorical story. Gunn shows nicely the extent to which Jean prefers *amplificatio* to *narratio*, how he sustains his poem not with a narrative flow of his hero's experiences—as did his imitator Deguilleville—but with the wealth of illustrative, exemplary materials which have threatened to categorize him misleadingly as an encyclopedist. While it is true that many of the *exempla* require mythographic, and therefore allegorical, understanding, there is no indication that Jean de Meun was interested in constructing ingenious allegories, dark conceits.

The account of the *Roman* which follows, therefore, does not

[3] Alan M. F. Gunn, *The Mirror of Love* (Lubbock, 1952), p. 505.

for the most part depend upon controversial methods of interpreting the allegorical plot; the problem of interpreting the *Roman* begins rather than ends with the unveiling of the surface allegory. The rose quest is a sexual metaphor, slightly less blatant with Guillaume de Lorris than with Jean de Meun but always obvious. The few emblems within the poem of any allegorical difficulty— e.g., the carbuncle in the Heavenly Garden—are explained by Jean de Meun himself. So far as I know, no medieval reader ever had any trouble in "getting" the historical sense of the seduction, but the absurdities of the interpretations *in bono*, like those offered by Jean Molinet and Clement Marot, which were enough to shock even such an enthusiastic and naïve allegorist as Winckelmann, testify that by the end of the fifteenth century the poem was no longer clearly understood.[4] Indeed Marot's pious fumbling with the fourfold method of interpretation, like much of the writing about traditional sacred art after the Council of Trent, is a poignant reminder of the changes in intellectual style which hid the great figurative arts of the Middle Ages from the eyes of the Enlightenment.

Merely to explain the central metaphor of the poem and call the *Roman* an "Art of Love" is not much more instructive than to describe *Paradise Lost* as an "Art of Eating Apples." The interpretive problem remains: to gloss the poem, to explain its meaning rather than to rehearse its plot. To apprehend the greatness of Jean's poem is to share with his medieval audience an appreciation of its ironic structure.

To use the term "gloss" in reference to the *Roman* is no abuse. Paré has shown that the dominant thirteenth-century pedagogical concern of the *glossatio* or "search for the moral or philosophic as opposed to the literal sense of texts," including secular poetry, has imposed a scholastic vocabulary on Jean de Meun's poem.[5] The chief glossator or exegete in the *Roman* is Lady Reason, who explains at some length the principles of poetic fiction and moral allegory (ll. 7153ff.).

---

[4] "Von der Allegorie überhaupt," *Winckelmanns kleine Schriften zur Geschichte der Kunst des Altertums*, ed. H. Uhde-Bernays (Leipzig, 1913), p. 250.

[5] G. Paré, *Le Roman de la Rose et la scolastique courtoise* (Paris and Ottawa, 1941), pp. 26-27.

The Lover, to whom her explanation is addressed, denies any knowledge

> . . . des poetes les sentences,
> Les fables e les metaphores,
> Ne be je pas a gloser ores. (ll. 7190-92.)

Later, in the apology for his book in which he attempts to antici-
pate criticism, Jean himself promises to gloss (*gloser*) his text.
Paré goes on to mention the remarkable vogue of glosses to pagan
poetry—glosses to Ovid, to Virgil, the dull and easy glosses to
Horace—inspired, directly or obliquely, by the old text which also
inspired Guillaume de Lorris: Macrobius' commentary on the
Somnium Scipionis. We know that the vernacular poems of the
later Middle Ages had their glosses, their moral interpretations,
too. The *Divine Comedy*, with its extraordinary burgeoning of
exegetical satellites, is the most conspicuous example. Another is
the *Echecs Amoureux* whose exegete says that men value for their
moral sense "the stories of *Ysopet* and *Renart* and many other
love stories."[6] And the *Echecs* gloss, largely unexplored, is a con-
vincing moral reading of an allegory of love, a daughter poem to
Jean's *Roman*. Finally, there are numerous medieval references
to the gloss of the *Roman* itself.

The technical term "gloss," of course, by no means always refers
to the allegorical unveiling of cryptic meaning. One of its com-
mon medieval meanings is simply *explication de texte*, amplifica-
tion or paraphrase on the literal level. Few mysteries are revealed,
for example, by Chaucer's imitative glosses to his translation of
Boethius or by E. K.'s old-fashioned glosses to the *Shepherd's
Calendar*. It is clear that many of the early references to the gloss
of the *Roman de la Rose* are little more than catch-phrases exploit-
ing the convenient rhymes of *rose* and *glose*. When a scribal
explicit tells us

> Cy gist le Romant de la Rose,
> Ou tout l'Art d'Amours se repose,
> La fleur des beaulx bien dire l'ose,
> Qui bien y entend texte et glose . . .[7]

[6] Paris, Bibliothèque nationale, MS fr. 9197, fol. 13ᵛ.
[7] Cited by E. Langlois, *Les Manuscrits du Roman de la Rose* (Lille, 1910),
p. 211.

we can probably be sure only that the anonymous rhymer is taxed by the demands of four endings in -*ose*. Such allusions to the gloss of the *Roman* are very numerous, though it would be risky to conjecture too much from them; at most in such references the word *glose* carries the generalized definition of "meaning" or "sense."

Some references to the gloss of the *Roman* go beyond this, however. A fourteenth-century French poem of the popular *débat* type provides the following example. A married and an unmarried man debate the satisfactions of their respective states. The unmarried man, refusing to credit the glowing reports of matrimony offered by his married antagonist, congratulates himself on his celibacy. He claims thus to avoid the notorious infidelity of women, an infidelity widely celebrated by the *Roman de la Rose*. The married man counters in a surprising way:

> Quant est du livre de la Rose,
> Il n'en parle que bien a point,
> Et, qui bien entend la glose,
> Des femmes il ne mesdit point.[8]

In other words, he says, if we understand the gloss of the *Roman*, one of the most notoriously misogynous poems of a misogynous age does not say anything against women. The married man is debating, of course, and one must be wary of verbal tricks. Still, what he says makes it clear that for him at least the sense of the *Roman* does not always lie on the surface and that the sense can be understood through a gloss.

The gloss in question can hardly be an actual written document like the scores of glosses to the Bible, Boethius, classical poetry, and other texts, which were the chief product of medieval scholarship. It is not a gloss to pick up and read, but an instructive metaphor. Elsewhere, however, the term seems to be used in another sense. The narrator of the *Book of the Duchess* tells us of a garden with unusual walls:

[8] *Recueil de poésie françoise*, ed. Anatole de Montaiglon (Paris, 1865), ix, 161. It is interesting that the reference to the "gloss" was lost in the version of the poem published by Vérard about 1501 in the *Jardin de Plaisance*: "Quant est du livre de la rose / Il nen parle que bien a point / Et qui bien entend la *chose* / Des femmes il ne mesdit point. . . ."

And alle the walles with colours fyne
Were peynted, bothe text and glose,
Of al the Romaunce of the Rose.

Here is a copy of the *Roman* painted not on vellum but on stone, a copy not of the poem only but also of its gloss. What is this gloss of "colours fyne"? Chaucerian scholars seem agreed that it probably is just what we should expect to find in an aristocratic copy of the poem dating from the late fourteenth century, namely a sequence of finely executed painted illustrations of the text.[9]

Chaucer's reference to painted textual illustrations as a gloss, if that is indeed his meaning of the term, would not have been unusual. Such a meaning follows directly from the principles of medieval book painting. There is almost no medieval discussion of the theoretical bases of illumination, if by that we mean aesthetic theory divorced from the practical concerns of the artist. Medieval documents concerning the painter's art are by no means lacking, but they are unapologetically practical in content, giving instruction for drawing a Wheel of Fortune or whipping glair. For discussions of the Beautiful we must turn to the Order of Preachers rather than the scriveners' guilds. At the same time even a casual reader must note the commonplace theological assumptions about the nature of the visual arts which lie behind the treatises of the Anonymous of Berne and Cennino Cennini. What might be called the pedagogical implications of textual illustrations are suggested by the *double entendre* "illumination."

According to the extremely influential analysis of beauty by Dionysius, which became a set text for aesthetic discussion in the later Middle Ages, beauty is associated with the good: beauty is like the light of God. St. Thomas, in his commentary on Dionysius, makes it clear that this beauty, this illumination, is intellectual and, in Augustinian terms, utilitarian. It is something to be understood and something to be used. It is the "light which lightens our footsteps" and its use, of course, is to illuminate the path to God, its source. For medieval theoreticians, color was an aspect of light; and panchromatic tendencies in various media reveal a preoccupation with "illumination." The principal mani-

---

[9] See, e.g., Joan Evans, "Chaucer and Decorative Art," *Review of English Studies,* VI (1930), 410.

9

festation of concern with "illumination" in the painting of the Gothic period is the lavish use of gold, a precious metal, rich as well in allegorical properties, and a substance which actually does reflect a kind of yellow brilliance. Surface light produced by gold and vivid colors was much admired, and it characterized medieval sculpture and architecture to an extent now often forgotten. Much statuary, and many church interiors which are now prized chiefly for their contours and linear form were, in the Middle Ages, decorated with gold and bright colors in a way which must have altered the apprehension of form. The painted light of this kind was not preserved in parchment, and most of it has long since faded or been scraped away; but where something like it remains or has been restored, as in the panchromatic interior of Albi cathedral or even in the chaster northern style of the Sainte Chapelle, the effect is at first startling to the modern eye. The fact is that much of medieval decoration, including the most carefully produced, is to our eyes garish, characterized by a tinsel glitter, a flashing of exterior light.

The tendency toward the lavish use of gold is nowhere more noticeable than in the painted books of the fourteenth century. The chief means of lighting a picture (as in Fig. 1) was the use of gold leaf border and background. The actual representation of light as subject matter was common enough at this time, but, radiating in solid halos or solid gold beams, it was by no means illusory. It is only in the fifteenth century that painters develop a convincing representational technique, and "realistic" sunlight begins streaming through windows. Indeed, one leading art historian has persuasively argued that the development of illusory beams of light, not the development of linear perspective, is the chief technical advance of fifteenth-century painting; and he shows that the newly perfected light soon took on the kind of symbolic significance suggested by Dionysius' simile.[10] Whatever may be the general relationships between the artistic preoccupation with light and the Dionysian aesthetic, there is no doubt that, at least in theory, the illumination of medieval books is meant both to brighten the page and to enlighten the reader. In St. Bonaventure's discussion of *lumen*, which he takes to be one of the

[10] Millard Meiss, "Light as Form and Symbol in Some Fifteenth-Century Paintings," *Art Bulletin*, xxvii (1945), 175-81.

three kinds of light, he makes the point that the exterior (i.e., artificial) light creates the *claritas* or *splendor* of the artifact. "Both as a radiance and as a perspicacity . . . the illumination of a manuscript, as also its rubrication, both makes it bright or gay, and at the same time illustrates or throws light upon its meaning."[11] It is one of the functions of manuscript illustrations to gloss their texts; the narrator of the *Book of the Duchess* saw such a gloss of the *Roman* painted in bright colors upon a garden wall.

In the Middle Ages art was not its own excuse for being. It was a didactic and pedagogical technique, joining with a number of other techniques to explain and celebrate a divinely ordained and revealed world order. The masons truly did construct sermons in stones, and St. Gregory was able to call holy images the Bible of the laity; in the later Middle Ages, with the *Biblia pauperum*, Gregory's metaphor became a literal reality. There is strong evidence, however, that the illustrations of secular texts are also meant to teach as well as to delight. When Francesco da Barberino wrote a Latin gloss to his allegory of love, the *Documenti d'Amore*, he explained that he had also, under interesting and unusual circumstances, produced his own illustrations. He traveled in Provence during the composition of the *Documenti* but was unable to find illustrators for it there; disappointed, he took the job on himself and, incidentally, did a quite creditable job. Considering the very high quality of French painting at the time, it seems odd that he should have encountered difficulty in finding a suitable artist. It seems probable that French artists were unable to produce pictures with meanings compatible with his rather bizarre use of familiar iconographic materials.[12] That the pictures were meant to have meaning is attested to by the Latin gloss.

[11] Ananda K. Coomaraswamy, "Medieval Aesthetic II: St. Thomas Aquinas on Dionysius and a Note on the Relation of Beauty to Truth," *Art Bulletin*, xx (1938), 72-73n. For a convenient brief discussion of the meaning of "light" in medieval aesthetics see the remarks on "Schönheit und Licht" by M. Grabmann in the introduction to "Des Ulrich Engelberti von Strassburg O.P. (+ 1277) Abhandlung De Pulchro," *Sitzungsberichte der Bayerischen Akademie der Wissenschaften, Philosophisch-philologische und historische Klasse* (1926), pp. 58-59.

[12] See Francesco Egidi, "Le miniature dei codici barberiniani dei 'Documenti d'Amore,'" *Arte*, v (1902), 1-20; and, with caution, R. Freyhan, "The Evolution of the Caritas Figure in the Thirteenth and Fourteenth Centuries," *JWCI*, xi (1948), 77.

Indeed, they form a gloss in pictures, even as the Latin commentary is a gloss in words.

An explicit statement of the idea that textual illustrations are a kind of gloss can be found much closer to Jean de Meun's own intellectual milieu—not that Francesco was many miles away—made by a secular priest, a humanist, and man of letters in the Ile de France: Richard de Fournival. The prologue to the *Bestiare d'amours* says that there are two ways of learning, by word and by picture, and that in his courtly bestiary the author uses both methods of teaching.[18] The gloss of the *Echecs Amoureux* demonstrates the same principle. In two of the five extant copies of this work of poetical exegesis, elaborate illustrations form an important part of the poem's critical apparatus. As a final example of this pervasive medieval habit, we may note that the "layout" of some manuscripts emphasizes the glossing functions of the illustrations. A number of sumptuous fifteenth-century manuscripts of Christine de Pisan's popular *Epitre d'Othea*, one of the works recently rehabilitated by Rosemond Tuve, are striking in this respect. The *Epitre* is a sequence of a hundred short verse histories, each of which is followed by a brief exegetical commentary, called a "glose," "moralite," or "exposicioun" in the English translations. In the composition of the manuscripts the text of the story is written on the recto of the leaf. Immediately following it, on the verso, is the painted illustration of the text accompanied by the written gloss. In this case the practice continued right into the printed editions.

My point is simply this: in many illuminated manuscripts of the Middle Ages the illustrations are more than merely decorative. There is an intimate relationship between the painted picture and the written text, a relationship which is suggested, in purely formal terms, in a variety of ways. The artist attempts to weave the "text" and the "gloss" into one fabric. The most conspicuous such attempt is the historiated initial, as in Fig. 5, in which the letter of the text and its decorative illustration are inseparable. More amusing perhaps is the kind of visual pun by which the illustrator arranges his composition to echo the form of a letter, or several letters, in the text which it accompanies. In Fig. 6, for

[18] *Li Bestiares d'Amours di Maistre Richart de Fornival e li Response du Bestiaire,* ed. Cesare Segre (Milan and Naples, 1957), pp. 4-5.

example, the artist has meddled with the normal posture of Viellesce so that she stands holding her single elongated crutch in such a pattern as to echo the *A* which initiates the line beginning her description below the illustration: "*A*pres fu vieleche portraite." The aim of this kind of wit is to stress the union of the icon and its meaning, of the text and its gloss.

The relationships between painting and poetry were no less complex and compelling in the Middle Ages than at other periods, but it will not be necessary for my purposes to go back and take up the quarrel with Lessing; for I do not propose to study a relationship between the "autonomous" arts of painting and poetry, but one between a specific poem and some specific paintings dependent upon it. The contingency of medieval miniatures cannot be seriously questioned, although it is frequently ignored. There cannot be book paintings unless there are first books, but the implications of the dependent relationship of textual illustrations have been largely obscured by the very methods of art history which have taught us so much about medieval art. Art historians generally have been concerned with the technical problems of medieval painting, with defining and tracing stylistic changes, and with cataloguing and explicating a rich and diverse iconographic tradition. Books about medieval illumination are as often as not monuments to the ruthless vandalism of photography which snips the illustrations out of manuscripts to be used in a way they were not meant to be used. It is of course impossible, practically speaking, to discuss medieval book illustrations without abusing them in such a manner, but the abuse should be conscious and reluctant. Kurt Weitzmann writes that "in miniatures the content or what is called the iconography and which is the equivalent of the reading of the text, is fused with the style, i.e. the element corresponding with paleography, to form such a close artistic unity that the one cannot be considered apart from the other."[14] Such is the integrity of the union of the text and illustration.

Whatever else a medieval reading of a medieval poem implies, it must suggest a reading in manuscript; for it was in manuscript, not in modern critical editions, that poems were read in the

[14] *Illustrations in Roll and Codex: A Study in the Origin and Method of Text Illustration* (Princeton, 1947), p. 182.

Middle Ages. It is to the textual illustrations which are the glory of the medieval copies of the *Roman*—and which have not survived, not even one, in the only modern critical edition of the poem—that I wish to direct attention. For Jean's great poem the manuscript materials are particularly rich. In a catalogue which is by no means complete, Ernest Langlois was able to list well over two hundred manuscripts which have survived to the twentieth century. Most of them are decorated to some degree. Many are lavishly illustrated, and the iconography of the *Roman* is far richer than that of the accumulated remainder of medieval secular literature. In spite of a fine preliminary stylistic study of a substantial number of the illustrated exemplars of the *Roman* a half-century ago by a young doctoral candidate, the manuscripts have received too little attention. Though they must represent a considerable portion of the work of the ateliers in northern France in the fourteenth century, they are not discussed in detail—indeed, they are hardly mentioned—in any of the standard works on Gothic illumination. Although a number of individual manuscripts are of unusual interest because of their style or content or both—e.g., Douce 364 in the Bodleian Library at Oxford (Fig. 13) or MS 387 in the University Library at Valencia (Fig. 7)—only one manuscript, an admittedly fine but not exceptional fourteenth-century copy in Vienna, has ever been published. Several other *Roman* manuscripts merit the attention of art historians. As for the iconography of the illustrations in the more limited sense of Professor Weitzmann's definition as "content . . . which is the equivalent of the reading of the text," the manuscripts are virtually unexplored. It is my intention in this book, which by no means pretends to be an exhaustive iconographic study of the poem, to suggest some of the implications which the content of the illustrations have for the interpretation of the poem. To this end it is possible to construct a useful analogy between figurative painting and figurative poetry.

A principal issue to which the study of iconography in the visual arts has addressed itself is the identification of subject matter; indeed, iconography means subject matter. From such iconographic study, pursued now for more than a century by art historians, literary scholars have much to learn. Few literary critics would admit that it is quite possible to make sophisticated critical statements about works of art when the very subjects of those works are unknown or universally and radically mistaken; art historians, on the other hand, have long since concluded that it is not only possible but, in some cases, necessary. To take a convenient and well-known example, there has been considerable discussion for some time about Titian's so-called "Sacred and Profane Love," and the discussion has centered on the subject of the picture. The interpretations of Titian's allegory—that is, the proposed definitions of its subject—have been as diverse as they are numerous. The matter may not yet be settled. An inability to identify the subject of the painting correctly, however, has not meant that criticism of it has been entirely sterile. On the contrary, art historians have felt capable of offering quite intricate criticisms of the formal qualities of the work—balance, color, shading, and the like—and placing it meaningfully in Titian's *oeuvre*. Such critical statements, we may note, ignore the subject and therefore the allegory or figurative meaning of the painting and concentrate on its surface meaning (formal composition) and artistic techniques. They are statements about what the painting "literally says" and not about what it "means"; they describe its iconography but do not explain it. The past three or four decades, an exciting and fruitful period in the field of iconology, have produced demonstrations that a number of Renaissance paintings which had been thought lacking in emblematic content, including still-life and genre paintings, are in fact allegorical. That we may still have much to learn is suggested by the numerous vague and unidentified "Allegories" which hang in our galleries today.

I have chosen examples from the Renaissance merely because the study of Renaissance iconography has been rather more flamboyant than that of the medieval period. Renaissance icons are more complicated, ingenious, literary, and classical than the most common medieval ones and present rather greater challenges to iconologists. Schematic, well-ordered medieval iconography leaves few new worlds for scholarly conquest; but such was not always the case. A little more than a hundred years ago Mrs. Jameson, whose importance in the history of iconographic studies is much greater than her dated Victorian prose might suggest, could write: "It is curious, this general ignorance with regard to the subjects of Mediaeval Art, more particularly now that it has become a reigning fashion among us."[15] She goes on,

> In the old times the painters of these legendary scenes and subjects could always reckon securely on certain associations and certain sympathies in the minds of the spectators. We have outgrown these associations, we repudiate these sympathies. We have taken these works from their consecrated localities, in which they once held each their dedicated place, and we have hung them in our drawing-rooms and our dressing-rooms, over our pianos and our side-boards—and now what do they say to us?

Mrs. Jameson's diagnosis was correct, and the question she asked was the pertinent one. It has now been answered, for the most part, in the great works of Künstle, Mâle, and other scholars of our own century, and in the continuing work of the monumental Index of Christian Art directed by Rosalie Green. As far as the predominant religious iconography of the Gothic period is concerned, few monuments remain totally undeciphered, and modern iconographic study has come increasingly to be centered on questions of national schools, specific literary sources, dating, and the like. Nonetheless it remains true that much, or even most, nineteenth-century discussion of medieval religious art—some of it really quite good, quite illuminating—reveals an appalling ignorance of the very subject matter of the works involved. I know there are those who will argue that we have learned little about art when we discover, for example, that a group of Gothic statues represents not the kings of France, as long supposed, but the kings of Judah; or that the Correggio frescoes at Parma are informed with emblematic meaning and not merely capricious imagination. That argument bears no force here, if indeed it does anywhere, for my point is simply that the subjects of works of art of earlier periods have often been elusive, and that the subject matter can chiefly be identified through a knowledge of iconographic conventions. We must regain "certain associations and certain sympathies."

My own argument is that what is true of the visual arts is, within limitations, true also of literature and that it is possible to

---

[15] *Sacred and Legendary Art*, 4th ed. (London, 1865), p. 10.

construct a useful analogy between the two which suggests that the criticism of medieval literature has hardly reached the point of iconographic sophistication represented in art history by Mrs. Jameson. Literary criticism seldom addresses itself to the definition of subject matter in a direct fashion. Certainly no literary critic is likely to begin an analysis of a medieval poem with the frank admission that he has no notion, or only a dim one, of what the poem is about. Nevertheless the current controversy over medieval poetic allegory proves that there must be a number of critics who might well begin with some such candid statement of ignorance or at least doubt, since the controversy is in reality centered on the question of subject matter. If Professor Kaske is correct, the Old English "Husband's Message" is about neither a husband nor his message, but the Cross of Christ. If the medieval masons of Angoulême were right, the *Chanson de Roland* is essentially about the spread of the Christian Faith. And if I am right the subject matter of the *Roman de la Rose* has been almost entirely ignored for the past five hundred years. As a result, literary criticism of an interpretive nature has been understandably debilitated, in spite of the many good things written about the poem's structure and rhetorical techniques. Alan Gunn's vast book on the *Roman*, while advancing a blatantly unhistorical reading which in my opinion devastates it utterly, makes a valuable and effective defense of its unity. It would appear, heresy though it may seem, that the knowledge of the subject matter of a work of literature is not strictly necessary to its critical discussion. The Horatian injunction of *aut placere aut docere* presents a real option.

Modern definitions of the subject of the *Roman* by no means correspond with medieval statements concerning the poem's meaning; and an amusing and dramatic example of sensational difference of opinion between modern and medieval critics concerns the comparison of the *Roman* with the *Divine Comedy*. Most modern critics, with the honorable exception of C. S. Lewis, have taken pains to assert that the *Roman* is a very different kind of poem from the *Comedy*, indeed that it is antithetical to Dante's great work. Typically we hear that "The *Roman de la Rose* was written in the very opposite spirit to that of Dante. Jean de Meun . . . wrote with a vision completely filled with the things of this world,

17

of life as it was being lived around him."[16] So too write the historians, for whom Jean's *Roman* "n'est pas une *Divine Comédie,* bien loin de là, c'est simplement une Comédie humaine."[17] In fact the polarization of these two famous poems, products of the same generation, has become a kind of ritual commonplace for books on medieval literary and intellectual history; time and again they are produced to attest to the clashing ideals of the late medieval intellectual world. Such a judgment should, however, be tempered by comparison with some quite different medieval testimony. Laurent de Premierfait was perhaps the leading "Romance philologist" of his day (ca. 1400). An enterprising humanist who was the first to translate Boccaccio into French, he can hardly be characterized either as stupid or monkish. Laurent claims that Dante's model for the *Comedy* was Jean's *Roman,* which the Florentine poet had encountered on a trip to Paris. "Cestui poete DAUT . . . ," says Laurent de Premierfait,

> rencontra le noble livre de la Rose, en quoy Jean Clopinel de Meung, home d'engin celeste, peigny une vraye mapemond de toute choses celestes et terreines; DAUT donques, qui de Dieu et de Nature avoit receu l'esperit de poeterie, advisa que ou livre de la Rose est souffisammant descript le paradis des bons et l'enfer des mauvais en langaige francois, voult en langaige florentin, soubz aultre manier de verys rimoiez, contrefaire au vif le beau livre de la Rose, en ensuyant tel ordre comme fist le divin poete Virgile ou sixiesme livre que l'en nomme Eneide.[18]

We cannot dismiss this testimony, once we have said that it is quite probably unreliable as to fact. Laurent may well have sacrificed factual detail to patriotic enthusiasm or dubious tradition, or simply to the passion for the French source so well known to modern philologists; but we have no reason to suspect that he

---

[16] F. W. Bourdillon, *The Early Editions of the Roman de la Rose* (London, 1906), p. 2.

[17] Henri Pirenne *et al.*, *La civilisation occidentale au moyen âge du XIe au milieu du XVe siècle* (Paris, 1933), p. 229.

[18] I follow the transcription made by Henry Martin in *Le Boccace de Jean Sans Peur* (Brussels, 1911), p. 11.

was a knave or a fool. On the face of it, it seems unreasonable that such an eminent literary scholar should have misunderstood, totally, the two most famous poems in the Romance vernaculars in which he so assiduously worked. Yet he unmistakably and overtly states that Dante's poem is a "copy" of Jean's, and that a principal subject of the *Roman* is the "Heaven of good men and the Hell of bad men." He does not speak of "courtly love" or "scholastic love" or "Christian phallicism" but of eschatology. It matters not a whit whether Dante had in fact ever been to Paris, whether he had ever read the *Roman*, or whether he had ever even heard of Jean de Meun. The relevance of Laurent's testimony to my argument is that a learned humanist of Gerson's generation, a specialist in allegory, as any close disciple of Boccaccio must be, found the *Roman de la Rose* and the *Divine Comedy* so much alike that he was prepared to say that the latter was a "copy" of the former. What Laurent has done is to place both poems in a context of eschatological dream-visions beginning with the *Somnium Scipionis*, Amant's bed-time book. In his account of the principles of poetic fiction the exegete of the *Echecs Amoureux* says that the meaning of Macrobius' dream-vision is that the good and faithful go to Heaven, while wrongdoers go to Hell. "Et cest che que nous voulons dire quant nous disons que les bons et les justes apres la mort sen vont en paradis et les maluais au contraire en enfer. Et aussi fu ce par aduenture fait le rommant de la rose."[19]

Laurent's comparison of the *Roman* and the *Divine Comedy* ceases to baffle when placed in its medieval context rather than juxtaposed to modern opinion. The commentators of the Middle Ages frequently make odd comparisons of this sort—indeed, what are the great works of medieval typology and allegory if not catalogues of comparisons, mostly very odd indeed? Some strange comparisons, rather like Laurent's, relating to early medieval architecture have been brilliantly discussed by the art historian Richard Krautheimer. Observing that medieval documents sometimes describe two churches as being alike, when to the modern student of architecture they may seem radically different in form or style, Krautheimer concluded that "mediaeval men must have

[19] Paris, Bibliothèque nationale, MS fr. 9197, fol. 14ʳ.

19

had *tertia comparationis* utterly at variance with those to which we are accustomed."[20] He found that the bases of these comparisons were not necessarily formal but iconographic; that is, they refer to a common meaning of function or dedication rather than to formal architectural similarities. Clearly a comparable mental habit lies behind Laurent's literary gossip. He may be wrong, but he is no fool. He knows the two poems are formally dissimilar— the *Comedy* is written in "a different kind of rhyming verse." The clear implication, indeed the overt statement, is that the poems are alike in meaning.

The comparison of these two poems which Laurent de Premierfait makes is a kind of gloss, and it can serve to bring us back to a consideration of those visual glosses, the manuscript illustrations, which are our present concern. The difficulty with a statement like Laurent's is, in part at least, that it is not literally true. There is, to be sure, a description of Heaven and Hell in Genius' sermon toward the end of the *Roman*, and it was a fairly common subject for illustration (Fig. 7); but the principal literal subject of the poem is the quest for a rose. The illustrations, however, like the testimony of Laurent, invite our attention to the figurative, rather than the literal, meaning of the poem.

Consider four miniatures (Figs. 1-4) which all illustrate the same text, the opening lines of the *Roman*. The simple action is as follows. The fictional first-person narrator tells us that he had a dream about a beautiful garden. He admits that some people maintain that dreams are all nonsense, but he cites the example of Macrobius' commentary against them. In his own dream, he wakes to full daylight, dresses, and walks out of the town. He comes to a garden wall on which are painted pictures of various allegorical personages, Hate, Envy, and others. Eventually he is admitted to the garden by a beautiful young woman named Oiseuse. The garden is characterized by strange trees, and by its abundance of animals and birds, particularly the latter. The well of Narcissus is in the center of this garden, and it is while staring into the well that Amant first sees the rose, or rather rosebud, which he will achieve only in Jean de Meun's continuation of Guillaume de Lorris' beginning some eighteen thousand lines later.

[20] "Introduction to an 'Iconography of Mediaeval Architecture,'" *JWCI*, v (1942), 3.

Of the illustrations under consideration, Fig. 1 is undoubtedly the least useful for explicating the poem. It adorns its page with a certain amount of crude fourteenth-century color and *splendor*, but throws little *claritas* upon the text. Against a stark and overbearing geometrically patterned background, and within the severely architectural spatial organization of the barbed quatrefoil, the narrator is in bed asleep. There is no indication of any of the details of the dream, or even of the fact that he is dreaming. Yet even in this flat picture the technique is figurative rather than literal. Even allowing for the obvious technical limitations of the artist, it is clear that the figure in the illustration is not meant to be in a realistic sleeping position, but in a conventional attitude inherited from antique art. Such a posture signifies sleep, however uncomfortable it might in fact be to sleep in such a position. As a conventional pictorial demonstration of a dream, the iconography of Fig. 1 was already steeped in antiquity by the thirteenth century. In the very ancient Vatican Virgil the illustration of Hector's appearance to Aeneas *in somnis* is strikingly similar to any number of pictures in *Roman* manuscripts which present an *incipit* illustration of the recumbent Dreamer with Danger standing at the foot of his bed.[21]

In Fig. 2, a less pedestrian production, it is the predominantly Gothic religious iconography which dictates the form. This four-part *encadrement* characterizes a family of fine fourteenth-century French manuscripts. While the subject is still caught in the stasis of the architectural quatrefoils, the action represented is much fuller; there are four episodes organized chronologically. The first quarter shows the Dreamer in bed with a rosetree swirling up behind him. In the second quarter Amant sits on his bed dressing; next he is walking, basting his sleeve; and finally he enters the walled garden. There is marginal decoration—medallioned heads and some animals from the garden.

Figures 1 and 2 are both literal illustrations of the text, and in them the surface action of the picture can easily be correlated to the letter of the text. There are elements in Fig. 2 which may at first seem puzzling—the swirling rosetree, or the Lover's tonsure, for example—but as a whole the illustration is an entirely coherent

---

[21] See J. de Wit, *Die Miniaturen des Vergilius Vaticanus* (Amsterdam, 1959), Plate 9, Fig. 15.

and correctly ordered temporal sequence of complex action. In Fig. 3, the range of superior fifteenth-century techniques has produced another kind of illustration. In fact, Fig. 3 really consists of two illustrations, perhaps designed by two different illuminators. Below, in what is now a decidedly fifteenth-century bed triumphing in the technical details of relief work and a canopy, Amant is iconographically sleeping. His dream fills the top half of the page. According to Guillaume de Lorris the garden is square, but our artist has made it round, following a convention begun in some quite early manuscripts which exploit the earliest and simplest successful French attempts to create pictorial space. The artist has managed to crowd a good deal into the picture. Beside the stream flowing from the garden, Amant stands at the open gate shaking hands with Oiseuse. Around the garden's wall, not painted, as in the text, but carved in relief, is the cycle of allegorical portraits. Within the garden are a number of trees, splendidly differentiated, including a magnificent pine which grows by the Fountain of Narcissus, where, incidentally, Narcissus himself gazes at his image in the water. There are rabbits, a roebuck, a large variety of birds and flowers. At the extreme left Danger, destined to be one of Amant's chief adversaries, leans laconically on the wall, his club over his shoulder, guarding a rosebush like the one growing beside the Fountain of Narcissus. In this illustration the artist is still quite close to the text, but he has reorganized the material. He needs the icon of the Fountain of Narcissus, so he actually shows Narcissus in the garden at the same time Amant arrives at the gate. He wants Danger, who does not appear in the poem for more than three thousand lines, so he puts him there too. These are, of course, selective details. Although we see nearly all of the interior of this *hortus conclusus*, there is no sign of the god of Love and his numerous minions, the bright dancers, the warriors against chastity. Such an illustration gives us some idea of how the illustrator read the poem, for in its very center he has put the well of self-love. But the action represented is still quite close to the text, and its value as a gloss is limited. Like Erasmus, we must seek those glosses which depart most of all from the letter.

Such a gloss is Fig. 4, from a third manuscript of the fourteenth century. The illustration has no obvious connection with the literal action of the *Roman* at all, and to study it is at first to play a medieval version of "What's Wrong with This Picture?" Leaving aside for the moment the question of its style, which is rather unusual, there are several odd things about its content. In the first place, it presents ambiguities of time and space more perplexing than those of Fig. 3. The Dreamer is in bed in town, but he is also in the middle of the garden. It is not clear whether he is asleep and dreaming, as his position would suggest, or awake within the dream, so to speak, as his open eye would suggest. Furthermore there are a number of details in the picture which immediately capture the attention and curiosity. There are four lighted candles behind the bed. The man on the bed is tonsured, as in Fig. 2, and he holds a very large glove in his left hand. On either side of the tent is a tree, markedly different from the others in the picture, which has fleurs-de-lys for leaves. In the trees there are many birds—this, at any rate, we have seen before. There is a fox trying to get at the birds in the tree on the right side of the picture, and there are also a couple of animals, possibly grotesques, at the foot of the other tree. Finally, of course, the most prominent and surprising detail is the nest of birds at the top of the picture. The converging sides of the tent point to it like an indicator arrow, and it rises right out of the composition as defined by its elaborate gold border. Within the nest a mother bird is feeding her young with blood from her breast.

We cannot, of course, really separate the iconography of the illustration from its style, which may explain some of its apparent peculiarities. The style is not realistic. In the illustration, no less than in the text, we are in a world which does not operate under the familiar coherences of space and time. In the center of the picture it is night time, and this explains the burning candles. Outside the tent we are on the other side of the dream, and it is day time. Against the swirls of green and etched gold which are the foliage of the dream garden, the fleur-de-lys trees, though still striking, are not entirely out of place. On the other hand, the literalism of some of the details in the garden jars slightly against the delicate suggestiveness which is the impression of the picture as a whole: the birds and animals seem almost pasted in.

Indeed, it is impossible to account for the iconographic peculiarities of the picture by reference to the literal text of the *Roman*, or to explain them as artistic reorganization of literal details. It is true that there are birds in abundance in the garden of Guillaume de Lorris, but none of them bleeds. There are animals in the garden too, particularly rabbits and roebucks (cf. Fig. 3), but our illustrator has put in the fox, which does not appear in the text. According to Guillaume the trees have been imported from the land of the Saracens, but here they seem to be very like the royal emblem of France. Finally, the text says nothing about the Dreamer's having a tonsure or holding a glove.

As far as that goes, it may be argued that the text says very little at all about concrete details. All men, after all, must be either tonsured or not tonsured. Our artist has had the difficult task of drawing a picture of a dream. He has had to use his imagination, filling in the background for the situation provided by Guillaume de Lorris. Is it really fair to him, or for that matter to ourselves, to drop dark hints about trees and tonsures and to look for allegories in every bush? The answer to such argument must be unequivocal. Not only is it fair to attempt to explain details which cry out for explication, it is necessary. The introduction to Guillaume's poem, the exposition of the situation and the description of the garden, is by no means sketchy. We have seen in the cluttered composition of Fig. 3 the attempt of a fifteenth-century artist of no mean skill to do partial justice to the richness of its detail. The visual scene is quite complete in the poem. It requires of the illustrator not imaginative detail, but selective and coherent organization.

Such organization is in fact manifest in Fig. 4, in spite of the wealth of competing details which the illustrator has introduced. For Fig. 4 becomes immediately intelligible as an illustration of the *Roman* when it is realized that it illustrates the allegorical, rather than the literal, meaning of the poem. The illustrator has not, as in Fig. 3, taxed himself with an attempt to show what is literally in the garden. He has instead made a kind of summary painting, a summary of what he thinks the *Roman* is about. To do this he has introduced into his little painting a number of emblematic elements which would have been transparent to any sophisticated fourteenth-century reader, however arcane they may initially seem to us. We may begin with a consideration of a simple yet striking detail of this picture, namely the little fox, barking, so to speak, up the fleur-de-lys tree.

The fox attacking the tree is, figuratively, a friar; he represents a major theme of the *Roman* which previously has too often been considered peripheral. Like most of Jean de Meun's antifraternal material, the fox can be traced to William of Saint-Amour and the University strife of the 1250's in Paris, though the background of the fox image is much older. In origin such foxes are probably the *vulpeculas parvulas* of the Canticle of Canticles (2:15), which were given various "bad" interpretations in the vast exegetical literature which burgeoned about that biblical love-song. The most common gloss on the "little foxes" was probably "heretics," as in St. Bernard's famous sequence in the *Sermons on the Canticles*. Haskins mentions an amusing example of the pervasion of that interpretation, which was apparently appropriated by the heretics themselves.[22] William of Saint-Amour, however, glossed them as hypocrites and false preachers, along with the execrable *penetrantes domos* of II Timothy 3:6— that is, friars. According to William the foxes of Luke 9:58, together with the *lupi rapaces* of Matthew 9:15, are also friars. William applied to the mendicant orders some of the natural history of Isidore of Seville which had become popularized in the bestiaries. According to Isidore (*Origines*, XII, ii, 29) foxes feign death to deceive the birds which fly down within reach of their supposed carcasses. Likewise, says William, the friars pretend to be "dead to the world" in order to seduce the gullible laity, i.e., the birds.[23]

Much of this material had already been appropriated into vernacular poetry by Rutebeuf by the time Jean de Meun set out to attack the friars, and it is reasonably certain that Rutebeuf was Jean's immediate source for much of his antifraternal material. The earlier poet had turned the popular figure of Renart into a friar; he had also appropriated the bestiary image from Isidore. The friars "Aussi nous prenent et deçoivent / Com li gorpis fet

[22] C. H. Haskins, *The Renaissance of the Twelfth Century* (New York, 1957), p. 79.

[23] *Opera Omnia quae repereri potuerunt* (Constance, 1632), p. 300.

les oisiaus. . . ."[24] That the fleur-de-lys trees represent the king-
dom of France is too obvious to require argument in the light of
the commonplace allegories of the *Dit du Lys* variety. Opposition
to friars began, on a significant scale, in France, and although
antifraternalism in the thirteenth and fourteenth centuries was
not a peculiarly French phenomenon—as the great English
poets among others attest—the movement was certainly more
pronounced and better organized in France where it was indeed
midwife, if not mother, to Gallicanism. It was widely believed in
certain quarters that Saint Louis was being hoodwinked by friars,
to the detriment of the fleur-de-lys;[25] and the specific point that
it is the friars who spoil the fleur-de-lys trees is made in the clos-
ing lines of that splendid fourteenth-century satire the *Roman
de Fauvel*.[26] In short there is no doubt whatever that the back-
ground of Fig. 4 is meant to suggest what Jean de Meun himself
calls the "renardie" of the friars. Jean's antifraternalism, often
misleadingly called "anticlericalism," is a major and relevant
theme of the *Roman*. In an appropriate place I shall argue that
it is intimately linked to the central concern of the poem, that it
is not an irrelevant graft. The illustrator has here indicated what
he believes to be its importance by including it in his composition.
Illustrating what the poem means, not what it literally says, he
feels free to turn to scriptural exegesis, patristic authority, contem-
porary theological polemics, and vernacular poetry to select the
emblems of his composition.

So much for the little fox, which is merely one small element
in this extraordinary *incipit* illustration which attempts with con-
siderable success to compress within a few square inches the content
of four volumes of poetry. The detailed explication of medieval
iconography frequently becomes highly technical and pedantic.
There are those who characterize it as "puzzle solving," a rather
poor substitute for aesthetic criticism; but for the modest aim of
this book, the definition of the significant content of the *Roman*

[24] *Oeuvres complètes de Rutebeuf*, ed. E. Faral and Julia Bastin (Paris, 1959),
pp. 534-35.

[25] See, for example, the violent sermon of William of Saint-Amour from
Erfurt MS Amplon Q 170, cited by Lester K. Little, "Saint Louis' Involvement
with the Friars," *Church History*, XXXIII (1964), 23-24n.

[26] *Le Roman de Fauvel*, ed. Arthur Langfors (Paris, 1914-19), pp. 116ff.

de la Rose, questions of content must take precedence over questions of form. That there is a puzzle to solve about the poem, or about any other medieval work of art which depends for its meaning upon conventional iconography, is the accident of time, not the vice of man or the *trahison des clercs*. If a little fox, or the glove and the pelican, which will in their own places be explained, can help us recover the meaning of the greatest vernacular poem of medieval France, let us by all means talk about them. Such discussion may in the long run be more valuable than that of the grander, though wholly imaginary, modern graven images of "naturalistic mysticism," *scolastique courtoise*, and bourgeois effulgence which are our modern glosses to the poem.

One cannot, however, merely rampage through manuscripts ransacking icons, whether one chooses to call it puzzle solving or literary criticism. Recall what Weitzmann has said with regard to the iconography of the medieval miniature; his dictum must become a rule of work. Iconography and style are "fused," says Weitzmann, "to form such a close artistic unity that the one cannot be considered apart from the other." This is entirely lucid. The iconography, or content, of an illustration of the *Roman* must be examined within the context of its style. It is accordingly necessary to speak of stylistic considerations.

II

The word "style" is used here in its general sense, to mean the set of predominant technical characteristics of a general period, region, or school of illumination, rather than in its narrow sense of the minutiae by which some art historians have been able to identify individual illuminators—as, for example, Millard Meiss was able to identify the artist of the Stuttgart *Roman*.[27] A picture of Oiseuse painted in the fourteenth century (Fig. 8) is stylistically very different from one painted a century or so later (Fig. 9), though their content is, of course, the same. Such an example underscores a principal problem of this iconographic study, and that is the sheer immensity of the project. The materials for an iconography of the *Roman* are enormous, indeed staggering. The

[27] "The Exhibition of French Manuscripts of the XIII-XVI Centuries at the Bibliothèque Nationale," *Art Bulletin*, xxxviii (1956), 196.

present study is based on the examination of well over a hundred illustrated copies of the poem, and there are others which I have not seen. Although most of them are products of the fourteenth century—the heyday of the poem's popularity and of the international Gothic style—they range in date from MS fr. 1559 in the Bibliothèque nationale in Paris, probably produced within a few years of Jean's completion of the poem, to the sumptuous Harley 4425 in the British Museum, dating from the turn of the sixteenth century, "after at least three printed editions had appeared."[28] From the point of view of art history, no less than from that of other aspects of intellectual history, this period is one of enormous and vital stylistic change. It ranged from the last days of the cathedral builders through the international Gothic, the flamboyant, the English "perpendicular," and, in particular reference to painting, through what John White has nicely called "the birth and rebirth of pictorial space." Jean de Meun's great poem, sealed forever within its thirteenth-century text, was for at least two more centuries gazed upon from many different perspectives, with the stylistic vision of ages other than its own.

While the *Roman* was still being avidly read, if with decreasing comprehension and increasing dilettantism, there burst upon Europe that technical change which was so radically and rapidly to alter her intellectual world. The coming of the printing press meant the virtual death of book painting—a slow and brave death, to be sure—but certainly not the end of the poem's textual illustration. Rich, if derivative, cycles of woodcuts decorate the proliferation of printed editions of the poem which began to appear about 1480, and these illustrations, as Lebeer has remarked, are entirely medieval in spirit.[29] Throughout the late Middle Ages there were in existence *Roman de la Rose* tapestries. Philip the Bold had one, and while no medieval examples have survived, so far as I know, there is a splendid and iconographically suggestive sixteenth-century set in the Hermitage.[30] In addition many chests, combs, ivory cases, and so forth, dating from the fourteenth and

---

[28] Bourdillon, *Early Editions of the Roman de la Rose*, p. 75.

[29] Louis Lebeer, *L'esprit de la gravure au XVe siècle* (Brussels, 1943), p. 15.

[30] Georges Doutrepont, *La littérature française à la cour des ducs de Bourgogne* (Paris, 1929), p. 329; and N. Y. Birykova, *The Hermitage, Leningrad: Gothic and Renaissance Tapestries* (London, 1965), pp. 107-16.

fifteenth centuries, are decorated with scenes much influenced by the poem's iconography; indeed these carved scenes are frequently, if dubiously, described as illustrations of the poem.[31] No other work of the "secular" literature of the Middle Ages can rival the poem in the richness of its iconography.

From a purely stylistic point of view, there are a great many changes in the illustrations of the late fifteenth-century manuscripts of the poem when compared with those, say, of the early fourteenth century. Such changes are likely to be called "developments" by art historians and, by art historians of a certain school, "advances." Kuhn's study of the *Roman* illustrations, for example, gives the impression that the stylistic history of the manuscripts follows a course from modest to major "advances." Actually, what he means is that the history of the illustrations is one of increasing spatial freedom, increasing verisimilitude, and increasing degree of exemplification. Terminology here is no mere matter of taste, for it is important to realize that stylistic change does not always lead to something "better" or, in matters of art, to something "more artistic" or "more advanced." Misleading analogies of artistic change and biological selection of the sort which continue to plague the study of medieval drama (to cite but one example) are pernicious. To the organic school of stylistic history, art presumably must end with technicolor motion pictures viewed through stereoscope spectacles—at least until the advent of Aldous Huxley's "feelies."

It is a scholarly convention to speak of the stylistic changes discernible in the vernacular poetry of the late Middle Ages as movements toward "realism" or even "naturalism." Literature becomes more "life-like." Yet neither the word "realism" nor the word "naturalism" is to be found in the ample vocabulary of medieval literary criticism, and neither one, so far as I can judge, adds anything distinctive or necessary to the discussion of poetry in a medieval context. A more useful term to describe such stylistic tendencies, one which at least has the virtue of not being an anachronism, is "verisimilitude." Both the literature and the visual arts of the late Middle Ages are characterized by an increas-

---

[31] It seems safe, however, to describe them as "in the spirit of the *Roman de la Rose*," as does Louis Grodecki, *Ivoires français* (Paris, 1947), p. 113.

ing degree of verisimilitude, which is to say increasingly complex exemplification.

As a general statement, easily enough faulted in specific exception perhaps but still true enough in the main, the history of medieval allegorical poetry is one of an increasing degree of literary exemplification. There is in the history of this poetry— so diverse in its sources of inspiration, so rich in its achievement— a movement from broad intellectual abstraction to concrete example and, hence, to verisimilitude. In Prudentius' *Psychomachia*, an early and influential Christian allegory which has left its mark on the *Roman* in more than one place, the characters are almost purely abstract, little metonymies. Pride, meeting Humility in deadly combat, rides a spirited mount, and has a few other proud iconographic attributes: a lion's skin, a fancy coiffure, an expensive scarf. Aside from this, "she" (since *Superbia* is feminine) has no character whatsoever. The essence of her opponent, Humility, is simply the negation of the attributes of Pride. In the *Roman* there are, to be sure, such characters as these: the walk-ons who do psychomachic battle at the siege of the castle; Seureté, who fights Peur; Franchise, who takes on Danger. They engage our attention on the level of verisimilitude no more than do the abstract vices whose portraits decorate the exterior of the Garden of Deduit. Such, essentially, is the allegorical tone of Guillaume de Lorris' part of the poem. It is enriched to some extent by episodes of Ovidian myth (Oiseuse, the well of Narcissus), but it is in no way strikingly verisimilar in its stylistic technique. In Jean de Meun's continuation of the poem, however, there are a number of characters who can, off and on, be encountered on the level of verisimilitude. They engage our attention as exemplifications of real life. Faussemblant is both abstract False-Seeming or Hypocrisy, and a specific exemplification of that vice at work in daily life—i.e., that kind of hypocrisy which William of Saint-Amour claimed was being practiced by the friars, particularly the Dominicans at the University of Paris in the 1250's. Both in speech (for example, his long confession) and in action (for example, his treacherous violation of the confessional), Faussemblant *exemplifies* as well as *is* Hypocrisy.

In terms of the stylistic changes under consideration here the once-famous pilgrimage poems of Guillaume de Deguilleville occupy a kind of middle ground between the *Roman* and the *Canterbury Tales*, the best known of the longer allegories of the fourteenth century. Guillaume was a fervent admirer of the *Roman*, however much he may have been offended by the poem's puzzling slurs on Norman probity, and he repeatedly used its techniques in his own works, which are dream-visions populated with abstractions clothed in a variety of iconographic garments. But while the *Pèlerinage de la vie humaine* uses both the dream framework and abstract characters—some very abstract, like my favorite, Hagiography—it also includes a number of details from ordinary everyday life: street scenes, scenes from shop life, and the like. Among the most verisimilar details for his fourteenth-century audience was the pilgrimage itself.

The allegory of Chaucer's *Canterbury Tales* is almost entirely exemplary in technique. Indeed, the verisimilitude is so marked that it is all many critics can see. Instead of telling us that he had a dream in which representatives of the various estates of England paraded before him—which is, in essence, the poetic fiction used by his contemporary, Langland, in *Piers Plowman*—Chaucer feigns a pilgrimage, a common event in his time, in which the author himself takes part. The other pilgrims are described with stunning verisimilitude, modified by the demands of conventional iconography. A number of the characters from Jean's *Roman* are there, both as pilgrims and as characters in the tales, though this is by no means apparent to the casual reader, for they have undergone a marked change in style. To a certain point the verisimilitude of detail seems to carry all before it. In spite of the fact that she is a pastiche of motifs from the Bible, scriptural exegesis, classical and vernacular poetry, the Wife of Bath is verisimilar—that is, she is highly exemplary. When the hypocritical Pardoner, who owes not a little to Faussemblant, casts aside the veil of literary verisimilitude to reveal in his confession an allegorical abstraction, he raises a critical question vexing to Chaucerians, who feel obliged to discover ingenious explanations for what has happened. (The Pardoner is drunk—on a single glass of ale! —or hubristically overconfident.)

The parallel transition in pictorial art—that is, from iconographic abstraction to verisimilar exemplification—can easily be seen in the handling of the portraits of the vices which decorate

31

the exterior façade of the Garden of Deduit: Hate, Envy, Avarice, Old Age, and the rest. Though ten in number, these abstractions are clearly based on the concept of the seven capital vices and, within the ironic economy of the *Roman* as a whole, form a part of the self-mocking trappings of the religion of carnal love. They are glossed differently by fourteenth-century readers. One says that they are "ymages la figure Des quex li dieu d'Amours n'a cure."[32] Another is more clinically theological: "Nota quod ista vicia sive defectus non participant ad actum de dilectione et ideo dicitur esse extra murum."[33] The lengthy description of these allegorical figures by Guillaume de Lorris may seem little more than self-indulgent imitation of Ovid. Actually, the vices become rather amusing when one realizes that most of them actually are involved in the *actum de dilectione,* as Jean de Meun goes on to explore it, albeit in a disguised way. At least one medieval reader of the poem, Geoffrey Chaucer, seems to have enjoyed the joke: the Merchant's Tale, one of the most uproarious moments in the *Canterbury Tales,* shows what happens when Viellesce, or Old Age, gets into the garden.[34]

But the aspect of these vices which I wish briefly to explore here is their popularity with the illustrators of the poem. That popularity was immense. In sheer bulk the number of individual miniatures runs well into the hundreds. With the exception of that small class of manuscripts which Kuhn disdainfully calls *Kitschhandschriften,* I know of only one unmutilated illustrated manuscript which does not portray all, or most, of this cycle of vices. They surely must be some of the most frequently illustrated subjects of late medieval book painting, not excepting the commonest scenes in religious art. They thus present an unusually rich and perhaps unique body of materials to approach from the point of view of stylistic and iconographic mutation.

During the two centuries of the poem's illustration in manuscript, the treatments of these figures vary enormously. They are

[32] Florence, Biblioteca Riccardiana, MS 2775, fol. 140ʳ; cited by Langlois, *Les manuscrits,* p. 187.

[33] Paris, Bibliothèque nationale, MS fr. 1560, fol. 1ʳ.

[34] *Preface to Chaucer,* pp. 256-57; see further, George Economou, "Januarie's Sin against Nature: The *Merchant's Tale* and the *Roman de la Rose,*" *Comparative Literature,* XVII (1965), 251-57.

wash designs, niched statues, sepulchral effigies, seated figures, figures in a garden, figures in *tableaux vivants*. In short they are, at one time or another, practically anything within the range of the illustrators' imaginations and technical abilities except that one thing which Guillaume de Lorris says they are—figures sculpted and painted (*portrait . . . e entaillie*) in gold and blue (*a or e a azur*). The allegorical nature of the figures represented presents no problems. These are patent abstractions, the capital vices of the religion of Love. Hate, Poverty, and Tristitia are no more three masks in a *roman à clef* than Faith, Hope, and Charity were a trio of St. Paul's friends. Their descriptions, of course, contain many elements typical of hateful, poor, or sorrowful people —as well as a number which are not—but they remain characterizations of abstractions, not of personalities. The stylistic history of these allegorical paintings parallels that of allegorical literature from Prudentius through Jean de Meun to Geoffrey Chaucer. That is, the paintings also become characterized by an increasing degree of exemplification, an increasing degree of verisimilitude.

Consider the figure of Envy. As Guillaume tells it, Envy has no description, merely a complex of characteristics. The only physical details on which a would-be illustrator of Envy could put his finger are that she is ugly and shifty-eyed. Indeed, in most illustrations of the early fourteenth century, that is all she is— a shifty-eyed, ugly woman sitting on a bench, shiftily eyeing nothing in particular off to one corner of the boxed-in illustration. Within Guillaume's text, however, there is an exemplification of envious conduct, as opposed to abstract Envy, to which the interested illustrator could turn. Envy does not like to see other people loved or praised, says Guillaume, and here the illustrators picked up their cue. Thus it is that in the oldest surviving illustration of Envy, in MS fr. 1559 in Bibliothèque nationale, and in increasing numbers of manuscripts through the mid-fourteenth century, there is an object for Envy's shifty-eyed envy: a young couple in conversation or, more amusingly in the context of the sexual metaphor of the *Roman*, a couple in amorous embrace. In the fifteenth century, Envy is likely to be found in very complicated social situations indeed—as in Douce 364 in the Bodleian Library at Oxford, analyzed by Robertson, where she is an old hag surrounded not only by the couple but by a musician playing for them and a servant offering them bonbons. Tracing the stylistic change exemplified by such an illustration, Robertson points out that the picture not only conveys the idea of envy but places it in a setting of easily verifiable human experience. "This kind of representation requires a spatial continuum rather than an idealized background, and this continuum is afforded by means of perspective."[35] The development of pictorial space in the visual arts is usually accounted for, in large part, in terms of increasingly refined technique. The fifteenth-century artist is simply able to do what the fourteenth-century artist could not—but what, by implication, he would have wanted to do. The premise is extremely dubious.

The matter of illusory pictorial space is, of course, the key to increasing exemplification in visual narration after the turn of the fifteenth century, just as verisimilitude (a public pilgrimage rather than a fantastic dream) is the key to such exemplification in literary narration. To this subject I shall shortly return, after offering an important parenthetical warning concerning the allegorical nature of even the most "realistic" events and exemplifications in the *Roman*. The dangers implicit in thinking of some figures in the poem as "more" or "less" allegorical than others is illustrated by another picture of the abstract vice of envy. In MS Egerton 1069 in the British Museum (Fig. 3) the illustrator has executed a piece of particularly felicitous visual wit, which immediately draws attention to the theme of sexual cupidity at the heart of the poem. In this *incipit* illustration he has arranged the garden door so that the painting of Envy—here a classical bas-relief—is next to it. Her jealous pointing is directed toward a couple, but not a pair of stick figures within her set. Here she is jealous of the lubricious hand-shaking of the Lover and Oiseuse at the gate. Such an illustration has something to say about Envy and the Lover, to be sure, but it also has something to say about the nature of allegory. Its clear implication is that the intellectual abstraction Envy and the intellectual abstraction Amant operate on exactly the same plane of being, however different they may be in their degree of exemplification.

Similarly the Ellesmere manuscript of the *Canterbury Tales*,

[35] *Preface to Chaucer*, p. 208.

the single green bough on the sadly barren tree of Chaucer iconography, presents us with illustrations of the Canterbury pilgrims together with some allegorical figures from the Parson's Tale. The Wife of Bath with her heavy crop, the simian Miller with his bagpipes, and the flaming heart of Caritas all share the same stage, the same pictorial continuum; for they are all allegorical representations. The Wife of Bath is no more and no less *real* than the abstract virtue of Charity. As an exemplification, she may have certain qualities of verisimilitude. Indeed certain details of her description must have been suggested to Chaucer directly from "real life," just as the burning heart may have been suggested by the "real life" warm-heartedness observed in the charitable. Yet the interest in reality shared by Jean de Meun, Geoffrey Chaucer, and the illustrators of both poets is an interest in abstract moral reality, handled with varying degrees of exemplification from situations of daily living.

Jean de Meun, in an attempt to make significant statements about abstract concepts such as Fortune, also turned to real life, as in the *exemplum* which provides the scholarly *terminus ab quo* for his part of the poem. The story of Charles of Anjou and Manfred is a topical and potentially moving *document humain*. There is here, indeed, a kind of appeal to felt experience. Jean's readers are invited to see exemplified in this story and those of other real people, like Héloïse and Abelard, the workings of certain immutable and transcendent moral principles. The question is eventually one of what Jean de Meun, and his readers, thought real. The clear implication is that they believed Fortune, although illusory, to be quite as real as Charles of Anjou; quite as real as the gat teeth, warty noses, and syphilis scabs which have been hailed in Chaucer as the triumph of literary realism. Literary realities of whatever pretensions invite verification, generally by comparison with the reader's experience of life and human nature. Gat teeth are real, for we have all seen gat teeth. But what man hath seen God? Medieval men, including, incidentally, nominalist philosophers of the fourteenth century, seem to have been capable of referring literary fictions and historical events to abstract moral concepts for verification. The reality of the story of Charles and Manfred was not that it concerned real people and actual events, but that it exemplified a real principle. For such exemplification stories from classical mythology, from a wide variety of authorities, or from Jean's own imagination served quite as well.

To discuss these ponderous matters superficially is to skate on thin ice over deep water. It is clear that the matter of increasing exemplification in literary and pictorial art, as well as the question of the focus of reality, has many important ramifications in medieval intellectual history. It has everything to do, for example, with the growth of science. A system which sees no pressing demands for *visibilia* is likely to produce neither birdwatchers nor biochemists. It is much less clear, at least from the case so far made by literary historians, that these matters have much to do with the technological and materialistic concerns of a rising burgher class. In the long run, it is also true, the techniques and methods of exemplification by experimentally verifiable detail are inimical to the arts which they were first meant to serve. It has repeatedly been pointed out that what might be called the allegorical method in its broader aspects—that is, the Augustinian view of the material and the literal as contingent upon the intelligible and the spiritual—was the great enemy of the scientific method for more than a thousand years. It confounded Copernican astronomy and sound philological criticism alike in its dramatic rejection of solipsism. Increasing exemplification has something to do with changes in theological style as well: with academic debates between realists and nominalists, the preaching of the friars, the agony of the *corpus* on the crucifix, and the attempts to prove the existence of God. For my own present purposes, fortunately, the question need be considered only within a narrow intellectual spectrum suggested by one medieval poem and its illustrations.

Among Kuhn's many acute observations about the illustrations of the *Roman* is the realization that the predominantly religious iconography of the thirteenth century impressed itself upon the illustrations of this great secular poem in two ways. In the first place, we shall find a certain amount of outright appropriation of Gothic icons. The standard treatment of Villenie in the manuscripts is very like that which we find in the medallions of the virtues and the vices of Amiens cathedral.[36] Oiseuse, as we shall

[36] Émile Mâle denies that the Amiens relief represents "Baseness," contending instead that it signifies "Harshness"—see *The Gothic Image* (New York, 1961),

see in the next chapter, is nothing more to the illustrators than a slightly pastoralized Luxuria. The various altars at which Amant from time to time prays are the Gothic altars of the fourteenth century (albeit adorned with pagan idols). In short, whenever the illustrators have at hand traditional iconographic materials to fit the theological drift of the poem at any given point—and there is always a theological drift, as well as the unrolling of the love story—they borrow them freely.

Secondly, influence of another sort, of a purely formal nature, can also be detected. For example, Kuhn noted that the *incipit* illustration in a number of manuscripts, showing the Dreamer in bed with Danger standing behind him, is strikingly similar to the formal arrangement of one of the commonest scenes in the religious iconography of the Gothic centuries: the Nativity. In Fig. 10, for example, the Dreamer corresponds to the typical form of the Virgin in her *accouchement*, with minor modifications, while Danger hovers nearby even as Joseph, in the cognate religious scene, stands guard over his wife. Other such formal echoes are not difficult to find. The Dreamer in bed with the swirling rose-tree—the substance of his dream—behind him is obviously formally influenced by the tree of Jesse motif, in which a tree swirls up from Jesse's reclining body. Other traditional religious scenes which Kuhn shows to be obvious formal antecedents of a number of the poem's more common illustrations include the Ascension, portraits of the Evangelists, Fortune's Wheel, and several others.[37]

The detection and documentation of such influence was, for Kuhn, a legitimate art-historical end in itself. It is regrettable that he failed to distinguish between significant iconographic borrowing and mere formal cliché, but his discoveries nonetheless suggest new ways of thinking about the stylistic history of the fourteenth century which deserve pursuit. From a purely negative point of view, as a sound lesson in iconographic exactitude, Kuhn's analysis of thirteenth-century Gothic influence provides a warning against making too much of any particular illustration

---

pp. 123ff. Such a contention seems very doubtful in light of the ample and unambiguous iconography of the figure of "Villenie" in the *Roman*, with which Mâle was apparently unfamiliar. A similar picture, borrowed no doubt from some copy of the *Roman*, appears in the illustrated MS of the *Roman de Fauvel*.

[37] "Die Illustration des Rosenromans," pp. 57ff.

without first examining it for signs of cliché. From a positive point of view, it provides a valuable touchstone for the kind of stylistic analysis necessary to examine the changes in painting and in literature which I have been discussing. For what Kuhn discovered about the legacy of thirteenth-century art to that of the fourteenth suggests a general truth about the art of the Gothic period viewed as a whole and about the stylistic difference between the *Roman* and the *Canterbury Tales*. One is lapidary, implastic, static, abstract; the other is fleshy, malleable, verisimilar.

Early Gothic art is an art of stone. The dominant artistic concerns in the north of France in the thirteenth century were those of ecclesiastical architecture, its structure and its decoration. It was the age of the great cathedrals, and the major art of the cathedrals was masonry. In its service were the other arts, painting and sculpture in particular, and their role was to decorate the stone with complex patterns of meaningful beauty. As arts, they were hardly less contingent than book painting itself.

The dominance of architectural techniques had important implications for manuscript illumination of all kinds right up until the fifteenth century. This dominance especially influenced the form of book illustration. "Thus it was long before French Gothic painting freed itself from the former dominant technique of architecture, and Gothic painters ceased enclosing their scenes and figures in little decorative frames of pinnacles and flying buttresses only in the fifteenth century."[38] A good example of this kind of influence can be detected in Fig. 11 (Bibliothèque nationale MS fr. 1567), which reproduces a number of the most striking features of Gothic architectural detail in the painted frames which encase and for the most part separate Amours, the Dreamer, and Danger. Even more common is the practice of framing the illustrations in quatrefoils of various kinds (Figs. 2 and 12), a device strikingly reminiscent of one of the most popular forms of decoration in the Gothic cathedrals, the quatrefoil medallions. As is the case with some of the architectural decoration itself, book paintings of this sort frequently display a playful tendency toward the spatial strictures of the frame. In Fig. 11 the Dreamer's bedclothes fall out and over the frame, while in Fig. 12 both pairs

[38] Robert Grinnell, "The Theoretical Attitude towards Space in the Middle Ages," *Speculum*, XXI (1946), 146.

of feet, as well as the god of Love's bow and wings, violate the encirclement of the quatrefoil in a way which pushes it into the background without the techniques of linear perspective.

Characteristically, the illustrations of the earlier fourteenth century present frozen abstractions against a tight, unyielding, panchromatic background composed of geometrical designs (Figs. 1, 2, 6, 12). Such illustrations are idealized in that they present concepts in the abstract rather than in exemplification in a spatial continuum. Indeed there is no possibility of such "realistic" exemplification in the early part of the century, since the illustrations provide neither spatial continuum, as Professor Robertson pointed out, nor any suggestion of finite duration. The figure of Hate with her knife to her breast in the beautiful Geneva manuscript which once belonged to the Duke of Berry is captured forever within the vise of her idealized background. She has always been there, and she always will be. She is not merely timeless—"older than the rocks among which she sits"—but, since there are no rocks or any explicitly verifiable context of finite duration, she is outside time. She is an idea. Not so with the pitiable Tristesce who sits within a little *hortus conclusus* in Douce 364. She, too, is an idea, but an idea with a local habitation, an idea married to the finite and temporal exemplification of the poor girl in the garden. She may, we feel, one day grow old and perhaps less sad. She may even get up and walk out of the garden. She is no longer a lapidary figure, a decoration from a Gothic cathedral. She is, instead, a very *triste* girl, a figure from Chaucer rather than from Guillaume de Lorris.

Kuhn, in common with many art historians of his generation, put a high premium on the illusion of movement which the development of pictorial space made possible. Such movement was in his eyes the great technical achievement of the end of the fourteenth century. "MS 19195 in the Bibliothèque Nationale makes a step forward," he says. "The figures really begin to move from left to right."[39] While it is difficult to agree with Kuhn's implication that the late Gothic painters of the *Roman* sought above all to create the illusion of motion in their pictures, there is no doubt

[39] "Die Illustration des Rosenromans," p. 36. Kuhn presumably means Bibliothèque nationale, MS fr. 19156; MS fr. 19195 does not contain the *Roman de la Rose*.

that in special circumstances they were interested in representing complex action. The special case was the initial folio of the manuscript, the "frontispiece" as it were, frequently the most carefully illustrated page of the book. It was here that the illustrators often undertook to show the entire sequence of action of the poem, from the time the Dreamer lay asleep in bed until he reached the Garden of Deduit. To do this, they employed two discrete but cognate techniques.

The first technique was continuous narration, in the manner of the so-called Vienna Genesis. The principle of continuous narration is that a series of temporally successive events is illustrated within the frame of a single picture, or in sequence without any frame.[40] Kuhn thought the first example of continuous narration in a manuscript of the *Roman* to be the *incipit* illustration of MS Gg. IV 6 in the Cambridge University Library, a manuscript of generally indifferent quality. The illustration takes up both columns at the top of the first folio. At the left the Dreamer lies in bed with the usual rosebush in the background. Next, in the same spatial continuum, he stands sewing up his sleeve. Finally, he stands holding a glove in his right hand, pointing up at the garden wall on which seven murals can be seen. As the language of my description probably suggests, the scene is to be "read" in a temporal order corresponding to the spatial order, from left to right —that is, in the linear direction of the reading eye. In spite of the fairly early introduction of the technique into the illustrations of the poem, however, there is a mere handful of fourteenth-century manuscripts which employ continuous narration, though its flamboyant use may be considered one of the hallmarks of the sumptuous manuscripts of the fifteenth century. It is difficult to account for Kuhn's high praise of this ancient technique, which is not characteristic of the most careful and expensive manuscripts of the poem during its heyday, except in terms of his inflated regard for pictorial movement.

In fact the typical fourteenth-century *incipit* illustrations convey the impression of complex action in a way which betrays no interest in movement at all: by means of the encadrement

---

[40] For a convenient discussion of the technique, see Kurt Weitzmann, "Narration in Early Christendom," *American Journal of Archaeology*, LXI (1957), 83-91.

sequence, the technique of modern strip cartoons. In the illustrations of the *Roman* the common four-part encadrement was obviously based on the practice, developed quite early, of having two parallel illustrations at the top of the first page—one showing the Dreamer in bed, the other Oiseuse seated in the garden. On one hand this diptych developed into the kind of elementary continuous narration found in two parts in the *incipit* illustration to MS Additional 31840 in the British Museum. On the other, it expanded the series into four parts—the Dreamer in bed, dressing, walking (or sewing up his sleeve), and coming to the garden wall—sealing them into four individual quatrefoil compartments in a block at the top of the page. A good example of this very common technique can be seen in Fig. 2, dating from mid-century. Here the spatial strictures inherent in the quatrefoil frame are in no way relieved; they are, on the contrary, made more severe by placing the individual illustrations together like tightly fitting tiles and surrounding them not with one heavy frame but with two. In light of the general technical sophistication of the illustration, such a technique can only reveal the deliberate choice of stasis over movement.

Both continuous narration and encadrement blocks were in fairly common use in various kinds of book illustration in the middle of the fourteenth century. Kuhn considered the former technique a great advance; yet his own evidence suggests that both techniques were being used during the same period in the ateliers of northern France. Kuhn's evidence also suggests that the finest, most careful, and most lavish *incipits* were being executed in block encadrement in a style which devalued movement and suggested static abstraction—a style, in short, which clearly did not prize complex exemplification and verisimilitude. It is only in the fancy manuscripts of the fifteenth century, perhaps under Netherlandish influence, that the "forward step" of continuous narration—actually a step backwards from the historical point of view—became the dominant technique in *Roman* iconography. Yet in some notably "realistic" illustrations of the high fifteenth century, such as those in MS fr. 24392, the most heavily illustrated exemplar of the poem in the huge collection of the Bibliothèque nationale, the encadrement technique survives.

The expected results of movement in continuous narration, the exploitation of pictorial space, and the depiction of realistic objects are logical relationships of space and time ill-fitted to traditional medieval allegory. The technique of pictorial abstraction, like that of literary abstraction, makes fewer such demands. For example, in Fig. 12 the literal action represented is the god of Love's firing on the Lover. In spite of the fact that Amours' bow is drawn, there is no tension of movement in the picture, and it is impossible to explain logically what is happening. The god's bow is drawn, yet it holds no arrow. The arrow is already in the Lover's breast. This is the logic of the dream-vision of Guillaume's poem, not the logic of Chaucer's verisimilitude in the *Canterbury Tales*.

I began this technical discussion of the broad stylistic history of the *Roman de la Rose* illustrations guided by Weitzmann's precept that iconography cannot be separated from style, and I shall in a moment attempt to invoke the style of the poem as well as that of its illustrations to correct certain misapprehensions about both. The question of style can lead us to examine the poem in that historical context which alone can offer the hope, at least, of its satisfactory understanding. The beautiful manuscripts of the fifteenth century, full of pictorial space, richness of detail, and a high degree of exemplification of action, are not better than their more primitive ancestors at illustrating the poem. They merely go about it in a different way. It may be argued, indeed, that they jut out like the Gothic mouldings in a reconstituted Norman church. We could wish for such a rich schedule of illustrations for the *Canterbury Tales* as we have for the *Roman* in the fifteenth-century Douce 364 or Harley 4425—alas, in vain—but with regard to the stylistic conventions of the poem they illustrated such pictures are anachronisms already. The fancy Renaissance courtier who is Amant in Harley 4425 is much further from Guillaume de Lorris' stylistic conception than the faceless, anonymous, universal *clerc* or *aucteur* of the fourteenth-century manuscripts, simply because he has ceased to be typical by becoming particular. He has a distinctive physiognomy, a distinctive wardrobe, and probably a distinctive personality.

It is, above all, the failure to discern the implications of incremental exemplification in Jean de Meun's part of the poem which has led to so much of the confusion about his handling of allegory. There is no question that the most elegant and influential attempt to deal with the love allegory of the poem remains C. S. Lewis' *The Allegory of Love*. One recent critic goes so far as to say that Lewis has "taught us how to read the poem"; it would probably be more accurate to call him our corrupting Aristotle. He has most recently corrupted, with regard to one specific and amusing aspect of the poem's iconography, even Rosemond Tuve, who in so many other respects has called us back from the siren voice of Lewis' brilliant *tour de force* to see the *Roman* as it actually is, or rather was. There is in the poem an abstraction named Bel Accueil who, according to Lewis, represents that aspect of the Lady's psychology receptive to the approaches of Amant. Guillaume de Lorris called Bel Accueil *un vallet*, a "young man," Chaucer's "lusty bachelor." Later on, in Jean's part of the poem, Bel Accueil, though still governing masculine pronouns, seems to be a lady. That is, Bel Accueil is incarcerated; Amant pines for "him" as he would for the Lady; and the Vekke teaches "him" the art of whores. Lewis uses this apparent discrepancy as an index of the difference in allegorical temper between the two poets, or rather as evidence that Jean de Meun knew nothing about allegory at all: "The one thing that he is not is an allegorist; he is as helpless with the dainty equivalences of Guillaume de Lorris as Dr. Johnson would have been among Pope's sylphs and gnomes." In particular Lewis chides Jean for confusing a psychological dimension of the Lady with the Lady herself. "He identifies Bialacoil with the heroine and describes female conduct accordingly: the name, with the masculine pronouns and adjectives which it demands, survives to remind us of the absurdity."[41]

Rosemond Tuve must have been pondering this judgment when she examined and described the lovely Douce MS 364 in the Bodleian. She ascribes to the brilliant illustrator of that manuscript, a delightful production unknown to Kuhn, the same "failures" and "ineptitudes" which Lewis had already ascribed to Jean de Meun and for precisely the same, or closely cognate, reasons. One of the illustrator's quirks in this manuscript is his love of labels; he puts little name-tags on his painted figures with a consistency found in no other manuscript of the poem. Fig. 13 shows, left to right, Bel Accueil, Amant, and Danger. Bel Accueil, though obviously a dandy, is a "lusty bachelor." The subject of

---

[41] *Allegory of Love*, pp. 137, 140.

Fig. 14 is the arrival of Venus, who forces the demure Bel Accueil to grant Amant's wish to kiss the rosebud as a pledge of hope. In the four folios which separate these two illustrations Bel Accueil, like an early-day Orlando, has changed sex. The illustrator, says Miss Tuve echoing Lewis, has botched Bel Accueil. He has painted him "not as the psychological abstraction he is, but rather as the Lover's lady, pure and simple." She then documents other alleged iconographic *gaffes* and argues, not entirely lucidly, that we have here an "obfuscation of the psychological allegory, precluding ironic implications or universalized meaning," a mingling of straight narrative with allegory.[42] The obfuscation, however, is of a different sort.

Anyone who looks at Douce 364 must be loath to see in its brilliant illustrator an uncomprehending bumbler. Has he really, like Jean de Meun, forgotten that Bel Accueil is a man, or, faced with Jean's botched allegory, is he simply making the best of a bad job? The temptation to explain unusual iconographic features of medieval illuminations as the artist's misunderstanding of the text seems to be almost irresistible to many students of medieval art and literature, although, on the face of it, it is likely that a medieval painter knew as much about how to read medieval poetry as a modern philologist. Kuhn, when he encountered a large number of examples of sexual metamorphosis like this one in Douce 364, was able to dismiss the problem with a single word: "nonsense."[43] It is true that examples of scribal sloppiness are common enough in medieval manuscripts, including manuscripts of the *Roman de la Rose*. Yet Douce 364 is no piece of hack work; the general impression which its rich iconographic schedule gives is one of sumptuous, loving care. Its pattern of illustrations follows none of the iconographic stereotypes established by the French artists of the fourteenth century. If the difference in the treatment of Figs. 13 and 14 is a mistake, a misunderstanding, or a "breakdown of the allegory," the aberrations of this otherwise painstaking artist are spectacular indeed. Not only does Bel Accueil appear both as a man and a woman, but he appears as four different people—an important fact which Miss Tuve failed to mention. He is one young man on folios 23 and 24, a completely

[42] *Allegorical Imagery*, pp. 322, 323.
[43] "Die Illustration des Rosenromans," p. 62.

different man on folio 95; one young woman on folios 28 and 92, another on folio 97. What the illustrator had in mind is perhaps difficult for us to grasp, but it certainly cannot be an equation of Bel Accueil with "the Lady, pure and simple." The illustrations are vivid testimony, in fact, that there is no "Lady, pure and simple." The "Lady" is Lewis' invention and a reduction of limited usefulness. Far from illustrating the artist's fumbling with the allegory, the pictures show an extraordinary sensitivity to the psychological abstraction of Fair Welcome which, after all, embraces a spectrum ranging from the shy friendliness of a school-girl to the "come hither" of a practiced siren. Though masculine in gender, such *accueil* is often distinctly feminine in implication and, consequently, is sometimes feminine when exemplified by the artist. Our illustrator seems to be tactfully respectful of contexts. Bel Accueil is a man when talking to Danger, a cowed girl before Venus, and both a man and a woman at school with the polymorphous Vekke.

Bel Accueil, may I repeat it, is a concept, an abstract idea. Ideas do not have "sex," though in Romance tongues they do have grammatical gender. Grammatical gender, as native English-speakers never cease to learn with amazement or amusement, need predicate no psychological implications—for example, *le hareng*, but *la morue*. The figure of Philosophy in Boethius' *Consolation* is called "Lady," but this is for grammatical, not psychological, reasons. "He makes Philosophy in the figure of a woman, because both in Greek and Latin the word is feminine."[44] The great Lady of the *Roman* is not, by the way, the rosebud; Lady Reason in the *Roman* is very similar, for both Guillaume and Jean, to Lady Philosophy in the *Consolation of Philosophy*. All the "characters" in the *Roman*, including Amant, are ideas, not people. Some of them are open to a degree of exemplification which permits, in the iconography, sexual metamorphosis. We can find, if we wish, a fourteenth-century manuscript, carefully done, depicting Bel Accueil both as a man and a woman on the same page.[45] Amant,

[44] *Saeculi noni auctoris in Boetii consolationem philosophiae commentarius*, ed. E. T. Silk (Rome, 1935), p. 7.

[45] Tournai, Bibliothèque communale, MS C. I., fol. 30ᵛ. On this MS see E. Langlois, "Gui de Mori et le *Roman de la Rose*," *Bibliothèque de l'Ecole de Chartes*, LXVIII (1907), 249-71; and Lucien Fourez, "Le Roman de la Rose de la Bibliothèque de la Ville de Tournai," *Scriptorium*, I (1946-47), 213-39.

a *fol amoureux*, has a firm sexual identity, as do many of the other abstractions: Amours, Venus, Faussemblant, Constrainte, Abstinence. But where there is no very firm guide of euhemeristic tradition—Venus has to be a woman, after all—or simple allegorical insistence—friars have to be men—the scribes choose their own paths, departing more and more from grammatical gender as part of the increasing pattern of exemplification characteristic of fifteenth-century style. It is no more possible to have a male concept than it is to have a pink equation, and the illustrators knew as much. Thus there are both male and female depictions of Viellesce, Papelardie, Povrete, Jalousie, Amis, Malebouche, Honte, and other characters in the *Roman* for whom grammatical gender and its pronominal paraphernalia have provided a kind of working sexual identification.

The difficulties which C. S. Lewis and Rosemond Tuve find in these Bel Accueils, one made of words and the other of paint, have nothing to do with the abstract nature of allegory, as they both supposed. It rather concerns these very questions of stylistic change which have engaged our attention in this chapter. For Guillaume de Lorris, Bel Accueil was a pure abstraction, a quality. Jean de Meun took up this same abstraction, along with its grammatical gender, and exemplified its behavior in a way that showed he really knew what it meant. Fair Welcome, that elusive and mercurial sexual response which Amant so desperately seeks, is today one thing, tomorrow another. It is perfectly true that Guillaume de Lorris, had he finished his poem, would never have shown us anything but the one stone icon of Bel Accueil. It is likewise true that no illuminator of the early fourteenth century would show us a half-dozen ways of looking at that icon. But this emphatically does not mean that Jean de Meun (and the fifteenth-century painter) knew less about allegory than Guillaume de Lorris (and his fourteenth-century illustrator), or that he misunderstood the allegory. We have here instead some striking testimony to the kinds of stylistic change evident in the exemplified verisimilitude of Chaucer and the Limbourgs. We do not say that Chaucer "misunderstood" Faussemblant when he exemplified that quality in the Pardoner and the friar in the Summoner's Tale, or that he destroyed Jean de Meun's "dainty equivalences." We remark instead a striking change in style.

III

The last generation of readers who could read the *Roman* for pleasure and profit without humanistic self-consciousness was that of Geoffrey Chaucer, through whose works Jean's old poem echoes and re-echoes. Even as Chaucer lay dying there was taking place one of those *affaires* for which the French are famous: the well-known Quarrel of the *Roman de la Rose*. I say well-known, not well-understood, for it still awaits a thorough explication of its historical setting and significance. The attackers of Jean de Meun at this time were two minor poets: Christine de Pisan, and Jean Gerson, the Chancellor of Paris. Christine's part in the Quarrel has been rather inflated, one suspects, by modern feminists and should probably not be taken too seriously. Rosemond Tuve, one of Christine's greatest admirers, could only consider that her part in the affair was a joke, a sort of whimsical pose. Taken seriously, her arguments and her manner show the acumen (in the words of Jean de Montreuil) of "the Greek whore who dared to write against Theophrastus."[46] But Jean Gerson is not joking when he says he would burn the last copy of the poem were it worth a thousand pounds.[47] Furthermore, he is no laughable person; on the contrary, in the intellectual history of his period he rightly deserves a position of prominence—he was a great moralist, a great preacher, one of the seminal minds of conciliar theory.

That, to any disinterested student, it is apparent that Gerson was thoroughly trounced in the Quarrel by Pierre Col and Jean de Montreuil is irrelevant. We can diagnose in him a marked case of another kind of stylistic change. He is the first modern critic of the *Roman*, the first person to whom it must patiently be explained that Jean de Meun was a "true Catholic, the most profound theologian of his day, versed in every science which the human mind can grasp."[48] With the passing of the *ancien régime*, Gerson's criticism lost only its direction, not its content, and there

---

[46] Jean de Montreuil, *Opera*, ed. Ezio Ornato (Turin, 1963), I, 220; Ornato cites Cicero, *De natura deorum*, I, 93.

[47] "Sermo contra luxuriam: Dominica IV Adventus," in *Opera Omnia*, ed. Ellies du Pin (Antwerp, 1706), III, col. 931.

[48] C. F. Ward, ed., *The Epistles on the Romance of the Rose and other Documents in the Debate* (Chicago, 1911), p. 29. The phrase is Gontier Col's.

is poignant irony in the fact that more than one leading authority on the *Roman* has extolled Jean de Meun for the very obscenities which the Chancellor of Paris execrated.[49] For modernists Jean's voyaging mind seems to break free from the strictures of bland medieval Catholicism to articulate brave new doctrines of life and love. For example, he is supposed to have believed that sexual intercourse is "the chief manifestation of the goodness, the love, the overwhelming bounty of God."[50] (The Incarnation, the Passion, sacramental grace, all this, presumably, was small beer for Jean.) Indeed why bother with God at all? "For Jean love is simply an expression of the reproductive instinct, and this he regards as wholly and necessarily good. In his view the reproductive instinct is something to be followed at all times and in all circumstances, something that ought not to be confined by any regulations or institutions."[51]

The superficial literary criticism of recent years has corrupted even serious scholars of the intellectual history of the thirteenth century, who, not without astonishment, stretch a putative Averroism or *scolastique courtoise* very thin indeed to cover the vast chasm of sensualism, "Christian phallicism," naturalism—in two flavors, ordinary and bourgeois—and mere heresy which their literary colleagues assure them is Jean de Meun's *Roman*. But the multitude of sins thus covered are not those of Jean de Meun.

Jean was a sinner and even, perhaps, a notorious one, though his personal moral failings have no particular relevance for his poem. He has, however, left a long and moving *Testament* which is in part a penitential meditation on his sinfulness. He there laments having in his youth written some little poems (*dits*), of which he now repents. With regard to the *Testament* and to this particular reference in it, critics have typically been tempted by alternative unlikely explanations. They have denied that Jean de Meun wrote the poem, or they have claimed that he is here confessing, in his monkish old age, the sin of having written the *Roman*. Two points need be made here, even at the risk of digression. In the first place, the *Testament* is almost beyond question the work of Jean de Meun, chief architect of the *Roman de la*

---

[49] See Robertson, *Preface to Chaucer*, p. 363.

[50] Gunn, *Mirror of Love*, p. 495.

[51] Norman Cohn, "The World View of a Thirteenth-Century Intellectual," Inaugural Lecture of the Professor of French (Durham, 1961), p. 16.

Rose. The manuscript evidence is massive, and by all methods of authenticating authorship save explicit internal evidence, the poem is Jean's. In dozens of fourteenth-century manuscripts of the *Roman*, with which the *Testament* is very frequently made up, it is ascribed to him, and its recent, careful editor agrees with the ascription.[52] The only negative "evidence" is that the *Testament* "impresses one [i.e., Professor Gunn] as inferior in poetic quality to the *Roman de la Rose* and as dissimilar in intellectual quality and attitude."[53] It impresses me, for what it is worth, as a fine poem which recapitulates in a formally theological manner all the major concerns of the *Roman de la Rose.* Secondly, the vain *dits* for which Jean de Meun apologized can hardly be imagined to include the *Roman*, as Pierre Col sufficiently pointed out more than five and a half centuries ago.[54] Petrarch, with heavy sarcasm, could call the *Roman* a *libellus*; none could call it a bagatelle.

A more interesting passage in the *Testament* concerns the manner in which Jean de Meun thought readers ought to gloss poets, whom he warmly if partially admired. It is indeed a plea, not without eloquence, on behalf of all Christian poets: he asks that the reader gloss their poems charitably unless they contain obvious errors, by which he clearly means errors of doctrine or morals:

> Nuls ne doit des aucteurs parler senestrement,
> Se leur dit ne contient erreur appertement,
> Car tant estudierent pour nostre sauvement
> C'om doit leurs dis gloser moult favorablement.[55]

Presumably the audience of the *Roman* was able to read it "moult favorablement" for something over a century, during which time Jean de Meun enjoyed a wide reputation as a moralist in morally conservative circles; and we must attempt to understand the nature of their reading. It clearly did not involve any farfetched allegorical interpretations. Molinet's understanding of the poem is as alien to Jean's meaning as that of later generations who too slavishly accept the fabliau which lies barely concealed beneath the botanical plot. Rosemond Tuve, with brilliant perception, has

---

[52] See the introductory discussion in the edition of Aimée Céleste Bourneuf, "Le Testament de Jean de Meun (The 'Testament' of Jean de Meun)" (Fordham diss., 1956).

[53] *Mirror of Love*, p. 30*n.*

[54] Ward, *Epistles on the Romance*, p. 61.

[55] *Testament*, ed. Bourneuf, ll. 77-80.

seen that all Molinet really succeeded in doing to Jean's poem by "moralizing" it was to make it what it had never been before— a dirty book.[56] It still is one, the lubricious French novel par excellence. No wonder the recent English translation can boast truthfully on its paper cover that it is the first to be published "complete"—all the juicy bits left in—when its learned editor assures the reader that the *Roman* is a veiled autobiography of a free-swinging, free-loving poet named Jean de Meun, an account of his exploits with "the first important pregnant heroine in European literature."[57]

The *Roman de la Rose* is ironic. It is the chronicle of a hero who is neither wise nor admirable, a young man who, overcome with carnal infatuation (Lechery, as the Middle English translation puts it), rejects Reason and embraces false courtesy, hypocrisy, and wicked counsel to achieve the sordid "heroism" of a seduction. His close friends and helpers include the most notorious old whore in medieval literature and a hypocritical friar of diabolically evil character. His sworn "enemy" (his word) is Reason, whom Guillaume de Lorris had called the "daughter of God" and who is obviously the close cousin of Lady Philosophy in the *Consolation of Philosophy*. The course of action which he follows in the poem is the typical path of sin as described by innumerable medieval psychologists. As Charles Dahlberg has shown, what happens in the *hortus deliciarum* of the *Roman* is essentially what happened in the Garden of Eden: Reason is overthrown by Passion, which has enslaved Amant.[58] As Milton puts it, rephrasing a tropological interpretation of the Fall of Man in currency since Origen's time,

> Reason in man obscur'd, or not obeyd,
> Immediately inordinate desires
> And upstart Passions catch the Government
> From Reason, and to servitude reduce
> Man till then free.
>
> (*Paradise Lost*, xii, 86ff.)

[56] *Allegorical Imagery*, p. 245.

[57] C. W. Dunn's Introduction to *The Romance of the Rose*, tr. H. W. Robbins (New York, 1962), p. xxv.

[58] "Macrobius and the Unity of the *Roman de la Rose*," *Studies in Philology*, LVIII (1961), 573-82.

The danger in writing about archetypal sin in a dramatic way, apparently, is that literary critics some centuries removed may not clearly grasp the moral hierarchies on which dramatic action must be grounded. Those who, with credible perversity, turned Milton into a Satanist are fortunately in full retreat; but Jean's raucous admirers (or attackers) who have hailed him as the "Voltaire of the thirteenth century" (or an "immoralist") are still firmly entrenched in the field, blocking access to his poem and obfuscating his poetic techniques.

For Jean's originality, such as it is, lies neither in his theology nor in his sexology, which are at least as old as St. Paul and St. Augustine. It lies rather in the breadth and boldness of his ironic intent, which can be compared with that, say, of Fielding in *Jonathan Wild*. In a typically suggestive remark, Lewis opined that Guillaume de Lorris meant to end his poem with the "traditional palinode"—that is, with the rejection of *fol amour* by the hero and his return to Reason. Jean runs in precisely the opposite direction, for all he is worth, extending the "greatness" of his Lover's activities out over thousands of lines of exemplary commentary until it culminates in the ludicrous obscenities with which the poem ends.

Of course the *Roman* never ceases to be a love story. Lewis was probably even right to praise the effectiveness of Guillaume's treatment of "falling in love," conventional as it is; while formulated in the terms of a commonplace medieval moral psychology, it remains largely accessible to the modern reader. Jean was able to take up the rosebud fiction where Guillaume left off, for it presented a discussion in depth of the stages of *fol amour* entirely suited to his end. For Jean such carnal infatuation was the perfect vehicle, the perfect icon, for the various kinds of rose gathering to which fallen human nature is prone. It was suited to his purposes, perhaps, because of its pervasive topicality, its ubiquity and, in literary terms, its conventionality. In the *Testament*, where Jean de Meun deals briefly in schematic fashion with the seven capital vices, he devotes as much attention to the vice of *luxure* as he does to all the rest put together. This is not, we may assume, because he considered lust more corrupting than pride, but because "Cilz pechies est a tous communaus et moiens." Through the five senses lust strikes us all, high and low, Christian and Jew, wise and foolish; it retreats only from the deathbed.

Jean de Meun cannot be credited with fathering "Christian phallicism," whatever that is, except as part of his comic exemplification of original sin. On the other hand, there is some originality in his method. Typically, the medieval dream-vision leads an at first uncomprehending narrator from ignorance to understanding or from despair to consolation. Such is the plot of the *Consolation of Philosophy*—the most important medieval dream-vision and the most pervasive in its literary influence—*Le Pèlerinage de la vie humaine* and *Piers Plowman*. Jean de Meun follows the typical course of the dream-vision in that he exposes his dreamer-narrator to the doctrines of various allegorical abstractions, but, atypically, he makes the hero seem increasingly stupid in his perverse rejection of good counsel for bad. Petrarch, who apparently found the device, and indeed the whole poem, tedious, makes a *bon mot* to the effect that the Dreamer never really wakes up: "Somniat iste tamen dum somnia visa renarrat/Sopitoque nihil vigilans distare videtur."[59] Lewis is again at least close to the truth when he says that Jean's *significatio* "is hardly worth the finding."[60] It is not that Jean has no *significatio*, or that it was a trivial one in the eyes of his contemporaries. It is simply that Jean's fame as a literary figure must surely rest upon his new bottle rather than his old wine.

So much for the relationship of this poem with the tradition of the dream-vision. Perhaps it may be fruitful as well to consider Jean's poem in the light of the developing conventions of medieval morality. In its basic structure, the *Roman* is at least as old as Prudentius' *Psychomachia*, with which it can be fruitfully compared.[61] The *Psychomachia* presents, with many extensive secondary diversions and rather fancier costuming, the kind of tug-of-war between right and wrong which Jean could have found

[59] *Opera quae extant omnia* (Basel, 1554), III, 114; Pierre de Nolhac suggests, in *Pétrarque et l'humanisme*, 2nd ed. (Paris, 1907), II, 228 and *n*, that Petrarch may have known the *Roman* only at second hand.

[60] *Allegory of Love*, p. 138.

[61] See in particular Hans Robert Jauss, "Form und Auffassung der Allegorie in der Tradition der *Psychomachia*," *Medium Aevum Vivum, Festschrift für Walther Bulst* (Heidelberg, 1960), pp. 179-206.

nearer home in the *Théophile* of his antifraternal colleague Rute-beuf. There is so much flesh on Jean's poem that we may forget it has bones; but the skeleton, when finally exposed, is that of a morality play. The god of Love in the *Roman* has an alluring mythographic exoticism about him, but his line is scarcely distinguishable from that of the vices in the *Castle of Perseverance*. Indeed Oiseuse, the keeper of the keys of Deduit's *société joyeuse*, actually makes an appearance in the French moral drama of the late Middle Ages. Along with various demonic siblings like Despit and Orgeuil, she is one of the members of Lucifer's train in the Burgundian *Passion de Sémur*.[62] Jean's Lover is a kind of picaresque Everyman, a Hercules at the crossroads who consistently chooses the wrong road. Unlike Everyman's final penitential awareness of his own perversity, however, Amant's drama ends with the obscene and blasphemous rape of a rosebush. Unlike Hercules he is a pushover for the forces of sensuality. All this suggests another aspect of Jean's irony which has been too long neglected, and that is its rich comedy. The scene in which the lecherous Lover reprimands Lady Reason for smutty talk achieves the comic *plateau* of the best of Chaucer.

Such, in essence, is the characterization of the *Roman de la Rose* which a study of its iconography suggests and supports. It is not, of course, a complete characterization. In spite of recent attempts to find in Jean's poem a taut, not to say remorseless, unity, I remain unconvinced that he has achieved, or indeed attempted, anything more than a loose poetic structure. There is much in the poem, it seems to me, that is half encyclopedia and half versified raree show. Dunn draws a nice analogy between the structure of a Gothic cathedral and the Gothic structure of this poem: all the stonework fits, but it does not all bear weight. The girders of Jean's poem have apparently been too long obscured by its façade or, perhaps, by too superficial a study of the façade decoration. In the following chapters I shall attempt to redirect attention to the main lines of Jean's poem—the bold, clear tracings which the miniatures suggest.

[62] Ed. Emile Roy, in *Mystère de la Passion en France du XIVe au XVIe siècle* (Dijon, 1903).

CHAPTER TWO

The *Hortus Deliciarum*

HE *Roman* begins with a conventional situation in medieval literature. The narrator tells us he is in bed reading a book, and then recites a dream which has been inspired or suggested by the book he has read. In the fourteenth century, the bedtime reading of the *Roman* itself would inspire more than one dream-vision, but Guillaume's dreamer has just been reading a rather severer work: Macrobius' *Commentary on the Dream of Scipio*. Against those who say that dreams are merely fables and lies Guillaume de Lorris offers the testimony of Macrobius:

> Mais l'en puet teus songes songier
> Qui ne sont mie mençongier,
> Ainz sont apres bien aparant.

In its context Guillaume's citation of Macrobius is not merely an invitation to see his poem as a moral allegory like the *Somnium Scipionis*; it is also a playfully ironic indication of his subject matter. For the definition laid down by Macrobius in the chapter cited by Guillaume makes it perfectly clear that from Amant's point of view the dream which composes the *Roman* is no dream at all, but a phantasm, a nightmare (*insomnium*).[1] According to Macrobius, erotic dreams, in which "a lover dreams of possessing his sweetheart or of losing her"—the very subject of the allegory of the rose—are without significance. Charles Dahlberg, who was the first scholar to make this important connection, argues persuasively that the *Somnium Scipionis* thus becomes a valuable index of the entire poem's unity; for Jean de Meun continues to extend the thin metaphor of the rose as an *insomnium*, culminating, with a grotesque flourish, in the rape of a rosebush.[2] What Guillaume has done rather cleverly in the opening lines of the *Roman* is to prepare his audience for serious moral allegory with

---

[1] *Somnium Scipionis*, i, iii.

[2] "Macrobius and the Unity of the *Roman de la Rose*." Cf. the crude humor about such erotic dreams which "ne sont que fantasies" in *L'Amant rendu Cordelier*, ed. A. de Montaiglon (Paris, 1881), pp. 22-23.

the citation from an eminent *auctor*, indeed the standard *auctor* on dream allegories, and at the same time to sow the seeds of the central irony of the poem—that the principal concerns of the hero are *interpretationis indigna*. There is a whisper of this same irony in Chaucer's Nun's Priest's Tale, where a lecherous rooster, despite his academic knowledge, refuses to believe in the figurative meaning of dreams just as the Lover in the *Roman* refuses to believe the allegorical meanings of poets—both Chauntecleer and Amant live out nightmares. Nonetheless, for the understanding of the poem, both the events of the dream and their setting invite interpretation.

The garden of the *Roman*, to borrow a figure of speech from another age, is a *paysage moralisé*. It is not a "setting" in the ordinary sense or even a "symbolic setting"; for not only is it outside the coherences of geographical verisimilitude, but also it has no important reality at all apart from the moral action which it circumscribes. It is a convention like a chessboard, briefly animated by the activities for which it serves as a background and control, yet rigid, implastic, unmoving—depending for its vitality on the intelligibility of its conventional components and the uncertain if regulated movement of the pieces upon it. The analogy of the chessboard, which was suggested to me by the reworking of the materials of the *Roman* in the fourteenth-century *Echecs Amoureux*, is an inexact one; but it will perhaps make the point that it is what happens in the garden, rather than the garden itself, which is of chief interest. In the *Roman* we may think of Amant's pursuits as a chess game with opposing forces and, of course, alternatives of possible action. Amant's free will is crucial to the poem, for it predicates a moral responsibility which cannot be waived by an appeal either to philosophical or biological determinism. His choices are schematically organized into schools of opinion represented by his various teachers and advisers. There are in the garden both those who encourage his pursuit of the *bouton* and those who oppose it—advisers of one and another persuasion: Reason, Danger, Amours, the Vekke, Amis. Yet it is Amant who remains responsible for his "moves" and the reader who must pass judgment on their wisdom. For this last task, that of the reader to appraise Amant's love, the iconography of the garden offers numerous valuable suggestions. Yet the reader will be required to go beyond the discovery that the garden in the poem is a literary convention.

That the garden of the *Roman de la Rose* reflects the widespread classical *topos* of "idealized Nature" or the *locus amoenus* is a hoary truth but not a particularly useful one. The critics, having isolated the poetic figure, give Guillaume de Lorris high points for humanism, though they thus unintentionally obfuscate what the poet is actually doing. The Garden of Deduit, taken as a whole, is not in fact very similar to any *locus amoenus* of classical poetry; it is merely suggestive of one. On the other hand, it is markedly similar in its iconography to two biblical gardens, both of which present images of the earthly paradise. Amant does say that the garden is a "pleasant place," showing an awareness perhaps of the classical *topos*; but he specifically compares this pleasant place with the *paradis terrestre*. For this reason we may move directly on to talk about the poetic *topos* of the earthly paradise, seen in Christian perspective, without distorting the poem or stripping Guillaume of any humanistic laurel.

Historians of Christian spirituality tell us that medieval men longed for paradise as the exile pines for a distant homeland. They filled their world with images of the paradise for which they yearned—the spiritual Church itself, the hidden garden of the monastery, the *paradisus claustri*, and so on. The early Fathers and, in particular, the monastic authors of the high Middle Ages speak of paradise as their *patria* from which they are for a time exiled as pilgrims and strangers, wanderers and seafarers, a distant homeland accessible only by "angelic contemplation" through types.[3]

The image of paradise most accessible to them was naturally the Garden of Eden, the historical earthly paradise, the *locus amoenissimus in Oriente*:[4] an enclosed garden (such, etymologically, is the meaning of "paradise"), filled with a rich and varied

---

[3] The implications of the medieval veneration of the heavenly *patria* are very broad for many different classes of medieval literature; see the stimulating remarks of Jean Leclercq in *L'Amour des lettres et le désir de Dieu* (Paris, 1957), pp. 55ff. and the study by Garcia M. Colombas, *Paraíso y Vida Angélica, sentido escatológico de la vocación cristiana* (Montserrat, 1958).

[4] This definition, showing the Christian appropriation of the classical term, is that given in answer to the question "Quid est paradisus?" in the *Elucidarium* of Honorius of Autun, *Pat. lat.* 172, col. 1117.

abundance of trees and animals, with a luxuriant spring at its heart. It is hardly surprising, therefore, that when medieval poets sought to hold up before the eyes of their readers a vision of paradise they turned to the iconography of the terrestrial Eden. The garden painted in words by Guillaume de Lorris fits into a long literary tradition in which it commands a special place of its own. "The image of the earthly paradise haunts the *Roman de la Rose*," the historian of the paradise *topos* has recently written, "and the *Roman* haunts the literature of succeeding centuries."[5] Guillaume's garden is indeed a convention; it was used by Andreas Capellanus before him and by Geoffrey Chaucer after him, among a host of others. Its affinities with the terrestrial paradise are everywhere apparent, but its interpretation always presents ambiguous possibilities. What does Guillaume's garden mean? Traditionally, says C. S. Lewis, the garden "means Love; in Guillaume it is changed slightly and made to mean the life of the court, considered as the necessary sphere or field for love's operations."[6]

The identification of the garden with the courtly life, which has been accepted without demur by more than one reader of *The Allegory of Love*, is very curious. Does what happens in Guillaume's rose garden really reflect what happens, or conceivably could or should happen, in "the life of the court"? Let us forget for a moment that we know absolutely nothing about Guillaume de Lorris save for what Jean de Meun tells us, and that the "forty years" time lapse between them of which Jean writes is probably about as precise a measure of duration as the "forty years" the children of Israel wandered in the desert. Let us further pretend, with the writers of innumerable literary histories and encyclopedia articles, that Guillaume actually was writing his poem in the late 1230's. A final leap of the imagination will place Guillaume de Lorris at court—his local court, that of the young French king, Louis IX, recently come into his majority. Our courtly Guillaume *could* have been there, since Louis' courtiers "were mostly Frenchmen from the Orléanais, the Ile de France, Picardy, and Champagne."[7] The young Orléanais poet, gathering materials

---

[5] A. Bartlett Giamatti, *The Earthly Paradise and the Renaissance Epic* (Princeton, 1966), p. 66.

[6] *The Allegory of Love*, p. 119.

[7] Charles Petit-Dutaillis, *The Cambridge Medieval History*, vi, 334.

for his book, observes, learns, and takes stock of "the life of the court." Of what does such a life consist? If we can believe the extraordinarily rich and diverse accounts of eyewitnesses, it consists largely of sermons, Scripture study, and deep theological consultations between the young saint who sits beneath the canopy of fleurs-de-lys and his courtiers. The royal family, including perhaps the King's sister, one day to be venerated as the "blessed Isabel," debates questions of abstract morality. The courtiers—some mitred, some tonsured, a few in civil dress—vie for the king's ear. Who are these men? Famous theologians like William of Auvergne or Matthew of Vendôme; pious souls such as Geoffrey of Beaulieu, William of Chartres or Eudes Rigaud; a future pope, Guy Foulquoi.

With this experience behind him, Guillaume concludes that "the life of the court" is the "necessary sphere or field of love's operations" and sits down to write about it. Understandably, perhaps, he describes what he has seen in terms of a paradisal garden. One is admitted to this life by Idleness. The king here is Mirth, or idle pleasure, and his courtiers spend their time in dalliance and dancing. Then everybody fornicates on the grass. Lady Reason, "God's daughter," is afforded all the respect in this sunny principality elsewhere granted to lunatics.

We can easily enough find poems in which the "joy of court" is used emblematically to suggest the vain pomps of the world, but the *Roman* is not one of them. The view that Guillaume's paradisal garden means the life of the court—any court, let alone the extraordinary French court under Louis IX—seems to me untenable, mistaking not only the nature of court life in the thirteenth century but also the nature of the terrestrial paradise from which the image of the garden of Love is taken. I am far from disagreeing with Lewis that the garden is a poetic façade for real discursive content, but its meaning must surely be sought in the realm of shared public myth rather than in private intuition.

In the first place, the garden of the *Roman* is not the same as the terrestrial paradise, merely like it in accidental ways. Amant says that he thought he was in *paravis terrestre*, but Amant is more than a little stupid. The pair of literary gardens are alike in two principal respects: in their formal iconography and in the drama which is acted out within their walls. Both are characterized by abundant and diverse sensuous *things*, and calamities occur in both gardens. Adam plucks an apple; Amant, the *bouton*. The strictures on the *Roman*'s unhappy garden, everywhere implicit beneath the glittering description of Guillaume de Lorris, are made explicit when Genius, late in Jean de Meun's continuation, condemns the garden as illusory, fading, and unreal. But how did Guillaume de Lorris think of the historical Eden with which his Lover confuses the Garden of Deduit at the beginning of the *Roman*?

To begin to answer such a question involves sketching the venerable exegetical tradition of the tropological Fall of man. According to this ancient spiritual interpretation of Genesis, the meaning of the parable of the Fall to the individual Christian is as a paradigm of all sins, revealing the seduction of Reason (Adam) by Sensuality (Eve) through sinful and idolatrous preoccupation with *things*. The garden is accordingly the world, the sphere of the individual Christian's daily contact, for good or ill, with things. How then are we to view the beautiful *choses* in the Garden of Deduit—the pursuit of which is the entire plot of the *Roman* —or for that matter, the beautiful things in Eden? How we interpret Guillaume's use of the paradise *topos* depends not only upon a tradition of secular poetry which he by no means slavishly follows, but also upon what he is likely to have thought about paradise, historical and tropological.

Guillaume might well have discussed such matters, during his hypothetical stay at the court of France, with no less a personage than William of Auvergne, Bishop of Paris and one of Louis' most trusted courtiers. At a recent French colloquy on humanism in medieval poetry it was suggested that reference to William's works—he was, seemingly, a strict contemporary of Guillaume— might help to elucidate the poem, and so, perhaps, it does.[8] For William wrote about the terrestrial paradise, and much else, at considerable length in the monumental *De Universo*. He discusses it not only from a purely theological point of view, but also as it appears in "the poets" as the Elysian Fields or Tempe. He sets out to explain why God did not repopulate paradise after the Fall, as he had created mankind to replace the fallen angels. The rea-

---

[8] See the remarks of R. P. Hubert in *L'Humanisme médiéval dans les littératures romanes du XIIe au XIVe siècle* (Paris, 1964), p. 166.

son he gives is that the physical delights of the garden "are extremely harmful to human souls, inebriating them and seducing them from truth and righteousness, and leading them to forget their Creator." In that case, why did he put Adam and Eve into the garden in the first place? Because until the Fall the physical delights of the garden were not harmful, being made so only in relation to the changed nature of man. At the Fall "all physical delights became for men the strong wine of drunkenness, aids to corruption, the sickness of our first parents." Thus "in the state in which men are, and have been since the time of the corruption of their first parents, dwelling in paradise has become extremely harmful and dangerous."[9]

In other words, the post-lapsarian terrestrial paradise—and we all, including Amant, live in a post-lapsarian world—is a type of testing ground in which each man succumbs to the temptations of "physical delights." Man's nature makes it dangerous for him; Guillaume de Lorris suggests the extreme danger of his garden with a variety of decorous yet obvious details: the sirens' songs, the trees from the land of Mahoun, the well of Narcissus. He reorganizes conventional materials for an immediate purpose, yet his garden remains the garden of the tropological Fall, the same garden which appears time and again in the poetry of "courtly love."

The main features of this literary garden in the *Roman* have been brilliantly analyzed by D. W. Robertson, who traces its classical and patristic background and shows how Guillaume moulds it to his purposes.[10] Of the essential correctness of Robertson's analysis of the poetic functions of this garden there is, in my opinion, no doubt, and I refer readers to its fuller explication in his pages. Since, however, his arguments have by no means been universally accepted and, with reference to this specific point, have even been controverted after a manner, it may be necessary briefly to deal with the objections raised against the tropological interpretation of Guillaume's garden. In essence these are two: such an interpretation implies the knowledge of "specialized"

[9] These opinions are expressed by William in the *De Universo*, I, pars I, cap. lviii, *Guillielmi Alverni Opera Omnia* (Paris, 1674), I, cols. 674-75.

[10] "The Doctrine of Charity in Mediaeval Literary Gardens," *Speculum*, xxvi (1951), 24-49.

Latin exegesis by vernacular authors, and it implies that the tech-
niques of spiritual interpretation applicable to the Bible can also
be used in the exegesis of "secular" literature. In short, his analy-
sis of the garden "involves such a radical revaluation" of the
Roman "as not to carry conviction."[11]

The critical ukase that radical revaluations lack conviction pre-
sumably admits no exceptions. I shall address myself instead to
the specific question of whether the garden *topos* which Robertson
claims to detect in the *Roman* could have been either accessible to
its authors or appropriate to their poem. Aside from what Jean de
Meun tells us we have absolutely no knowledge of Guillaume
de Lorris save that he had read Ovid and could write smooth
couplets. It seems likely that he came by his Ovid in the clerical
schools of Orléans, which made a specialty of confusing the secu-
lar and the religious in the explications of the great poet, but this
is speculation—an interesting speculation to which I shall shortly
return. About Jean de Meun we know rather more, indeed quite
a lot by comparison. Jean was a learned man, a clerk, a religious
poet of some merit, well grounded in Vergil, Ovid, Macrobius,
Saint Augustine, Boethius—all the giants of early medieval
culture.[12] Among the several scriptural exegetes whose works are
unquestioned sources of the *Roman* the most conspicuous is the
beatified Cistercian, Alain de Lille. (The most "specialized,"
presumably, is Guillaume de Saint-Amour, who made a kind of
specialty of antifraternal readings.) It is just possible through
strenuous exercise of the imagination and ruthless suppression of
historical probability to think of Guillaume de Lorris as a mono-
glot Frenchman who had never heard the Bible expounded, but
it is utterly fantastic to suggest that the tropological interpretation
of the Fall of man, which was still a commonplace to literate lay-
men in the seventeenth century, was somehow beyond the *maistre*
of the *Roman de la Rose.*

Granted that the authors of the poem may have been acquainted
with this "specialized" tradition of scriptural exegesis, what is

[11] K. Kee, "Two Chaucerian Gardens," *Mediaeval Studies*, XXIII (1961),
155*n.*

[12] The range of Jean's citation and allusion is impressive. See E. Langlois,
Origines et sources du Roman de la Rose (Paris, 1891), for a list, by no means
complete, of works used by Jean in the composition of the *Roman.*

there to suggest that they would bring it with them to the composition of a secular poem? To allow that the *Roman* is a "secular" work at all—Laurent de Premierfait, echoing Cicero on wisdom, called it a "vrai mappemonde de toutes choses humaines et devines"—is in the first place to yield to special pleading. Repeated assertions to the effect that Jean de Meun vigorously advances secular, bourgeois, anticlerical ideas reflect merely recent critical convention, not a mandate from the text. In any case Geoffrey Chaucer's Parson's Tale explains what I am here calling the tropological interpretation of Genesis, and the *Canterbury Tales*, while revealing a much deeper religious sense than has often been imagined, can hardly be called sacred art, pure and simple. In its context in Chaucer's poem, the Parson's account of the tropological Fall removes the flimsy veil from the love-in-a-garden *topos* which the poet has used with rich comic results in such tales as the Merchant's, where old January's garden is specifically compared to that of the *Roman*. Since, however, critics who will not grant a religious dimension to the masterwork of a Gothic theologian are unlikely to be convinced by the reworkings of his materials by a fourteenth-century lay follower, it may be necessary to consider more formal evidence. Fortunately, with specific regard to the allegorical meaning of the garden in the *Roman de la Rose*, such formal evidence does exist. First there is the witness of Pierre Col that Jean de Meun knew what Guillaume had been up to and that the characterization of the Garden of Deduit in Genius' sermon is therefore correct.[13] Since Pierre writes as a controversialist it may be argued that his testimony is partial, but it is at least suggestive. The unpublished prose gloss to the *Echecs Amoureux*, on the other hand, does not seem to be in any way a polemical piece; rather it seeks to explain and expound the vast humanistic riches of the *Echecs* in a context of moral instruction. This fascinating document, a major achievement of late medieval humanism which has been almost totally neglected by literary historians, discusses the "sens allégorique" of the Garden of Deduit in precisely the way Robertson's analysis of other literary gardens would lead us to suspect it might.[14]

[13] Ward, *The Epistles on the Romance*, p. 61.

[14] All five extant MSS of the *Echecs* gloss are in the Bibliothèque nationale in Paris: MSS fr. 143, 1508, 9197, 19114, and 24295. Of these the last appears

I have already made brief allusion to the Old French *Echecs Amoureux*, ascribed to the late fourteenth century. Still unedited and almost forgotten in histories of fourteenth-century French poetry, it can hardly be said to occupy a conspicuous place among the literary offspring of the *Roman*, though it does claim a modest footnote in the annals of English literature for having been "translated" by John Lydgate, who padded it extensively, as *Reson and Sensuallyte*. In close but not slavish imitation of its parent poem, the *Echecs* presents the situation of a young man walking through an allegorical garden of love where he is given good advice on one hand, and bad on the other. This garden is more obviously classical than many of its immediate forebears: Venus, Juno, and Pallas stand in its three corners. Amant, or rather L'aucteur, becomes a latter-day Paris. The learning of the *Echecs* poet, while no more profound than that of Jean de Meun, is flashier. He sticks closer to the mythographic handbooks, and his allegory begins to take on the schema often considered tedious in the great poets of the Renaissance. The only full manuscript of the *Echecs*, in Dresden, suffered very serious damage during the last World War, and it is unlikely that there will ever be a reliable edition of the poem.[15] But the long prose gloss, possibly composed by the poet himself, survives in five manuscripts; and it is of no less interest than the poem itself. Indeed this gloss is a crucial document in the controversy about the spiritual interpretation of secular poetry, for it is full of rich allegorical interpretations—hidden

---

to be the oldest (early fifteenth century) and the best text. mss 143 and 9197 are sumptuously illustrated, and I have as a rule made citations from the latter, despite its want of substantial portions of the text in 24295. Ernst Sieper, *Les Echecs Amoureux: Eine altfranzösische Nachahmung des Rosenromans und ihre englische Übertragung* (Weimar, 1898), p. 209, suggested the possible relevance of the gloss to the *Roman*, and published bits of it in the notes to his EETS edition of Lydgate's *Reson and Sensuallyte* (London, 1901), but it has generally been ignored by literary scholars. Art historians have shown greater interest in it—notably Jean Seznec in *La survivance des dieux antiques* (London, 1940)—but have confused the gloss with the poem itself. I have been greatly aided by the kind and expert advice of Dr. Marc-René Jung of Basel, who has recently examined the mss.

[15] There is, however, a fairly detailed summary of the poem from the Dresden ms by Stanley L. Galpin, "*Les Echez Amoureux*: A Complete Synopsis with Unpublished Extracts," *Romanic Review*, xi (1920), 283-307.

moral meanings to be harvested with the tools long used by scriptural exegetes—of the poem which it sets out to explain. Furthermore, it makes frequent and illuminating reference to our own poem, the *Roman de la Rose*.

The Picard exegete—he spent his youth, at least, in Arras—begins his book with an elaborate exposition of the principles of poetic fiction. There is little new in what he says, at least for anyone who has ever read Boccaccio's *De genealogia* and cognate works on exegetical theory stemming from *De doctrina christiana* of Saint Augustine. He sets out to explain why the author of the *Echecs* "says so many things which are not to be interpreted literally," and this leads him to the types of moral allegory, of which there are several: imaginary visions, as in Plato; ordinary dream-visions, like the *Somnium Scipionis*; and so forth. The principal type of allegory is that in which the poet can "introduce several characters who speak in turn according to their natures, as is done in the *Roman de la Rose*." (It is this elementary principle of Ciceronian decorum which has proved the *pons asinorum* of *Roman* criticism, beginning with Jean Gerson.) It is clear that for the exegete the content of the secular poem before him, like the content of those parts of the Bible which require spiritual understanding through exegetical analysis, is moral: the devices of scriptural allegory are the devices of secular poetry.[16] Likewise he maintains, echoing St. Augustine speaking of the interpretation of the difficult parts of the Bible, that truths hidden beneath the fiction of the poem are the more pleasant for the work involved in understanding them. That is why men so love "the fables of Isopet and of Renard, and a good many love poems as well."[17]

Thus does the exegete approach his task, giving us some idea about the flavor of secular exegesis as it was practiced by at least one learned clerk at the end of the Middle Ages. What does he have to say about the specific question of the Garden of Deduit? Like John the Scot, in his tropological analysis of the Garden of Eden, he thinks of the world of human nature as one large garden. Within this there are three smaller gardens, as it were, belonging

---

[16] "De ceste maniere meismes de parler par paraboles et par figures faintes use souvent lescripture sainte comme il appert es canticques salomon et en lapocalipse et en pliuseurs aultres lieux." Bibliothèque nationale MS fr. 9197, fol. 14ᵛ.

[17] MS fr. 9197, fol. 13ᵛ.

to Pallas, Juno, and Venus; and representing the three modes of life. He discusses all three gardens at some length, but it is to the garden of Venus which he directs his most penetrating exegesis. Venus' garden is called the Garden of Deduit, and its doorkeeper is Oiseuse. We are once again in familiar territory, and he says as much: this garden of Venus is the same garden written of in the *Roman de la Rose*. "Venus is not forgotten, for she has a gracious and pleasing garden where all those who seek the delights and vanities of the world can amuse and enjoy themselves. Oiseuse keeps the gate of this garden, which is the real Garden of Delight of which we would speak."

All of this is to say that the Garden of Deduit is a post-lapsarian Eden, a specific and accessible image pregnant with rich possibilities of interpretation. Plurality of meanings is a common-place of medieval scriptural exegesis. I do not here refer to the much discussed—and, with reference to vernacular poetry, much execrated—fourfold method, but rather to the tendency of exe-getes to shift the focus of a text so as to make it susceptible to a whole new series of meanings. Such a device is employed by the exegete of the *Echecs*, who now considers the Garden of Deduit itself as the world. What was a moment ago but a part now becomes the whole. "Thus the whole garden is like the world, even more so the Garden of Deduit of which we are speaking." Here there are many wonderful and beautiful things, yet they are transitory and mutable. Flowers wither, day turns to night, and so forth. "For the comforts and pleasures of the world—the joys, loves, honors, wealth, and all sorts of worldly prosperity which one enjoys in it—are all vanity, transitory things, accom-panied by difficult labors and pain, intermingled with sorrow, as has been said many times before, and as Fortune has so often shown."[18]

The *Echecs* gloss is to be nibbled, not devoured whole. It is not without its own kind of reductionist tedium, and I have no desire to impose upon the patience of the reader by making more extensive citation. Hopefully, however, it can help us to see that the rose garden in Guillaume's poem is neither "love," nor the "court," nor any kind of never-never land of "courtly love." It is tropological Eden. At the same time, it is more than Eden. I

[18] MS fr. 9197, fol. 237ᵛ-238ᵛ.

have promised two scriptural gardens and have so far produced but one. The walled garden *in Oriente* was not the sole paradise of the sacred texts, and by the late Middle Ages another was vastly more popular with exegetes and writers of devotional tracts alike: the *hortus conclusus* of the Canticle of Canticles. The exegesis of this erotic poem was consistently *in bono* throughout the Middle Ages and, after the eleventh century, increasingly Marian. The good garden of the Canticles offered fruitful possibilities for contrast with the old dangerous garden of Eden. Just as it was from the first paradisal *hortus* that the old Adam had been expelled, it was from the paradisal *hortus conclusus* of the Canticles—i.e., the Blessed Virgin Mary—that the new Adam, Jesus Christ, was expelled in sinless conception and miraculous parturition. In the staple exegesis of the late Middle Ages, Christ is, so to speak, the Amant of the Canticles; Mary or the Church, the *sponsa*, the *rosa sine spinas*. Now if one brings to the garden of the *Roman* the iconographic associations *in bono* of the *hortus conclusus*—associations which abounded internationally in the late medieval lyric and which formed a sort of central metaphor for the *Devotio Moderna*—one is likely either to be shocked, as apparently Gerson was, or to impose incompatible meanings on the elements of the poem, as did Molinet. Such impositions seem to have been the recourse of at least one serious modern scholar as well: H. H. Glunz, the great authority on the Vulgate in England.[19] His fantastic reading of the poem (the rose is "göttliche Liebe"), while disturbingly naïve, stems directly from his ready familiarity with twelfth- and thirteenth-century exegesis of the Canticles.

Glunz's perception that such exegesis is of undoubted relevance to the *Roman* is an important one by no means invalidated by his own clumsy handling of the discovery. It is possible to speculate—nothing more—that Glunz presents us with a valuable clue for understanding the peculiarly obdurate and obtuse stand against Jean de Meun's poem taken by Gerson; for Pierre d'Ailly, perhaps Gerson's old teacher, had written a particularly lush commentary on the Canticles and used a good garden in his neglected

[19] *Die Literarästhetik des europäischen Mittelalters* (Bochum-Langendreer, 1937), pp. 344-45.

66

vernacular poetry.[20] Gerson himself was a commentator on the Canticles, and, while his exegetical exposition is largely conventional, there are flashes of illumination for our understanding of the *Roman* in his commentary. At one point Gerson even seems to be making oblique reference to the poem he so much despised.

The Canticle of Canticles, like the *Roman*, is a dream-vision: "Ego dormio, et cor meum vigilat" (Canticles 5:2). For Gerson this *ego* is Jesus Christ, as we would expect, but a special aspect of Christ, Charity incarnate: Amor. Gerson does not want any of his readers to confuse the two dreams of the two lovers, Amant and Amor. Speaking of the first he says, "Quantum putas differat a somno veteris hominis & carnalis?" The "dream of the old man" presents a garden filled with fading "fantasies" of carnal beauty, seductive but illusory. Amor, on the other hand, "experiences the dream of the new man," a prophetic dream in which real things (*res verae*) are seen and known and where "the fantasies of things mutable cease to deceive."[21] Such is, in part, the interpretation which Gerson gives to the dream in the Canticles. It involves a contrast between two dreams and two gardens, a contrast strikingly similar to that which Jean de Meun's allegorical abstraction, Genius, discovers in the text of the *Roman* itself; though such a connection Gerson himself appears never to have made. There would seem to have been nothing in the allegory of the *Roman* which he could not perfectly well understand. On the other hand, there was perhaps a great deal he did not find appropriate in its ironic formulation. One wonders whether he could have better appreciated the Merchant's Tale, in which Geoffrey Chaucer

[20] Pierre d'Ailly may perhaps have shared Gerson's antipathy towards the *Roman* as an art of carnal love; for a work attributed to Pierre, the "Jardin de l'ame devote," contrasts this false art with the "art" of charity. Ceste art ne sceurent oncques Virgille, ne Ovide, ne les autres qui enseignerent a folement ou faulsement amer et a folement honorer Cupido le faulx dieu damour, et sa fole mere Venus. A cette faulse amour fuir forment nous semonce et encline foy maitress de vraye amour." Cited by L. Salembier, "Les oeuvres de poésie française du cardinal Pierre d'Ailly," *Mémoires de la Société d'émulation de Cambrai*, LXVII, 462. P. Glorieux has, without comment, ascribed the "Jardin" to Gerson himself; but on the whole the case for Pierre's authorship seems stronger.

[21] "In Canticum Canticorum," IV, 6, 3ff., *Opera Omnia*, ed. Ellies du Pin (Antwerp, 1706), IV, 67.

reworked the materials of the "dream of the old man" with theologically trenchant, yet hilarious, effect.

It is now possible, thanks to the recent work of Eleanor Greenhill on the iconography of the *Speculum Virginum*, to document the enormous influence which Marian exegesis of the Canticles could have on popular religious literature even before 1150.[22] She demonstrates that the key to the meaning of the pictures in the *Speculum*, which have long fascinated art historians, is to be found in the abundant exegesis of the Canticles, exegesis which had itself been influenced by the iconography of the *locus amoenus* of classical poetry. Furthermore, the psychomachic scheme of the trees of the virtues and vices forms only a small part of the ambiguity of the "double view" of the *hortus*—the old (*terrenus*) as opposed to the new (*caelestis*), the lovers of the world (*amatores mundi*) as opposed to the lovers of God (*amatores Dei*), the two wells, the two Adams, and so on.

It becomes clear that Guillaume's garden manipulates classical and scriptural elements in a similar way, though the implication is that the classical *locus amoenus* came to him in an already "Christianized" form. As a classical scholar he certainly cannot be given such high marks as, say, Thomas the Cistercian, whose commentary on the Canticles is a sort of classical florilegium; but he handles his materials tactfully and discreetly.[23] To follow what Guillaume is doing with the garden *topos* requires some awareness of the exegetical principle of ambiguity outlined by St. Augustine in the third book of *De doctrina christiana*, the principle around which the entire iconographic schedule of the *Speculum Virginum* and numerous other works is structured. According to St. Augustine Biblical signs can be used either in a bad sense (*in malo*) or in a good sense (*in bono*). The ambiguity is resolved by careful attention to context. The *Roman* which Guillaume began was to be no straightforward *Speculum Virginum*; quite the contrary, Jean de Meun was later able to make a joke of the matter by

[22] Eleanor Simmons Greenhill, *Die geistigen Voraussetzungen der Bilderreihe des Speculum Virginum* (Münster, 1962).

[23] The wide scope of Thomas' use of classical poetry strikingly illustrates the mingling of imagery from Latin love poetry with that of the Canticles; see B. Griesser, "Dichterzitaten des Thomas Cisterciensis Kommentar zum Hohenlied," *Cistercienser-Chronik*, L (1938), 11-14, 118-22; LI (1939), 73-80.

saying that his book ought to be called the *Mirrouer aux Amou-
reux*. When Amant says, in the Chaucerian translation, "For wel
wende I ful sikerly / Have been in paradys erthly. / So fair it
was that, trusteth wel, / It seemed a place espirituel" he postu-
lates an amusing ambiguity fraught with ironic implications:
"paradys erthly" is not at all the same as a "place espirituel." It
is a very different place, and while the rosebud therein is ironi-
cally a *rosa pudoris* it does not come from the same bush as that
rose which the exegetes of the Canticles borrowed from Latin
poetry and transplanted into their *hortus deliciarum*. Though
Guillaume is willing to posit ambiguities with ironic possibility,
he is less content to let them stand alone for very long. In a not
unpleasing way, his iconography is rather obvious. No attentive
reader can really think that the garden which has as its source
the well of Narcissus is the same garden as that of the Church,
whose wellhead is Jesus Christ, any more than one can fail to
distinguish between the clearly posted cities of Babylon and Jeru-
salem. When Jean de Meun's Genius schematically analyzes
Guillaume's *hortus terrenus* he merely makes explicit what was
already implicitly obvious.

Of Genius' contrasting of the two gardens I shall have some-
thing more to say presently. Recent explanations of this and other
aspects of the *Roman* have been tainted by Gérard Paré's
really quite extraordinary notion that Jean de Meun is "anti-
Guillaume," that, in effect, the second part of the poem is a
counter-blast to the first. However admirable the principle of
the *lectio difficilior* may be as a canon of textual criticism, it is
seldom a safe guide to literary interpretation.

We may perhaps best see Guillaume's garden with medieval
eyes by examining the ways in which the poem's illustrators organ-
ized, or rather reorganized, his iconographic materials in the
translation from word to picture. It is hardly surprising that more
than one fourteenth-century poet would speak of this garden as
the *ne plus ultra* of literary artifice, for it is a *hortus deliciarum*
of extraordinarily complex and varied beauty; the enamel imagery
urgently appeals to all the senses. Amant hears the sweet music
of singing birds—of "nyghtyngales, alpes, fynches, and wod-
wales." The trees are laden with an abundance of fruits and
spices. Fragrant blossoms daub the air, and even the turf has been

perfumed to give up a "ful good savour." The grass, downy and sweet, is pleasantly pliant, yielding—the perfect place for a man to tumble in amorous play with his *lemman*. Things "fair to the eye" are ubiquitous: bright colors, the glint of precious metals. In short, all five of Amant's sensory faculties are immediately and insistently engaged.

I have attempted to show that beneath the glittering surface of Guillaume's description lie, not very well hidden, a number of commonplace theological statements which the sensuous element of his verse only serves to accentuate. The schematic nature of Guillaume's aesthetics hints that the imagery of the garden is meant to be cautionary as well as exciting. Amant's "windows," his five senses, are wide open, and he is implicitly in danger that Death will enter through them (Jeremiah 9:21) unless with Melibee, at the feet of Ovid, he learns the dangerous ambiguities of the "delices and honours of this world." To the modern reader, unfamiliar with the conventions of medieval literary psychology and the Scriptural tradition out of which it springs, the surface elegance of Guillaume's style, his "courtly" tone, presents a number of problems which serve as distractions to the understanding of the poem. Delighted, as we should be, by the golden chaff on the threshing room floor, we are loath to leave it for the duller-hued grain. Guillaume's elegance presented problems to his earliest illustrators as well, but problems of a different sort.

The literary techniques used in the description of the garden represent an achievement considerably in advance of anything analogous that book painters of the thirteenth century could have achieved on the literal level—i.e., the level of verisimilitude— even if they had been interested in trying. In fact no miniaturist in France was able to approach this degree of achievement until the end of the fourteenth century. The scene is, after all, one of unusual visual complexity; to illustrate it literally demands not only the spatial continuum of perspective but also a number of advanced draughtsmanly techniques capable of handling the rich variety of specific details which is the flesh, in Guillaume's description, on an otherwise rather overworked set of bones. The early illustrations take it back to the skeleton, as it were, and the sumptuous nature of the garden is not suggested in the manuscript paintings until well into the fifteenth century with magnificent productions like Bibliothèque nationale MS fr. 19153 and British Museum MS Harley 4425. The earliest attempts to handle the garden lack the quality of verisimilitude entirely, and in the most common French style of the fourteenth century, there are few illusory techniques. It is certain, for example, that Chaucer never saw anything like the fifteenth-century illustrations of the *Roman* which have been produced, from time to time, to illustrate his works or essays about them.

The conjunction of the verbally dazzling garden of the *Roman* with its flat fourteenth-century Gothic illustrations may create a kind of bathos to the modern eye, which is as incapable of suppressing the illusory or abstractionist expectations to which it has been trained as the modern mind is of suppressing knowledge of Rousseau, Darwin, or Freud in the study of medieval intellectual history. In Bibliothèque nationale MS fr. 1559 (ca. 1300), the earliest extant illustrated copy of the poem, the garden is reduced to a couple of flat trees, mere swaying trunks with bulbs of foliage attached. Furthermore, even in such a reduction as this there is little attempt at verisimilitude. "Pink and blue trees are the rule," Kuhn observed with some incredulity;[24] and the contempt for realistic color parallels that for the shape and proportion of the trees. "Paradise," says St. Augustine, "is a place where there are trees growing." So says this early French illustrator, and little more; for his interest in paradise, like St. Augustine's, has little to do with verisimilar description. The allegorical figures on the wall are here, as elsewhere for the next hundred years, painted in completely discrete segments of space which are neither on the wall nor anywhere else in a verisimilar continuum. The wall itself, when it appears in an illustration on folio 6, is little more than an unconvincing gate with greenery sprouting over its top. The greatest detail attempted is variation of the kinds of trees, odd oversized flowers, and birds. A similar treatment can be examined in Fig. 15, from British Museum Add. MS 31840, dating from about 1330. The garden here is almost ludicrous, a trapezoidal, crenellated carton, on which some huge birds are perched. What is most noticeable, however, is the lack of depth in the backgrounds.

Guillaume's description, for all its detail, is not realistic either; but it does have depth, or at least the suggestion of depth. With

24 "Die Illustration des Rosenromans," p. 20.

him it is this suggested background, rather than the vague personalities (if they could be so described) pasted upon it, which is of striking dimensions. In the early illustrations of this part of the romance there is no comparable background—no landscape, no depth to the texture. The characters are pressed out against a two-dimensional background of solid gold or, more commonly, against regular patterns of brightly colored squares or lozenges. During the course of the fourteenth century, hints of perspective begin to appear. Toes squeeze over the heavily marked edges of the illustrations, or the material climbs out of its confines at the top. Grassy ledges are built up under standing figures (see Fig. 16) or the little Villard de Honnecourt benches on which they sit appear in oblique, dimensional perspective. In a few rare exceptions, like Fig. 3, the garden is presented as a satisfying whole, similar to a mosaic without the notable illusion of pictorial space. But nowhere, until after the death of Chaucer, is there any technical achievement of the glossy fineness of Guillaume's verbal picture.

The fact that none of the early illustrations of the Garden of Deduit show it as being, on the literal level, immoderately attractive to the eye is a result of the limited painting techniques before the fifteenth century; but this historical accident can be of use to us in approaching the poem. Much of the surface distraction or, from Guillaume's point of view, ornamentation, which is in the literary description of Deduit's Garden, is lacking in its visual realization; and the primitive nature of the pictures immediately strips the scene to its iconographic skeleton.

While it is impossible, within the confines of a book of reasonable length, to catalogue and study the entire iconographic schedule of a typical fourteenth-century manuscript of the *Roman*, it will be instructive to examine in a schematic way the initial episodes in Guillaume's poem which the illustrators, almost to a man, chose to gloss. The *incipit* illustrations, we have already seen, usually picture the Dreamer in bed. Then comes the static parade of the wall paintings. The next three illustrations, which are to be found as a series in almost every illustrated copy of the poem before 1400 (and most after that date) are of Oiseuse, the carol of Deduit, and Narcissus or Amant at Narcissus' well. As literary tableaux the episodes thus illustrated activate the garden by simultaneously adding texture to its superficial beauty and mystery and by unmasking the moral inversions which characterize it. Each of the three episodes, in the poem itself as well as in its iconography, strongly suggests Guillaume de Lorris' artistic strategy and his moral viewpoint. Taken together, they present evidence so persuasive that it is difficult to believe that Guillaume's intention has been so frequently mistaken.

We may begin with Oiseuse, the beautiful young woman who opens the door of the garden to the importunate knocking of Amant. Oiseuse, which means Idleness, is an abstraction familiar to readers of Chaucer, who, undoubtedly borrowing the figure from Guillaume, put her into the Prologue to the Second Nun's Tale in a context free of moral ambiguity. "Ydelnesse" is there called the "ministre and the norice unto vices," the porteress of the *hortus deliciarum*. Critics of the *Roman*, however, have implied that, for Guillaume, Oiseuse is a kind of genteel and courtly relaxation rather than the capital vice of sloth in secular garb.[25] The moral allegory of the *Roman* is of course only one layer of the poem's figurative richness, and to speak of it is to cut only one swath through a broad field. One must respond with tact to the courtly tone of the poem; and, since sound criticism demands strict attention to contexts and to speakers, among other considerations, it might seem at least arguable that there is a substantial difference between Guillaume's Oiseuse and Chaucer's Ydelnesse. The *chapeleyne* to even so worldly a Prioress as Chaucer's might be expected to have less liberal, more ascetic, views than a courtly young Orléanais poet. Guillaume, who could playfully make a vice of the ascetic aspiration of Poverty, could also perhaps make a virtue out of Idleness. The spirit of one poem is held to be hagiographic; the other, courtly.

In fact, however, the evidence of the literary history of Oiseuse, as well as significant textual details in Guillaume's description, deny the possibility of any such radical distinction. Chaucer neither misunderstood her nature nor transformed it in the Second Nun's Tale, and if his Idleness is easier to understand than Guillaume's, so is the Second Nun's Tale easier to understand than the *Roman*. The difference between the two treatments is not one of contrasting clerical and secular values. The difference is, emphatically, a

---

[25] Alan Gunn, e.g., maintains that "Oiseuse represents the leisure necessary for a courtly lover." *Mirror of Love*, p. 105.

literary one. Chaucer's nun decorously pulls no punches in her characterization of the "norice unto vices"; Guillaume makes greater demands on the reader, inviting him to make the moral judgments implicit in the ironic and uncomprehending behavior of Amant, challenging him to grasp the critically fashionable dichotomy between appearance and reality. To understand Oiseuse correctly from Guillaume's point of view does not require great theological or iconographic expertise. Her literary history, as Langlois noted, begins with Ovid's *Remedia Amoris,* where the connection between idleness and the life of *luxuria* finds witty expression: "Otia si tollas, periere Cupidinis arcus."[26] Guillaume sounds an Ovidian echo and reveals an Ovidian spirit, implying that the reader may expect the life of love described in the *Roman* to be viewed in the same light as that analysed in the *Remedia.*

It is foolish, and therefore a little funny, that the Lover should wish to follow Oiseuse. He is hardly seduced; at his first sight of the garden wall he beats upon its gate for admittance, suggesting the single-minded inclination toward folly which is his primary characteristic. Oiseuse is "fair to the eye"—indeed she is the corporeal representation of the sensuousness of the garden itself, described as she is in terms of tactile titillation and olfactory allure. The Lover's initial encounter in the garden becomes, in short, an encounter with the type of deceptive and phantom female beauty which is his chief goal in the broader field of the poem as a whole.

To critics who maintain that the richness of great poetry arises from "multivalence" and "double vision," it may seem a particularly blatant reduction to strip Oiseuse of her courtly glamor and give her another name as one of the seven capital vices. It is doubtful, however, that seeing double—which is, after all, usually symptomatic of a marked disorientation of needed faculties—is an adequate gauge of artistic success. I readily admit a richness in Guillaume's treatment of Oiseuse which is not to be found in Chaucer, but I cannot attribute it to any befuddlement of Guillaume's moral eyesight nor to Chaucer's simplism. The Second Nun talks like a nun; Amant talks like a literary lover, like a fool. That physical beauty is no necessary indication of moral probity

[26] *Remedia Amoris,* l. 139. See Robertson, *Preface to Chaucer,* p. 92.

74

we have already learned, if nowhere else, from the *Echecs* gloss. Guillaume could have learned it from a hundred different medieval psychologists. Amant describes Oiseuse as beautiful but clearly indicates, to the wary reader, that she is to be shunned. There is here a kind of irony, but no confusion of values and no refusal to arbitrate claims on the reader—in short, no double vision.

Traditional iconography can once again help make clear what at first may have been dark. Among the courtly details of Guillaume's description of the beautiful Oiseuse are two attributes which, to anyone familiar with the elementary iconography of the virtues and the vices in Gothic art, expose her physical beauty as an illusion which masks rather than adorns her true nature. Guillaume says that she holds a mirror in her hand (l. 557), and that she spends her morning adorning herself and combing her hair (l. 568). The mirror and the comb are, of course, precisely the attributes of the Gothic Luxuria figure, and it was upon them— rather than the green dress, the rose chapelet, the white gloves, and so on—that the early illustrators of the poem immediately seized (see Figs. 8, 9, and 17). The scribal instructions to the illuminators, often left unerased in the margins of manuscripts, especially in manuscripts where the illustration cycle was never completed, frequently merely say something like "[paint] a beautiful girl with a mirror."[27]

So it was that the scribes of the fourteenth century saw in Guillaume's Oiseuse not "the leisure necessary for a courtly lover," as Alan Gunn would have it, but the same abstract quintessence of lust which looks down from the quatrefoiled rose window in Notre Dame de Paris. Kuhn recognized this at once and discussed the relationship convincingly without, however, drawing the obvious conclusion that the iconographic kinship of Oiseuse and Luxuria reflects a blood relationship between the two and not merely the operation of artistic cliché.[28] Oiseuse *is* Luxuria, reshaped and recast in an allegorical and Ovidian alloy. Like the sirens who share her iconographic attributes, she is "fair to the eye"; but it is bizarre and debilitating critical optimism alone which can make us fail to see that she is beautiful only to the "eyes of the flesh," only to Amant's eyes.

[27] Paris, Bibliothèque nationale MS fr. 25523, fol. 6ʳ.
[28] "Die Illustration des Rosenromans," pp. 33-34 and Fig. 38.

75

The problem of the comb and mirror in Oiseuse's hands raises the larger question of the strategy and validity of iconographical analysis of a secular work of art. To say that in medieval art a mirror means *luxuria* and that, acordingly, Guillaume's lady bearing a mirror is to be associated with that capital vice and was so associated by most of the poem's illustrators, needs more support than I have so far adduced. As a matter of fact the mirror means a great many things—*luxuria, prudentia,* self-knowledge, vanity, pride, Venus, truth, the contemplative life, and not a few more. The mirror of Oiseuse in Fig. 17 does not bear the same connotations as the mirror in the hand of Jesus Christ in Fig. 18, or as the looking glass in the hand of Prudence as painted by Giotto in the Arena Chapel at Padua.[29]

In general there are two broad methods of verifying an iconographical reading. The best of these, of course, is the adduction of a specific text which comments upon or explains a painting. Such texts abound, with specific reference to the *Roman de la Rose,* in the gloss of the *Echecs Amoureux,* which is in effect a kind of mythographic digest of many of the commonplace literary configurations reflected by the *Roman.* A second method is to examine the qualifying context of an icon. In the rose window at Paris, Luxuria has a mirror and a comb. In the murals at Padua, the mirror is in the hand of a woman explicitly named Prudentia who is also clearly one of a series representing the four cardinal virtues.

As far as Oiseuse is concerned there is little difficulty in supplying either text or qualifying context. The mirror and the comb, elements of Guillaume's description, are well documented attributes of Luxuria. Furthermore they appear in selective conjunction in the illustrations, and they are amply qualified by similar illustrations of known meaning in other literary texts. For example Carnalité, in the *Roman de Fauvel,* is shown holding a mirror and a glove—giving us, incidentally, an important clue for interpreting the mysterious gloves which abound in the iconography of the *Roman.*[30] In another self-explanatory illustration of the fourteenth century we shall find Fleshly Beauty (*Corporal bel-*

[29] The chief significations of the mirror in medieval iconology are documented by G. F. Hartlaub, *Zauber des Spiegels* (Munich, 1951).

[30] Paris, Bibliothèque nationale MS fr. 146, fol. 12ʳ. There is a facsimile edition by Pierre Aubry, *Le Roman de Fauvel* (Paris, 1907).

lezza) holding a mirror and a small lap dog like the "little furry creatures" from the iconography of the *Roman* and elsewhere so amusingly analyzed by Robertson.[31] In a beautifully illustrated "Tree of the Ages of Man" in the *Tesoro* of Brunetto Latini, a work which shares many interests with the *Roman*, the folly of youth is pictured as an amorous couple sitting on the grass holding hands.[32] That the young man is not looking at his beloved, but rather at his own fair image in a mirror he holds before his face, will surprise no one who has read Brunetto on *fol amour*, or who has understood the significance of Guillaume de Lorris' *exemplum* of Narcissus. A final example will show us, in the splendid fourteenth-century Angers tapestries of the Apocalypse, both mirror and comb in the hands of the great whore.[33] In short there is a large and various tradition linking the iconography of the mirror and comb with young love in one or another of its medieval aspects, and the tradition both qualifies and illuminates the iconography of the *Roman*.

Erich Köhler has recently drawn attention to interesting iconographic parallels between the Garden of Deduit and Dante's Earthly Paradise. Unfortunately, his iconographic analysis remains superficial, and gives the unfortunate impression that

[31] Florence, Biblioteca nazionale centrale, MS Palat. 600, fol. 5ᵛ.

[32] Florence, Biblioteca Laurenziana, MS Plut. XLII 19, fol. 96ʳ. Such an illustration probably sheds light on why the narrator of the *Roman* experiences his erotic dream at the age of 20 ("el point qu'Amors prent le paage des jones genz") and writes about it at a distance of "bien v. anz ou mais." According to the common teaching of the later Middle Ages and Renaissance, man's life was composed of seven ages: *infantia, pueritia, adolescentia, juventus, virilitas, senectus*, and *decrepitus*. There is considerable variation in the actual span of years assigned to each age; but the third, *adolescentia*, was commonly said to run from ages 15 to 25, and it was associated with Venus, lechery, and the frivolous pursuits of love. Shakespeare's emblem for the third age is "the lover / Sighing like a furnace, with a woeful ballad / Made to his mistress' eyebrow." See further Franz Boll, *Die Lebensalter* (Leipzig, 1913), especially pp. 40ff. and Plate II. Thus, the action of the *Roman* is typical of unreasonable *adolescentia*, and is placed squarely in the center of that age. On the other hand, it is narrated from the maturer and severer point of view of *juventus*. With the rise of the 'teenager, L. *adolescentia* and MnE. *adolescence* have become false cognates. There were no "adolescents" in the Middle Ages, nor for a long time after, according to the stimulating book of Philippe Ariès, *Centuries of Childhood*.

[33] See Jean Lurçat and Jacques Levron, *L'Apocalypse d'Angers* (Angers, 1955), Plate lxviii; cf. Brussels, Bibliothèque royale MS II, 282, fol. 42ʳ.

Oiseuse is to be associated with the *vita contemplativa*.[34] This is, of course, a most misleading suggestion. As a matter of fact there is a widely published illustration which shows the "three lives" lounging in the rose garden of the *Roman*; needless to say it is Venus, not Juno, who holds the mirror in her hand.[35] If the study of traditional iconography is to be useful to the literary scholar, surely it must be handled delicately, with deferential tact and, of course, with some tentativeness.

The point about the beauty of Oiseuse is that it is fleshly, fading, phantasmic. Only her moral nature is durable. When dances end and dancers fail, Oiseuse will once again take her place as Luxuria or one of her sisters in the rose window at Paris, or in Antichrist's train in the *Passion de Sémur*. We cannot feel sorry for the mad Lover who willfully ignores the clear message of Guillaume's iconography to spurn Reason and wander the paths of unreality. There is in the *Faerie Queene* a situation which parallels the Lover's encounter with Oiseuse; and its contrasts with the *Roman*, presenting an alternative not chosen by Guillaume and Jean, are full of suggestion for the *Roman*. Early in the first book of Spenser's great poem, Red Cross Knight, "his eye of reason . . . yblent" by a phantasm, dumbly follows the False Duessa, who has Oiseuse's essential nature—not to mention her mirror.[36] Unlike Red Cross Knight, the Lover never regains his "eye of reason." In fact he wanders through twenty thousand lines of his erotic dream in a state of spiritual blindness from which, as Petrarch noted, he never recovers. Oiseuse is one with the garden; she is the appropriate, indeed the perfect, keeper of the keys for this false and evanescent paradise. Stripped of her apparitional beauty, the False Duessa becomes a mound of hideous and emetic corruption; for Spenser likes to tie the dangling threads of his allegory into tidy bows, to move from implicit to explicit judgments. The authors of the *Roman* as a rule show more poetic diffidence, and Guillaume does not unmask Oiseuse

[34] E. Köhler, "Lea, Matelda, und Oiseuse," *Zeitschrift für romanische Philologie*, LXXVIII (1962), 464-69.

[35] Bibliothèque nationale MS fr. 143, fol. 198ᵛ. This illustration from the *Echecs* gloss has been frequently published. See Jean Porcher, *Medieval French Miniatures* (New York, n.d.), Plate lxxxix, and Seznec, *Survivance des dieux antiques*, pp. 98-99.

[36] *Faerie Queene*, 1, iv, 10, 6.

in the manner of the Second Nun or the author of the *Passion de Sémur*. Instead he implicitly invites that careful reading and moral sensitivity, that willingness not only to comprehend but also to assess, which Boccaccio insists is the fruitful labor of all readers of allegory.

The further evidence of the *Echecs Amoureux* gloss, while it should be sufficiently predictable to anyone who has ever had an informed glimpse of an illustration of Oiseuse in the *Roman*, is useful for its schema and for its perception of Guillaume's Ovidian spirit. The *Echecs* borrowed from the *Roman*, hardly changed, Amant's encounter with Oiseuse; and the *Echecs* exegete is quick to point out the folly of Amant's subjection to the lady with the mirror and comb. He finds three reasons why the Lover should shun Oiseuse. The first is that Oiseuse is "the queen and nurse of all evils" and in particular (as Ovid points out) of *fol amour*. The second is that man alone of all creatures has Reason, and to follow Oiseuse is necessarily to abandon Reason. The third dissuasive, growing out of the second, is that in denying Reason man "denatures himself" and ceases, in fact, to be a man.[37]

It is fair to insist on such an interpretation of Oiseuse in the *Roman*, since it is the interpretation insisted upon by all the formal documents of the Middle Ages we have which talk about her. Of course the insistent claim that Guillaume de Lorris dealing with questions of practical morality may seem brittle, puritanical, and insensitive to critics who have learned from C. S. Lewis to subject the poem to an exegesis founded on the exotic mythology of courtly love; but I do not pretend just yet to defend Guillaume against such charges, nor even do I deny that his poem might have been a better one—more sensitive and ambiguous—had it been the poem which Lewis describes. It is not. It is rather the poem described by Deguilleville, Laurent de Premierfait, and Pierre Col, literary critics who, if they were entirely innocent of any knowledge of "courtly love," were yet capable of sensitive and sophisticated understanding of the *Roman*. Such an understanding was grounded in a traditional morality, and its method of *glossatio* was to explain moral meanings. This should not surprise us. Henri de Lubac has recently reminded us, with elegance

---

[37] Bibliothèque nationale MS fr. 9197, fols. 31ᵛ-34ᵛ.

and great authority, that for the Middle Ages the spiritual sense of the Bible par excellence was tropology, the *sensus moralis* which focused the meaning of a sacred text upon the individual moral problems in the daily lives of men.

Thus it is that the meaning of Amant's encounter with Oiseuse which was talked about in the Middle Ages was its *moral* meaning. The encounter with Oiseuse is a warning to the virtuous to flee idleness, a vice through which men are initiated to foolish, perverse, and sinful behavior.[38] Of course this is not the exclusive meaning of the passage, for the poetry is simultaneously up to other things. On the literal level it is talking about a young man called Amant and a young lady named Oiseuse. To find the allegorical meaning of all this (*quid credas*) is neither very difficult, nor terribly rewarding: it means a typical abstract lover has met and succumbed to the typical abstract vice of idleness. In terms of the familiar "meanings" of Scripture, which are neither more nor less appropriate to the *Roman* than to any other medieval poem, the commentators I have cited have shown little inclination to talk about the *littera* (what the text actually says) or the *allegoria* (what it means in an abstract or dogmatic sense). Their interest, typically, is in the workings of poetic tropes—the translation of the literary text into immediate, relevant, and practical moral significance.

Such a process is, clearly, reductionism, as is all medieval literary criticism with which I am familiar, with the exception perhaps of some technical rhetorical analyses of very limited interest. It should be pointed out, however, that most modern attempts to explain what the *Roman* means have involved self-indulgent reductions which make the prologue to the Scottish *Legends of the Saints* seem by contrast a very scrupulous and sensitive essay in literary criticism. When we hear from C. S. Lewis that the garden "means the life of the court," or from Alan Gunn that "Oiseuse represents the leisure necessary for a courtly lover," we are not merely being imposed upon with mildly fantastic conjecture. We are witnessing the operation of a modern hit-or-miss exegesis which reduces the literary text it examines to fit the dimen-

---

[38] Such is the meaning of Oiseuse in the *Roman* according to the prologue to the *Legends of the Saints in the Scottish Dialect of the Fourteenth Century*, ed. W. M. Metcalfe (Edinburgh, 1896), I, I, ll. 3-12.

sions of an *a priori* system: in this case, a quite hypothetical system known as "courtly love." *The Allegory of Love* has become the *Glossa ordinaria* of the *Roman de la Rose* for a generation of twentieth-century readers, but since my book is an attempt to explain what the poem may have meant to its medieval readers, I shall continue to prefer the exegetical insights of earlier periods.

Guillaume de Lorris took some care in preparing the first "dramatic" moment in his poem, an episode which at once establishes the urbane tone of the *Roman* and suggests the ambiguities and ironies around which it is structured. The psychological process by which Amant is to become entirely drunk and befuddled with the beauty of *visibilia* begins with his easy capitulation to Oiseuse, continues when he joins the dance, is confirmed when he falls in love with what he sees in the Fountain of Narcissus, and is formally ratified in his idolatrous homage to Amours. The Oiseuse episode is thus a critical one for the strategies of the poem, and for it Guillaume sought literary integuments of iconographic sophistication and precision. Oiseuse is Ovidian *otia*, but she is also more. There is in her nature something of the sirens whose sultry voices fill the garden of the *Roman* with enticing song, and something of lust, plain and simple. The iconographic details which Guillaume chose—the rose chaplet, the gloves, the mirror and comb—were prominently exploited by the illustrators in a way which leaves no doubt of the significant associations which they were able to see between the lady Oiseuse and her various abstract components. Oiseuse appears but for a moment upon Guillaume's stage, but she plays an important role. There is one whole family of fourteenth-century manuscripts in which an obvious Oiseuse-Luxuria shares the most prominent position in the illustration cycle, the *incipit* diptych.[39] At the left the Dreamer is in bed; at the right, in the position where the illustrators frequently attempted in some way to epitomize his dream, sits Oiseuse, mirror and comb in hand. The garden *tout carré* has been rounded to an architectural oval and swivelled on its axis to form a proper frame, like the quatrefoil at Paris, for its Gothic icon.

The next iconographic subject in practically all the illustrated

[39] See Kuhn, "Die Illustration des Rosenromans," pp. 20ff. for a partial listing.

manuscripts of the *Roman*, after the allegorical figures painted on the wall and the encounter of Amant with Oiseuse, is the carol of Deduit, Mirth's dance. The emblematic significance of this dance is an important one to the poem, and the study of its illustration provides a valuable lesson in iconographic meaning. There would seem to be a common-sense logic at work in the development of much traditional Christian iconography, such as that of the seven capital vices. Hate is self-destructive, like a suicidal dagger in the heart, and avarice is tight-fisted and grasping like a miserable old man who holds his little purse to his breast. A woman who preens herself all day in a mirror, combing and recombing her hair, might really be lecherous; but she might also stare forever into a mirror, as does Giotto's Prudence, and do so virtuously. Iconographic logic is not inexorable, and iconographic meaning arises from context and changes with shifts in point of view. The "things" of iconographic composition in visual and literary art must be carefully discriminated, from the "things" of daily living from which they are frequently borrowed. Every man with a purse is not avaricious, nor is every man with a knife necessarily wrathful. Medieval men presumably did not confuse every village swineherd with St. Anthony simply because of the pigs.

Some such disclaimer is necessary if I am to forestall one kind of obtuse criticism concerning the iconographic meaning of the carol of Deduit which Amant joins, at first diffidently, then with increasing enthusiasm. The meaning of the carol in the *Roman de la Rose* is a bad one, but it is not necessarily connected with the well documented attitudes of the Church toward the dance. The iconographic carol must be distinguished from the historical carol, so to speak, though the latter can at least help us to unmask some popular critical misapprehensions about the former and to suggest how the carol became a type of sinfully frivolous behavior, as in the legend of the dancers of Kölbig.[40] The carol was not the peculiar property of an aristocratic or courtly class. In origin it was a peasant dance like other folk dances, and the Middle English exegete who set out to give a spiritual meaning to one of the

---

[40] For the relevant historical background see Margit Sahlin, *Etude sur la carole médiévale, l'origine du mot et ses rapports avec l'Eglise* (Uppsala, 1940).

secular carol burdens quite clearly suggests a peasant milieu.[41] In its context within the *Roman*, Deduit's carol may without prejudice be called courtly because the characterization comes from the context, not from any inherent nobility of the dance.

A common objection to carols and other dances, as evidenced by medieval tracts on morality, penitential manuals, and the like, was that they were an excitement to illicit sexual relations, as indeed they are in the *Roman*. Such opposition no doubt had some basis in actual pastoral situations, and it helps to explain how the carol could easily become a figure or icon for sexual cupidity. It does not, however, suggest that everyone who ever took part in the carol was a fornicator or woman of easy virtue. The Black Knight, in Chaucer's *Book of the Duchess*, saw his virtuous lady in a carol; and there were probably men among Chaucer's friends less frivolous than Froissart who, like him, loved "carols and dancing and to hear minstrels."[42] Nonetheless, the literary suggestions of Guillaume's carol, springing from its context in the poem, can hardly be missed by the careful reader. Oiseuse delivers Amant into the hands of the ambiguous Courtoisie, who invites him to a dance led by Deduit, which ends in polite fornication. The illustrators who set out to capture something of the bittersweet nature of this courtly dance were not without an iconographic tradition to support them.

Some of the associations the carol had for medieval artists can be seen in the illustrations to explicitly Christian works like St. Augustine's *De civitate Dei*. In the elaborate late fourteenth-century translation and commentary of Augustine's work by Raoul de Prelles—a work which specifically cites the *Roman de la Rose* as one of its authorities—the illustrators show a round dance, a carol, to represent the obscenities of the Roman stage which Augustine attacks.[43] The illustration in the *De civitate* would be difficult to interpret *in bono*: Folly sits on a ledge overlooking the

[41] "Kleinere mittelenglische Texte," ed. Max Förster, *Anglia*, XLII (1918), 152ff.

[42] Henry of Lancaster, father of the duchess whom Chaucer mourned, says that while dancing is not necessarily sinful, it is a dangerous occasion of sin. *Le Livre de Seynts Médecines*, ed. E. J. Arnould (Oxford, 1940), pp. 77-78.

[43] The Hague, Museum Mermanno-Westreenianum, MS 11, fol. 36ᵛ. See Alexandre de Laborde, *Les manuscrits à peintures de la Cité de Dieu de Saint Augustin* (Paris, 1909), III, Plate lxxxvii.

little *hortus conclusus* in which naked dancers cavort. Not all such illustrations give the game away. Sometimes a carol quite as courtly as any in the iconography of the *Roman de la Rose* is used to contrast with a picture of angels making music, presenting a discordant symphony of the "old dance" of cupidity with the "new song" of charity.[44] In such illustrations, as in those of the *Roman* and in Guillaume's description which they mirror, the moral meaning of the dance is not reflected in the surface detail of the picture. The dancers are handsome, sumptuously dressed, and arranged in graceful attitudes. The old dance is a purely intellectual concept, and to understand its inclusion in the *Roman* we must realize that it is really not a dance but an inclination to cupidity.

Guillaume does not describe the carol of Deduit in great detail, for he no doubt assumes that his readers are familiar with the dance. Few of the illustrators of the fourteenth century, however, visualized the same thing, though most agreed on its essential features. According to the majority (see Figs. 19, 20, and 21), the carol was a round dance in which the participants joined hands in a circle, sometimes facing in. For the greater part of the fourteenth century the northern French style was incapable of capturing such a multilinear concept with convincing verisimilitude. The artists' compromise typically shows only a single flat line of carollers facing outward; sometimes the idea of a circle is suggested by including in the line the backs of a few carollers' heads. The fifteenth-century illustrators are more realistic in their creation of spatial illusion, though, I suspect, less accurate in their reproduction of the archeological details of the dance. In many of the later pictures, such as the famous illustration from Harley 4425 in the British Museum, the dancers simply promenade in pairs.

The most interesting iconographic detail which we can learn from fourteenth-century illustrations of the carol can be seen in Fig. 20. Here the god of Love holds hands with his partner by means of a glove, which is used as a chain between them. This is not a universal characteristic of fourteenth-century carol illustrations, but it does occur in something like half of them. Archeologically, this detail is almost certainly correct; several surviving

---

[44] E. W. Tristram, *English Wall Painting of the Fourteenth Century* (London, 1955), p. 25.

European folk dances employ a glove, handkerchief, or scarf for a similar purpose. The glove also shows up in many illustrations of other subjects. The Lover often carries it quite obtrusively (see Fig. 12) and, as we noticed in our brief examination of Fig. 4, quite disconcertingly. Some of the Lover's friends—Amis, Deduit, and others—also occasionally carry a glove, but it is only the Lover himself of whom it can be said to be a fairly constant attribute. Wherever we see him with it, it is a striking reminder of his essential cupidity, the kind of love which impels him. The glove is, so to speak, his proper costume for the old dance.

As an icon the glove is not unequivocal. It is often used in a good sense as a symbol of authority, as in some documented examples of the medieval iconography of Jupiter.[45] Frequently it is impossible to assign it any iconological significance at all. Its qualification in the iconography of the *Roman*, both in the carol sequences and elsewhere, leaves little doubt of the glove's meaning there. I have already mentioned the character called Carnalité in the fourteenth-century *Roman de Fauvel*, a work which relies heavily on and specifically cites the *Roman de la Rose*. Carnalité is pictured sitting on a bench, a mirror in one hand and a glove in the other. It is this glove, a clear invitation to join hands in the old dance, which juts out so alarmingly from the garden doorway in another fourteenth-century illustration.[46] And it is the same glove —oversized, ostentatious, unpaired—which, in many manuscripts, Amant carries with him throughout the illustrative cycle.

The motif of the Lover's glove appears and reappears in illustrations of every date, and in widely separated sections of the text of the poem. One of Pygmalion's maneuvers in his frenzied attempt to make his graven image respond to his passion was to invite her to dance:

> E espingue e sautele e baie
> E fiert dou pie par mi la saie;
> E prent par la main e dance,
> Mais mout a au cueur grant pesance
> Qu'el ne veaut chanter ne respondre
> Ne pour prier ne pour semondre. (ll. 21053ff.)

[45] See E. Panofsky, *Renaissance and Renascences* (Stockholm, 1960), Fig. 89.
[46] New York, Pierpont Morgan Library, MS 324, fol. 1ʳ, published as the frontispiece in *The Romance of the Rose*, trans. Robbins.

The brilliant illustrator of Valencia 387 caught the spirit of the text in an amusing manner (see Fig. 22). In the center, Pygmalion is jumping up and down in front of his statue while on the wall in the background hang no less than fifteen different musical instruments. Here the motif of the offering of the glove —shown in the vignette in the lower left-hand corner—serves a double purpose. The text suggests that Pygmalion, giving up his authority to the statue, offers it as his gage of submission; but it is also an invitation to the dance. Several illustrators pick up this incident, though it is but a minor one in an unusually rich context; and in one manuscript, which does not actually illustrate the idea, there is a textual rubric summarizing the *exemplum* which says "How Pygmalion offered his glove to the image."[47] The same motif shows up again in ivory carvings, though there its connection with the *Roman* illustrations is uncertain.

Love's dance is not everywhere as stately and serene as, superficially, it is in the pages of Guillaume de Lorris. Submission to the god of Love is, as Reason points out, a kind of frenetic enslavement of man's higher faculties by his animal passions, and there is, accordingly, a grotesque element in the *topos* of the carol. For sheer moral terror, there are few grislier moments in medieval literature than that in the *Libro de Buen Amor* when the religious of a hundred orders, with elaborate minstrelsy and ceremonial dancing, leave their convents on Easter Day to greet and kiss the hand of Dom Amor during his and Don Carnalis' frightening progress through anagogic Spain. There is no evidence that the Archpriest of Hita ever read the *Roman*, although he clearly has much in common with Jean de Meun, both in theme and in poetic vision; and I document merely a poetic commonplace, not an example of literary influence.

On the other hand, direct literary influence is clearly at work in Pierre Michault's fifteenth-century *Dance aux Aveugles* which appropriates the theme of Love's dance, virtually unaltered, from Guillaume de Lorris for its own central metaphor. The obscurity into which the *Dance aux Aveugles* has fallen is not undeserved, for the poem lacks most of the qualities for which the *Roman* was apparently prized in the first centuries after its composition: metrical sophistication, ironic wit, encyclopedic knowledge, anti-

---

[47] London, British Museum, MS Egerton 1069, fol. 141^v.

fraternalism, and moral apothegms. It reduces the complex ironic structure of the *Roman* to a kind of simple homily, much as any moral paraphrase of the poem must do. On the other hand, Michault was no Molinet: he fully understood the older poem and did not abuse it with absurd allegorical impositions.

In the *Dance aux Aveugles* (L'Aucteur) is given a guided tour by (Entendement) of the three gardens of Love, Fortune, and Death. In each garden the appropriate presiding deity makes his, or her, subjects perform a stately dance, imagined by the illustrators as a carol. The garden of Love is entirely familiar. In it Cupid and Venus, with appropriate iconographic attributes, sit on a throne "moult bien preparé & aourné de toutes fleurs & mignoties." Dancing around them are men and women of all ages and all nationalities. The two chief minstrels are named Oiseuse and Fol Appetit, and they so befuddle "raison naturelle" that "doulceur y est jugée amertume & le contraire aussy." The lovers in Cupid's garden all suffer from the same symptoms experienced by Amant: they are unable to distinguish between surface and substance, they experience irrational and compulsive yearnings, they reject sound moral advice, and so forth. In the lengthy catechisms which follow, Entendement teaches L'Aucteur that all men must join the dance of Death, but that only those foolish enough to subject themselves to Cupid and Fortune—to be sure, practically all of mankind—need join the first two dances. God has given man both free will to dance or not to dance and the rational faculty which, given rein, will unerringly choose not to.

Those moral judgments, which in the *Roman* are only hinted at or ironically implied, are overtly and perhaps tediously stated in the *Dance aux Aveugles*. Nonetheless it should by now be clear that Michault's exegesis of the dance of Love has more in common with the famous carol illustration in Harley 4425 than do the rules of courtly love. It is the sterner moralist, Michault, who gives us the perspective on sexual misbehavior necessary to deal with the charge of puritanism which is apparently inescapable in dealing with the moral ideals, perhaps as opposed to the moral practice, of the Middle Ages. It is the moralist's concern to take these matters seriously; and the authors of the *Roman*, as well as Pierre Michault, did so. They all, no doubt, considered lechery a mortal sin. Furthermore, it was for them a mortal sin which almost everybody had committed and which a great many people continually committed—if not in the flesh, then in spirit—so that it therefore had a certain universality. In the *Dance aux Aveugles*, L'Aucteur asks in exasperation whether there can have been any man alive who at least in his youth has not taken "a few steps" in the dance of Love; Entendement answers to the effect that practically all, "if not all of mankind," has done so.

Now the implications of this exchange are decidedly not puritanical. The fact that lechery was a deadly sin did not imply, at least in the Middle Ages, that men did not know it was extremely common. Nor, conversely, did the fact that practically all men and women knew themselves to be guilty, at one time or another, of lechery mean that it was not a mortal sin. Few medieval Christians, so far as I know, considered themselves free from mortal sin either in practice or by right.[48] The *Roman de la Rose* neither puts the question of sexual morality into a never-never land of "courtly love"—a sort of playground for the nobly-born, full of sophisticated toys for older child—nor abandons Christian morality to turn a frequently abused pleasurable bodily function into a pseudo-religion. Amant is a fool and a sinner, as are most men: his ludicrous rose quest and his enthusiastic dancing before Cupid and Fortune, are not exceptional. Rather, his is a typical course of action, common to most young men; furthermore, it is full of tropological suggestion of that process of reason's seduction which, according to medieval moral theory, was characteristic of any sin whatever. In the Middle Ages man's sinful nature was considered a painful affront to God and a great nuisance besides, accounting as it did for all troublesome aspects of the human condition. I have, however, found no medieval theologians who were unaware that God died on the cross to relieve the "human condition" or who considered the sacrifice insufficient to achieve that end; and it seems to me probable that Jean de Meun, being a medieval theologian, considered the saving redemption of Jesus Christ (rather than sexual copulation, as Alan Gunn would have it) God's greatest gift to mankind. The long line of Love's dancers

[48] See D. W. Robertson, "The Historical Setting of the Book of the Duchess," *Mediaeval Studies in Honor of Urban Tignor Holmes, Jr.* (Chapel Hill, 1965), pp. 169-95.

can, if they choose, put up their gloves and tambourines to worship at another altar.

To move from the icon of the carol of Deduit to that of Narcissus and his well is to follow a path of logical thematic development in the *Roman*; yet the transition requires a certain degree of allegorical sophistication. Whatever usefulness the term "allegory" retains for the analysis of medieval texts is seriously compromised by the failure to make the obvious yet vital distinction that allegory can be considered either from the point of view of its reader or from that of its writer. This is essentially the distinction with which Rosemond Tuve grapples in the first brilliant essay of her *Allegorical Imagery*. No medieval allegory could ever be quite like the allegory par excellence of the Scriptures, where the sublime tropes of the Holy Ghost and the inspired exegetical understanding of the Fathers—the energies of writer and of reader—joined in mysterious and fruitful harmony. But remove the Holy Ghost and one is left with the *De laboribus Herculis* or the *Faerie Queene*, the allegorical mode as literary criticism or as imposed poetic structure. In the *Echecs Amoureux* and its gloss, probably written by the same hand, we see the poet both as reader and as writer of allegory, perhaps, in complementary yet markedly distinct functions. The friars who collected or made up the little tales in the *Gesta Romanorum*, and moralized them, were writing allegory; the preachers who found spiritual meanings in obviously secular lyrics were reading allegory.

The poets of the later Middle Ages are, typically, both readers and writers of allegory. Dante, who produced one of the most elaborate and scholastically tidy allegories of the period, filled with received allegorical readings of scriptural tropes; and Giovanni Boccaccio, a distinguished allegorical writer, became a distinguished allegorical reader with his great *Genealogia*, which interpreted a vast body of classical literature in order to provide authoritative imagery for Christian poets and painters. Guillaume de Lorris, of course, could not turn to Boccaccio's book, but he apparently did have at his disposal allegorical treatises from the school of Orléans which represented, even in the thirteenth century, a venerable academy of classical study and allegorical reading.

Medieval *allegoresis*, wrenched from its historical context and from the hermeneutic and historiographical principles of the Middle Ages, is generally spoken of as a ludicrous abuse, even by scholars sympathetic to the intellectual life of the period. "The history of this medieval practice of allegorical thinking has yet to be written," says R. R. Bolgar. "We may regard it as a curious divagation of the human mind."[49] Perhaps so; but we are spared the embarrassment of subjecting our own principles of literary criticism to the judgment of a St. Augustine or an Erasmus. In any case it remains a curious divagation without which there might well have been little classical heritage for us to be beneficiaries of, and it is certainly a technique and a mode of thought, which the student of medieval literary history can ignore only at his great peril.

It was not for want of wit or originality that the authors of the *Roman* exploited a conventional setting peopled with abstractions and men and gods of old. Rather, classical mythology, particularly Ovidian mythology, provided them with a rich body of emblematic materials, familiar certainly to most of their readers, which could be woven at art's command into the texture of their poem. The great shared myth of the medieval artist and his audience was of course the Christian faith. From the Christian Scriptures and the voluminous exegesis which surrounded them, the artist could draw materials for his poems, paintings, and statuary with considerable confidence that his audience would be able to recognize and respond not only to their forms but also to their accepted associations. But we know as well that the voracious hunger of the medieval doctors to relate all knowledge to the central fact of human and divine history took them beyond *the* book to the "book of nature" and the books of the ancients—the "Egyptian gold" of pagan literature.

Thus it is that the Ovidian materials in the *Roman* require attention from a Christian perspective—i.e., they must be examined from the point of view of their mythographic rather than their mythological significance. Mythography, or the attempt to explicate myth authoritatively from the point of view of a given set of cultural values, would seem to be as old as mythology itself:

[49] *The Classical Heritage and Its Beneficiaries* (Cambridge, 1954), p. 422.

the first great mythographers appear in classical antiquity.[50] Each age produces its own mythographers, its Frazer or its Freud. The fascinating history of medieval mythography, traced so brilliantly by Jean Seznec in *The Survival of the Pagan Gods*, is chiefly remarkable for its richness and the formal nature of its documents —catalogues, encyclopedias, "moralizations." Ovidian mythography was very widely practiced, and indeed forms an important discrete category of medieval letters, as we know from the studies of Rand, Ghisalberti, and others. Ovid, a great moralist to the Middle Ages, also became its chief mythologist.

The mythographic treatments of the *Metamorphoses*, varied as they are in scope and nature, demonstrate the salient features of medieval mythography in general. In the first place they are moral in intention; the mythographer seeks to expose the Christian truth which, for him, lies buried in the integument. Secondly, Ovidian mythography—like scriptural exegesis which, viewed from the point of view of a rationalist, is a mode of mythography proper—admits varying, and even contradictory, interpretations *in malo* or *in bono* depending upon the aims of the commentator. Thus, for example, Pygmalion is condemned by Arnulf of Orléans as a typical idolator but praised in the Ovidian commentary of Dante's friend Giovanni del Vergilio. There is a "good" Venus, and a "bad" Venus in the explications of Ovid, just as the serpents of the sacred text can be good or bad according to the Augustinian principles of scriptural exegesis. It is thus obvious that Ovidian mythography is, in the useful terminology provided by Miss Tuve, blatantly "imposed allegory." She draws many of her illustrations of "imposed allegory" from one of the most complete and schematic mythographic treatments of the *Metamorphoses*—the enormous fourteenth-century *Ovide Moralisé*.

What the author of the *Ovide Moralisé* did to the *Metamorphoses* was essentially what Jean Molinet, in his time, did to the *Roman de la Rose*. The poetic transformation attendant upon this kind of moralization will not find approbation from current canons of literary criticism, but this should not blind us from seeing imposition for what it is. At the end of the Middle Ages mytho-

[50] Carl Schneider, *Geistesgeschichte des antiken Christentums* (Munich, 1954), I, 333ff.

graphic imposition could be satirized in such a work as the *Epistolae Obscurorum Virorum*, and the practice has seemed a patently absurd abuse to most classical scholars since. The attempts to explicate medieval secular literature, partly in terms of mythographic tradition, and partly in terms of the medieval tradition of scriptural exegesis, have proved highly controversial. One recent critic, complaining of alleged allegorical abuses in the interpretation of medieval romances, says scornfully that such interpretations have about as much validity as Ovidian impositions. But to speak of the "validity" of medieval mythography is to address oneself to a question of little interest. (It is also to deny, by implication, our own critical impositions. Is there really more "validity" in finding Narcissus an archetypal sexual psychotic or Pygmalion a fashioner of "mature love" through art than in seeing them with the eyes of Arnulf of Orléans or John of Salisbury?) I do not seek to defend or apologize for medieval mythography or to argue its validity or want of it. Molinet's recension of the *Roman* tells us a good deal about Molinet and something about his intellectual milieu, and had it attained any widespread circulation or obviously influenced a great deal of major poetry of the fifteenth and sixteenth centuries, we could validly use it to study that poetry. In fact it did not; we can doubt that it was a more influential literary document than the *Ovide Moralisé*. Of mythographic treatments of the *Metamorphoses* in general, however, the opposite is true; they did have wide currency, and their influence on their literary posterity is easily demonstrable.

The first Ovidian episode, apart from the hint we have seen in Oiseuse at the gate, is the *exemplum* of Narcissus. After the excitement of the carol, Amant seeks the quiet of a solitary walk. (Silently, invisibly, Amours trails him, bow and arrow in hand.) The Lover comes to a pleasant place (*bel leu*) where, beneath a pine tree, the likes of which has not been seen since the time of Charlemagne, he finds a fountain with the discreet lapidary inscription: *Se mori li biaus Narcissus*—"Here died the fair Narcissus." Guillaume de Lorris here takes time out to give an abbreviated account of Narcissus, the *demoiseau* who scorned the loyal love of Echo and who, for this disdain, suffered a terrible but just retribution. He fell in love with his own beautiful reflection in the fountain and there died. Into this fountain the Lover will himself peer in a moment, and see the crystals and the rosebud which becomes the object of his single-minded efforts for more than twenty thousand lines of poetry.

Few episodes of the *Roman* were more popular with the illustrators than the *exemplum* of Narcissus. From the earlier illustrations, such as Fig. 23, in which the fountain is little more than a formless splotch against the hillside, to the elaborate hexagonal Renaissance wellhead of Fig. 24, there is a considerable degree of stylistic change but, so far as can be judged, no change in the quite unromantic intent of the miniaturists. That the well of Narcissus is, in one sense, the central concept of the whole poem can be seen in one of the fine *incipit* illustrations which show the entire garden (Fig. 3). Here the well is at the center of the garden and is, indeed, the source of the river which the Lover has had to cross to arrive at the gate. With the anachronism which the time scheme of allegory implies, the painter shows us a rather puffy and bourgeois Narcissus staring at his own reflection at the same time that Oiseuse greets the Lover at the door. The illustrator has by no means mastered all the techniques of pictorial space, but he has nonetheless clearly and consciously organized the space of his picture around the central framed configuration of Narcissus at the well.

The fountain in the Garden is not merely like the well of Narcissus; it is that well, and Amant like Narcissus before him sees therein his own fatal reflection. Nowhere in his brilliant analysis of the *Roman* is Robertson more perceptive in detail than in his contention, against Lewis and others, that the magical crystals which Amant sees shining back at him from the pool are not the Lady's but his own eyes.[51] Indeed the crystals would seem to present a real crux for the interpretation of Guillaume's psychology of love. One recent scholar, Köhler, maintains that these crystals, the eyes of the Lady, are magic because they reflect

---

[51] *Preface to Chaucer*, p. 95. The mirror image from Bernard de Ventadour, cited by Lewis to "prove" the correctness of his explication of the well of Narcissus, is quite different from that in the *Roman*. Cf. Guido Favati, "Il tema degli occhi come specchio," *Studi in onore di Carlo Pellegrini* (Turin, 1963), pp. 3-13.

clearly, *sanz decevoir*, the contents of the garden.[52] Yet upon examination, Guillaume's characterization of their supposed magical qualities (ll. 1560ff.) makes no extravagant claims. The crystals, without deception, show the entire contents of the garden to those who stare into the water. They can see half the garden and, if they turn, the other half. Indeed there is no physical object (*chose*) in the garden so tiny or well hidden that it does not appear as if painted on the crystals.

What is being described here by Guillaume is neither magic nor superstition, but physical sight. The eyes reflected in the pool —the eyes of anybody who looks into it—clearly see everything within the garden. Such is the excellence of the ocular part, the fleshly eye, which can perceive the fleshly world. The gift which Christ was disposed to give to the blind was no less highly regarded in the Middle Ages than it is now, and Guillaume's riddling description of its processes reveals a sense of wonder before the miracle of sight rather than oblation before the supposed magic of crystals. Köhler's contention that the crystals reveal the Garden "in its essence" misses all this. It is precisely the garden's essence which the crystals of the fleshly eye cannot reveal. When Genius later in the poem contrasts the heavenly carbuncle with the crystals, he makes the point that the latter cannot reveal anything without the aid of sunlight (ll. 20458ff.). They are the physical eyes of the physical world, not the inner "eyes of the heart" (Ephesians 1:18). Amant, like Narcissus before him, becomes unduly preoccupied with the fantasies of the insubstantial physical world, with the sight of the fleshly eye— that indeed is the point Guillaume wishes to make—but this is a matter of morality, not necromancy. Amant is one of those who "seeing, does not perceive"; but to explain this dilemma we must blame his own willful rejection of Reason, not the shimmering of bright stones in clear water.

Amant's eyes within the *mirreour perillous* become themselves the revolving mirrors which impress upon his mind the fantastic beauty of Deduit's garden. Peering at himself in the well of self-love, Amant experiences a transformation, by the stratagems of

[52] E. Köhler, "Narcisse, la fontaine d'Amour, et Guillaume de Lorris," *L'Humanisme médiéval dans les littératures romanes du XIIe au XIVe siècle* (Paris, 1964), pp. 156ff.

art, worthy of the great Ovid himself; after a time, he no longer sees those ocular crystals, but a rose. Like Narcissus, he becomes a flower as the images within the pool become confused. Frappier must be correct to say that Guillaume here suggests that in Amant the idea of love precedes love itself.[53] Yet the psychological process involved is emphatically not a movement from a platonic generality to the specific reality of a particular rosebud. It is no ideal progression at all, but rather the projection of self-love upon an external object, one of the *choses* in the garden. The illustrators of the poem once again offer useful suggestions: in their attempt to capture this mysterious mutation they illuminate the process of "falling in love." Figure 23 illustrates, according to its rubric, "How Amant looked at himself in the fountain so much that he saw a rosebush full of roses." It is clear from the illustration that what is reflected for Amant to see is Amant's own face (cf. Narcissus in Figs. 24, 25, 26). The vision of the rose, swirling up from the hillock above the fountain, comes only later.

Concerning the significance of the Narcissus episode, the mythographers down to and including Freud are virtually unanimous. Narcissus is the archetype of self-love, and wherever we shall turn in the medieval mythographic tradition, whether it be to Arnulf of Orléans, John of Salisbury, or Giovanni del Vergilio, we shall find the *exemplum* of Narcissus used as a striking condemnation of the folly of self-love. According to E. K. Rand, an authority with whom it is painful to disagree, the mythographic teachings rolled off Guillaume "like water from the duck's back."[54] But to say that Guillaume is not himself a mythographer—that is, that he does not give overt moral meanings to his Ovidian borrowings —is hardly to demonstrate the poet's disinterested attitude toward the classical myth he introduces so appropriately into his own poem. It is of course true that Guillaume exercises both tact and playful originality in handling the story of Narcissus. At the end

---

[53] Jean Frappier, "Variations sur le thème du miroir, de Bernard de Ventadour à Maurice Scève," *Cahiers de l'Association internationale des études françaises*, XI (1959), 151. The extended discussion of the Narcissus episode by Frederick Goldin, *The Mirror of Narcissus in the Courtly Love Lyric* (Ithaca, 1967) was not available to me in time for consideration in this work; I hope to consider it in another place.

[54] "The Metamorphosis of Ovid in *Le Roman de la Rose*," *Studies in the History of Culture* (Menasha, 1942), p. 120.

of the *exemplum* he adds a few lines proposing that the meaning of the story is a warning to the ladies to look after their men. As a reading of the Narcissus story this interpretation has much in common with that which sees *Othello* as a warning that ladies should look after their linen. It seems to me a great strain on the text to suggest that in this splendid *non sequitur* Guillaume is seriously offering his own mythographer's mite *à l'amour courtois*.[55]

As for Amant, he thinks the danger in the Fountain is not for the *dames*, but for himself, and, his guard for a moment down, he tells his fear. "That mirrour hath me now entriked. . . . For in the snare I fell anoon / That hath bitrasshed many oon." At least one illustrator took him seriously, for he marked the spring with a death's head, the sign of a poisoned well.[56] Guillaume was up to a little more than reverent plagiarism, for both the Narcissus *exemplum* and its mythographic overtones add richly to his poetic meaning. The very clear implication of the text is that the love born in Amant when he stares so tenderly on the crystals is much like that engendered in Narcissus by his own image in the well; and if we remove from the crystals their mythic magical qualities—qualities distilled by the critics, not infused by the poet—we shall see revealed the auto-erotic origins of his passion.

The random transference of Amant's interest from the crystals to the *choses* in the garden and finally to a particular *bouton*, and his quite marked difficulty in grasping the idea of postponed gratifications, suggest a pattern of infantile behavior with which modern psychologists may be not altogether unfamiliar. Nonetheless, what Guillaume describes is typical behavior seen from the point of view of an ironic moralist. He has, in his part of the *Roman de la Rose*, somewhat schematically traced the typical course of love, from the first tentative steps in the "olde daunce" until its final confirmation in the feudal rite of vassalage by which Amant becomes the god of Love's man. The formal plighting of Amant's troth to Amours anticipates, to a degree, the subjugation of Théophile to the devil in Rutebeuf's play; indeed, it would seem that

[55] See, however, Donald Stone, "Old and New Thoughts on Guillaume de Lorris," *Australian Journal of French Studies*, II (1965), 157-70.

[56] Alexandre de Laborde, *Les principaux manuscrits à peintures conservés dans l'ancienne Bibliothèque Impériale Publique de Saint Petersbourg*, II (Paris, 1938), Plate lxxxiii.

Rutebeuf has copied the detail from Guillaume.[57] (If so, the *Roman* presents the literary curiosity of having influenced a poet, with its first "half," who was to be a substantial influence himself on its own second "half.") Once Amant is interested in a particular rosebud and sets out to pluck it, he is ripe for plucking by Amours; and sure enough Amant's god, who like the devil is a hunter, finally shoots his quarry. The arrow enters the eye, lodges in the heart; and we are once again on the familiar ground of "literary convention"—the literary convention of Augustinian psychology. The formal ceremony by which Amant becomes the sworn votary of a pagan god has been described as an exquisite fancy of the courtly sensibility. It can be better described as fornication of the heart, alias idolatry, and it is entirely jejeune to suggest, as a recent editor of the poem has done, that the ten commandments of Amours involve no parody of the Ten Commandments of Jehova. Rosemond Tuve has correctly identified idolatry as a principal controlling theme of the poem; Guillaume gives us the phony "stone tables of the law," and Jean the carnal pilgrimage to the shrines of concupiscence so amusingly captured by fourteenth-century illustrators, as in Fig. 27.

Such austere judgments may at first seem harsh, for after all are not the commandments of love noble commandments? The injunctions of Amours seem no more sinister than the Boy Scouts' pledge—be reverent, be clean, be cheerful; but what of the fruits of these commandments, the toothache and the masturbation, the sordid lies and the hypocritical clean speech? It requires no unusual literary sophistication to perceive the ironies which lie behind the commandments of Amours, merely a knowledge, however vague, of those true commandments of love on which hang all the Law and the Prophets.

A little bit of such "courtly love" hanky-panky goes a long way, and I do not wish to bore the reader with a full summary of Guillaume's plot. Suffice it to say that the poet evolves a formal scheme in which the assault on the rosebud becomes another episode in the perpetual war between the forces of Venus and those of Reason. That this is not immediately evident, perhaps, arises

[57] Since the story of Theophilus' pact with the devil antedates Rutebeuf, the analogous passages in the *Roman* and the *Théophile* may simply arise from the treatment of a common theme.

in part from the fact that Amant's description of the psychomachic warfare is painfully tendentious. Like another Adam in his fool's paradise, he has the power of name-giving, and it is a power he abuses. Who, for instance, is his adversary called Malebouche (Wikkid-Tonge, in the Middle English) except the soothsaying unmasker of the god of Love's hypocrisy? Yet the essential nature of Lady Reason shines through her iconographic attributes and is, indeed, overtly recognized by Amant himself. She lives in a high tower, is of harmonious proportions, has two shining eyes, wears a richly decorated crown. She was created in Paradise and is not a work of Nature: rather, she is God's daughter (and therefore, by implication, the sister of Jesus Christ). Her job is to keep men from folly, and whoever follows her will be sinless.

Reason, who has come to recall Amant from his "folly and childishness," chides him for being stupid enough to come into Deduit's garden "whereof Ydilness bar the keye" and for joining in the dance in the first place. She is, however, tolerant and of course eminently reasonable about such behavior on the part of young men, provided that they are not obstinately perverse in their folly. She counsels penance, self-examination, and the abjuration of love. Her counsel contains some knowledge of things human as well as those divine, and she points out some common-sense aspects of Amant's predicament; there is nothing high-handed about her advice, which is simply charitable good counsel. Amant's reaction is angry recrimination. He announces, in a para-doxical boast, that he has no will power; furthermore, he hates those who would correct him. He ends by accusing Reason of wasting her words in idleness and asks her to go away. So she does, for Reason will not stay as an unwelcome guest. Amant, his guard down for a moment, just as it had been in his description of the well of Narcissus, recounts the situation thus: "Reason went away when she saw that nothing could bring me from my folly. I was left alone . . . like a madman."

Having rejected the good counsel of the daughter of God, Amant is left with the bad counsel of his Friend, of whom the Middle English text, revealing a kind of Chaucerian irony, says "A trewer felowe was nowher noon." Friend anticipates the worldly wisdom of La Vieille. He is solicitous for poor Amant, sympathetic to his problem. Friend knows a way, he says, to lull

Danger into pliancy: flattery. Immediately acting on Friend's advice, as he had not on Reason's, Amant goes to Danger and swears to him that his sole desire is now to do Danger's will and to make penance for having offended him. This is not merely a lie, pure and simple, but an ironic echo of the kind of penance he should be making. The ruse works, Danger is duped, and Venus appears on the scene with her blazing torch to win for Amant the inflammatory joy of kissing the rose. The forces of Chastity rally, and Bel Accueil, clearly not to be trusted when inflamed by Venus, is incarcerated in a tower built by Jealousy. On the grassy bank at the foot of the tower, which is for the illustrators the Castle of Jealousy, wretched Amant, like so many other literary lovers of the Middle Ages, cries out that he will die if he does not get what Bel Accueil alone can procure for him from the rose. On this not entirely elevating note Guillaume de Lorris' part in the *Roman de la Rose* ends.

According to one critic, Amant's lamentable behavior has revealed a "full, subtle exhibition of human psychology"; for Guillaume de Lorris is a notable "descriptive psychologist," as opposed to Prudentius, a man more interested in morality than in psychology.[58] There is something in this, but not much. Guillaume does in fact describe a psychological process, speaking very loosely, but he does so in a derivative way, acting out the literary ritual of an ancient classical topos. Indeed, the psychological action of Guillaume's poem conforms to at least two sets of traditional literary schema: one—the five stages of love—deriving from classical poetry and the scholiast tradition, the other—the three stages of sin—from Augustinian theology. Professor Robertson first pointed out the usefulness of approaching medieval literary love psychology from the vantage points of these schema and has provided an extended analysis of Amant's behavior in the light of the latter convention, the so-called three stages of sin.[59]

Every sin can be divided into the three typical stages of the sin of our first parents in Eden: suggestion, pleasurable thought, and consent. The terminology varies—sometimes it is suggestion, the sin in thought, the sin in deed—but the process to which it refers

---

[58] Charles Muscatine, "The Emergence of Psychological Allegory in Old French Romance," *PMLA*, LXVIII (1953), 1161.
[59] *Preface to Chaucer*, pp. 94ff.

is always a tropological Fall, always involves the rejection of Reason, and always results in the turning "upsodoun" of the divinely ordered hierarchies. Amant is first conditioned for his fall by the "suggestion" of Oiseuse, Deduit, and the old dance; he is inflaméd by the "pleasurable thought" counseled by Amours and Amis; and he sets out to execute in deed the design to which his will has already yielded unreasonable "consent." It is only the thick stone walls of Jealousy's castle which prevent Amant from gaining, through Bel Accueil, the floral favors he so desperately seeks and keep him, in short, from committing "courtly love" or "mortal sin."

Robertson's analysis, which awards no prizes either for Amant's probity or for the delicacy and originality of Guillaume's sentiments and psychological insights, may seem at first clinically theological and, therefore, an "imposition." The dubious criticism seems to be that one must not seize with the rude hands of theology the tender flower of poetry, though that there are less delicate ways of seizing that flower the *Roman de la Rose* itself amply demonstrates. We shall arrive at the same conclusions, following a perhaps more tactful literary path, by examining the classical *topos* which Robertson first suggested and to which Lionel Friedman has recently devoted a learned and amusing essay—the *gradus amoris*, or the "steps of love."[60]

The steps of love are five, according to Pomponius' commentary on Horace: *visus, alloquium, contactus, osculum, factum.* The Lover sees, draws near in conversation, touches, kisses, *facit.* Friedman gives a variety of examples, from twelfth-century Latin drama and elsewhere, of literary exploitation of the *topos* and charts its adaptation by the moralists of the later Middle Ages, who used it, not surprisingly, to describe the condition of *luxuria* or carnal love. The five stages of Pomponius are neither more nor less realistic, psychological, or delicate than the three stages of St. Augustine. They form a literary convention which places typical behavior at a distance suitable for detached observation, and this is doubtless why they were found so congenial by Alain de Lille, the greatest single source influence on the *Roman,* Frère Laurent, and Chaucer's Parson. Critics are of course free

[60] *Preface to Chaucer,* p. 407*n*; and Lionel Friedman, "*Gradus Amoris,*" *Romance Philology,* xix (1965), 167-77.

to find a "full, subtle exhibition of human psychology" in the *Roman de la Rose* if they wish, but the trophies they award belong not to Guillaume de Lorris but to the scholiasts or St. Augustine. For the perfectly clear fact is that in the thirteenth century there was no tidy distinction between the *gradus amoris* as literary convention and the *gradus amoris* as theological schema. When Amant first sees, draws near, touches, and then kisses the rosebud, it is patently obvious, as Professor Friedman has shown, that the next step, soon to come, is *factum*. It should also be clear that the moral context into which Amant's career must be placed is that of *luxuria*, or what the Middle English text of the *Romaunt* calls Lechery.

For all his Ovidian smoothness and urbanity, Guillaume de Lorris is eventually rather obvious. The sources of his iconography are diverse, but he knows neither extended irony nor complex exemplification. C. S. Lewis credibly, though I think mistakenly, suggested that Guillaume's *Roman* was meant to end with the "traditional palinode" (where traditional?), that Amant would in the end turn his back on his folly and embrace Reason. Beyond question Guillaume prepares his reader for a rigorous judgment of love. Oiseuse and Narcissus are, so to speak, notorious icons; and Amant's cavalier dismissal of Reason is irredeemable save by penitential grace. That such grace was to be received is implied in the opening lines of the poem, where the narrator tells us that everything in the dream subsequently came true, and prays to God that his "Art of Love" will be acceptable to her for whom it is written, she "who is worthy of being loved so much that she merits being called Rose." The object of this courteous dedication is probably the Virgin Mary, the celestial rose of that garden in Jean de Meun's continuation which contrasts in almost every detail with the Garden of Deduit.[61] Such a rose is indeed worthy of love; others, implicitly, are not.

[61] See M. Gorce, *Le Roman de la Rose* (Paris, 1933), pp. 32-33; cf. Jean Sonet, *Répertoire d'incipit de prières en ancien français* (Geneva, 1956), no. 643. The odd idea that "Rose" was the name of Guillaume's girl-friend began, so far as I know, with Claude Fauchet in 1571, in his notes on the *Roman* (Paris, Bibliothèque nationale MS fr. 14726, fols. 5^r-7^r). The notion is still around, and still nonsensical: it does not require lovableness to be called by one's own name.

Speculation about Guillaume's intentions for the continuation of his poem is fruitless. Langlois found a few manuscripts which contain an abrupt conclusion, by some rude hand, in which Amant *tout court* gets the rosebud for a night and wakes up. The sole interest of this doggerel is that it is possible, barely, that it suggested to Jean de Meun the broad path of irony along which he might pursue his brilliantly original design. He knew perfectly well where Guillaume was headed, and he knew how to get there more surely by a more scenic, though much longer, route.

The most detailed and schematic thirteenth-century exposition of the *gradus amoris* is by Gérard of Liège. Gérard's *Remedia contra amorem illicitum* has a special interest for students of medieval French literature, and of the *Roman* in particular, since he makes frequent allusion to vernacular literature, including the *Roman*, in the course of his purely theological work.[62] Speaking of the monastic state Gérard says that "dius nous a enfremés en son castiel de sainte religion par tres grant ialousie damour." If André Wilmart's dating of Gérard's work is correct, we have here a most unusual reference to the *Roman* during the period between the time that Guillaume left it off and Jean de Meun took it up. Gérard's analysis of the *gradus amoris*, which takes several pages, is chiefly remarkable for his insistence that the familiar five stages which the poet says are carnal love are identical for spiritual love. In other words, both *cupiditas* and *caritas*, can be analyzed by the *gradus amoris*—the first carnally, the latter spiritually, as in the Canticles. It is of further interest that Gérard alternatively analyzes *amor* by means of the tropological fall and the three Augustinian stages of sin.

When Guillaume left Bel Accueil locked up in the castle of Jealousy, his hero was four-fifths of the way to erotic *factum*, two-thirds of the way to the "sin in deed." The anonymous hand which in the middle of the thirteenth century executed the fifth *gradus amoris* in a bald seventy-eight lines carried Guillaume's poem to its logical conclusion; Jean de Meun took eighteen thousand lines to do as much if more, and when he described his part in the *Roman* he said simply "I taught the way of capturing the

---

[62] André Wilmart, ed., "Les traités de Gérard de Liège sur l'amour illicite et sur l'amour de Dieu," *Analecta Reginensia* (Città del Vaticano, 1933), pp. 181-247.

castle and of picking the rose."[63] In short, he taught the fifth step of love, but he did so in ironic fashion, exciting his readers to love worthily, to discover the double lesson of love and to reflect upon it. He certainly cannot have been without success in directing his first readers to the sentence of his "moult noble doctrine." No one who has ever worked with the manuscripts of his poem can fail to be impressed that it is Lady Reason's definition of love, with its praise of charity and its warning against cupidity, which has attracted underscoring, marginal glosses, and innumerable recommendations of "Nota!"

[63] "Boethius' *De Consolatione* by Jean de Meun," ed. Dedeck-Héry, *Mediaeval Studies*, XIV (1952), 168.

CHAPTER THREE

Love's Preceptors

EADERS familiar with conventional criticism of the *Roman* may have noticed that so far nothing has been said about the chief critical "point" usually made about it: namely, its dual authorship. The French critics in particular have been insistent on seeing the poem as two very unequal parts, even to the point of speaking of "Guillaume's *Roman*" and "Jean's *Roman*" as though the two parts were two entirely different poems. Guillaume is supposed to be courtly, smooth, aristocratic, and conventional; Jean is anticourtly, bumptious, bourgeois, and unconventional. The *Roman* becomes, as one such critic would have it, "the poem of a Charles d'Orléans, finished by a Rabelais."[1]

Such a diagnosis of schizophrenia, which has frequently been offered in place of any kind of serious discussion of the ideas of either man, might engage our interest and even tempt consent were it not so obviously a modern imposition. Despite marked, indeed sensational differences of style, emphasis, and poetic strategy on the parts of the two poets, their poem prosecutes a single and unified action. The *Roman* is not a seamless garment, but it is of one cloth. Alan Gunn has shown how medieval readers regarded Jean de Meun as by far the more important writer; but no medieval commentator ever remarked, as not a few modern ones have, that Jean did not understand what Guillaume had been doing, since it was, and should continue to be, obvious that he understood very well. Pierre Col, whose essay reveals a close reading of the poem, says merely that Jean brought to completion what Guillaume had begun.[2] One fourteenth-century reader, a marginal versifier who calls himself "Philibertus," wrote a poem of some historical interest on the subject of the neglect of Guillaume de Lorris resulting from honors lavished on Jean de Meun. He says that in praising Jean de Meun—and he is, beyond ques-

---

[1] André Bellessort, *Heures de parole* (Paris, 1929), p. 148.

[2] Ward, *The Epistles on the Romance*, p. 72. Cf. the remarks of Jean de Montreuil, *Epistolario* in *Opera*, ed. Ornato, I, 178.

tion, to be praised highly—the reader should not fail to give credit to "the first author," as he rather coyly refers to Guillaume. Simply because the *Roman* is so "beautiful that one would think it was all of one piece (*tout un*)," the "first author" should not be entirely neglected.[3] The remark suggests that Philibertus regarded the two parts of the poem in the same way that Laurent de Premierfait viewed the *Roman* and the *Divine Comedy*, that is, iconographically, from the point of view of discursive content and meaning.

It should not have taken a Philibertus to remind readers of the "first author," for it is Jean de Meun's reference to Guillaume de Lorris within the text of the poem itself which has taught modern philology absolutely everything it knows about him. The miniaturists often give us pictures of the two authors, busily at work at their *pupitres*; such portraits are, as Kuhn observed, based on the cliché of the portraits of the Evangelists in illustrated Bibles. They reveal neither an incipient cult of literary personality nor a concern with the problem of the poem's dual authorship. As a matter of fact, Guillaume de Lorris is frequently confused with his more famous namesake from Saint-Amour, championed by Rutebeuf and Jean de Meun; and the oldest surviving picture of Guillaume, dating perhaps from the last years of the thirteenth century, bears this puzzling rubric: "Ci dit laucteur comment Mestre Jehan de Meun parfist cest romans a la request Mestre Guillaume de Saint Amor qui le commencement enfist si ne le pot parfaire."[4] Many of Jean's fourteenth-century admirers probably would have liked to think that Guillaume de Saint-Amour was the "first author"; none, so far as is known, thought the question a crucial one for the unity of the poem.

The fact that no medieval reader of the *Roman* has commented upon the difference in style and tone between those parts of the poem which are Guillaume's and those which are Jean's does not mean that there are none; and there clearly are. To a large extent the stylistic disparity between the two parts of the poem can be explained in stylistic terms—rather than in terms of alleged polarities of the poets' moral or philosophical vision—and I have tried to suggest one possible kind of stylistic analysis in my first chapter.

[3] Paris, Bibliothèque nationale MS fr. 24389, fol. 27ᵛ.
[4] Paris, Bibliothèque nationale MS fr. 1569, fol. 28ʳ.

Alan Gunn's defense of the unity of the *Roman*, a pioneering effort which flew in the face of received opinion, has done much to clear the air, though a number of the more durable chestnuts still show up in print. There is the Lewis line which maintains, in effect, that Jean de Meun knew nothing about allegory in general and even less about Guillaume's in particular, and that he "ignored, perhaps despised, Guillaume's architectonics." The nineteenth-century sociological school, which explains the *Roman* largely in terms of the fabulous distinction between Guillaume's "courtly" origins and concerns and Jean's "bourgeois" vision of the world, flourishes still, and perhaps finds its culmination in the extraordinary notion of Gérard Paré that Jean is an "anti-Guillaume." We have come a very long way from Philibertus and the poem that is "so beautiful that one would judge it to be all of one piece."

Jean de Meun neither misunderstood nor despised what Guillaume had begun, and the poetic structure of the two parts of the *Roman* rests on the common keystone of psychomachic drama. Amant is confronted by a series of characters who present to him intellectual positions implying moral postures. Ovid called himself a "love teacher" (*praeceptor amoris*), and it is useful to follow Gunn and others in calling Amours, Lady Reason, Amis, La Vieille, and the rest "teachers of love." I see no evidence in the text of the *Roman*, as Gunn apparently does, that Jean seeks by this method to work out a synthetic pronouncement on love arising from the clash of polar theses and antitheses—Jean had not, after all, the opportunity to read Hegel—or that Amant receives anything like a proper education in his chosen syllabus. Rather, Jean presents a number of traditional ideas about love, decorously distributed among a number of traditional fictional types: he advances no new ideas of his own about love whatsoever. To be understood and evaluated, the attitudes put forward by the teachers of love must be held up against the moral and intellectual traditions from which they derive. It is the comedy of the *Roman*, as well as the tragedy of Amant, in a medieval sense, that he fails to learn, that he fails to make reasonable evaluations. His "education," as a result, is a fiasco. From Amours he learns a stilted code of false courtesy which maintains that nobility is based on external, and often hypocritical, appearance rather than inner virtue. From Amis he learns the utility of mendacity in the game of love as well as much other cynical worldly wisdom, while the most notorious old whore in French literature, his ally and emissary, preaches love's mercantile strategy. From the most profound of all his teachers of love, Reason, associated in the poem with the *Sapientia Dei Patris* or Christ, Amant refuses to learn anything, leaving himself quite literally without the tools of rational analysis necessary to understand and qualify the "philosophy of plenitude" of which most recent critics have attempted to make so much. His is no education, properly understood, but a kind of intellectual rake's progress.

The psychomachic architectonics of the *Roman* are commonplace, and it is difficult to explain why so few critics have grasped them. As the exegete of the *Echecs* said, the *Roman* is the kind of poem in which there are "several characters who speak in turn according to their natures." The critical principle here enunciated is, of course, the very ancient one of literary decorum: the actions and speeches of fictional characters should consistently reflect their feigned natures. The obligation which this principle implies for the critic is that he must carefully distinguish between creature and creator, unless there is substantial reason to think that the two share a common point of view. Hamlet hesitates, not Shakespeare; and his hesitation is to be explained in terms of his own nature, not in terms of Shakespeare's.

Yet the prevailing critical abuse of Jean's poem observes no such amenities, however elementary. The inanities of a befuddled lover, the lewd guffaws of an aging prostitute, the ludicrous self-exculpation of an evil friar, the ravings of a jealous husband—all this, and more, is passed off as the personal opinions of Jean de Meun. The dictates of unbridled concupiscence, free of all reasonable governance, are seriously presented as his "gospel of sensuality." That Jean emerges from this critical ordeal as "the Voltaire of the thirteenth century" is an act of the critic's mercy; he should emerge as a nincompoop or a lunatic or both. Even Gerson knew better, in theory, than to ascribe to a poet the postures of his purely fictional creations. Pierre Col, who shared Gerson's theory but, unlike the Chancellor, actually practised it, never forgot; and his reminder that the Lover in the *Roman* talks like a lover, the Jaloux like a *jaloux*, and so forth, is one with which all serious criticism of Jean's poem must begin, wherever it intends to end. Such a dictum may prove unacceptable to the "naturalists," so that the return to sanity will probably be difficult. When Lionel Friedman, in an excellent article dealing with the matter of the literary decorum of the Jaloux' speech, reiterated the operative critical principle, it was almost immediately labelled "unconvincing" in a book advancing the thesis that Jean's part of the *Roman* is one of the "four mainstreams of medieval naturalism."[5]

If we are willing to grant to Jean the license of fictive invention usually accorded to poets, it will not be necessary to find his own philosophy (contradictory, of course, but all the more excitingly *outré*) in the pronouncements of each of the teachers of love. Since they "speak in turn according to their natures," the preliminary task of the critic should be to attempt to understand, from a medieval point of view, what their natures are, rather than to evolve a synthetic statement from their conflicting opinions. Professor Gunn analyzed at length that "medieval *conflictus*" which he saw at the heart of Jean's poem, and around which spins the rhetorical orbit of the Lover and his preceptors. But for him apparently Jean is not the remote puppeteer of the *conflictus*, poetically arranging the materials of a drama of the mind; rather its victim, one who possibly has, like the Lover, known the violent and incompatible demands of Christ and Venus, Reason and La Vieille.[6]

There is indeed a *conflictus* at the heart of the *Roman*, but it has nothing whatsoever to do with its authors' putative sex lives, except insofar as it exemplifies what was to medieval psychology a universal truth and therefore as true of poets as of plowboys or prelates. It is the conflict of two different ways of loving: the conflict of charity and cupidity, Reason and Sensuality, the conflict of the "two ways" of Lactantius, the conflict implied by the spreading arms of the Pythagorean Y. But this conflict was not the kind of clash likely to give birth to a higher synthesis; and the battle could be dubious, its outcome uncertain, only if men turned their backs on divine grace. As the *Echecs* gloss explains,

---

[5] Aldo D. Scaglione, *Nature and Love in the Late Middle Ages* (Berkeley, 1963), p. 168*n*.

[6] *Mirror of Love*, p. 471*n*.

it is true that Sensuality is always rebelling against Reason; but Sensuality is a "secondary power," whereas Reason is a "principal power."[7] That a secondary power should overthrow a primary power implies an absurdity, the absurdity of Amant. To reject Reason is, tautologically, to act unreasonably, to be a fool; and so the *Roman*'s Lover was judged in the Middle Ages. Parties on both sides of the Quarrel, Gerson on one and Pierre Col on the other, label him *fol*. The conflict, which is essentially another manifestation of the false dilemma of the mutability and instability of Fortune, is a recurrent theme of medieval literature—including, of course, secular literature—and in its less imaginative forms it soon becomes tedious. For poets who shared with theologians, and indeed ordinary Christians, the boundless vision of a divine order which was the manifestation of one kind of love and a human disorder which was the manifestation of another kind, this conflict provided a meditation, a dramatic foundation, a formal cliché like those stereotypes so often borrowed and adapted by miniaturists. Jean de Meun neither invented the conflict nor, so far as we know, found himself particularly involved in it personally. He did write a poem around it which, while largely derivative, evolved creative reformulations of familiar ideas and provided a poetic model of extraordinary popularity and influence.

To adjudicate the arguments of the teachers of love, arguments which intellectualize and dramatize the conflict, it is first necessary to place in their medieval context the various positions taken by the four preceptors who dominate Jean's poem for more than ten thousand lines while the plot creeps and the arguments sprint: Lady Reason, Amis, Faussemblant, and La Vieille. Perhaps one could say that to place them in their medieval context *is* to adjudicate them, to reveal their rightness, sophistries, or ironic formulation. Theoretically, according to a popular school of literary criticism, it should not be necessary to move beyond the "text itself"—indeed, it is mistaken and dangerous to do so—in order to make judgments about poems; but, in practice, any scholar seeking to recapture the remote and elusive meaning of a thirteenth-century poem will of necessity use what Miss Tuve called "all tools . . . studies of sources, of manuscripts and editions, of

[7] Bibliothèque nationale MS fr. 9197, fol. 199ᵛ.

background and philosophical milieu, illustration, analyses."[8] The need to call upon "all tools" is particularly pressing with regard to the *Roman*, for the poem is largely ironic and *ironia*, like all other forms of Isidorian *allegoria*, is impossible to demonstrate convincingly by reference to the literal text itself since it involves what is not in the text. In any case, one of the most useful tools for explicating the *Roman*, though one which Miss Tuve herself did not use, might be a statement by Jean de Meun, speaking in his own right rather than animating fictional creations, of his own mature philosophical and religious position.

The search for such a statement will not be fruitless. The clear evidence of the *Testament*, as I have observed, has been summarily dismissed by scholars because of its incompatibility with currently fashionable interpretations of the *Roman*. The testimony of that fine poem is telling; in it Jean formulates a schematic and orthodox statement of Catholic belief in a satire illuminated with flashes of the same eclectic learning which characterizes the *Roman* itself. Nonetheless, it is unnecessary to depend for such a statement on a work in any sense questionable in its authorship, for there survives another document of unimpeachable integrity in which Jean, speaking in his own person, explains his motives in translating Boethius' *Consolation of Philosophy*. Addressing himself to his royal patron, Philip the Fourth, Jean immediately identifies himself as the author of the *Roman*. That he lists it first among his works—the others are, to be sure, all translations —and that he spends some time in speaking of it, suggests perhaps that he considered it his *opus magnum*; that he does not retract it, apologize for it, or consider it an odd bedfellow for the works of Boethius, Vegetius, or St. Ailred suggests that he perhaps did not share the view that his poem was a "gospel of sensuality." In any case, after listing his other works and mentioning the art and utility of translations, he makes a brief analysis of the *Consolation*, which, in the absence of complete or accessible editions of Trivet or Pietro da Moglio, remains, brief and general as it is, perhaps the most suggestive "humanist" commentary on Boethius of the later Middle Ages.[9]

[8] *Allegorical Imagery*, p. 249n.

[9] V. L. Dedeck-Héry, ed., "Boethius' *De Consolatione* by Jean de Meun," *Mediaeval Studies*, XIV (1952), 165-275.

According to Jean de Meun, the *Consolation of Philosophy* gives men priceless instruction on the proper relationship between them and the things which surround them in the world. Jean begins by citing Aristotle to the effect that "All things tend toward the good—*toutez chosez tendent a bien.*" That is, the world operates by a natural, ordered, and providential teleology. To this general rule, however, man, in his perversity, is an exception; and the cause of his confusion and his distraction from his proper end of true happiness is his disordered view of "things." Typically, man loses sight of what is absolutely and essentially good because his senses are captivated by what is only contingently and accidentally good—i.e., by material creation. Intoxicated by the *sensible*, he loses all capacity for the *entendible*. The strategy of the *Consolation* lies in the method by which Lady Philosophy leads Boethius to understand the vanity and mutability of things and their resultant false happiness, and to comprehend the nature of true happiness, which lies outside the gift of worldly prosperity and is unaffected by its caprices. The work's dialectic, according to Jean, is that of a dialogue between a doctor and a sick man. "Dom cist livre n'est pas de petit profit, mais de tres grant, car entre touz les livres qui oncques furent fais, cist est souverains a despire les biens vilz et decevables qui demonstrent le signe de la fausse beneurté et a eslire les biens pardurables qui nous adrecent et enforment a la vraie beneurté."[10]

It is this Boethian statement, so simple in its formulation but so profound in its implications for the medieval mind—and not, in my view, any putative "naturalism" of the School of Chartres —which motivates Jean and informs his book. Like many other medieval translators, Jean held that his task consisted more of faithfully rendering the general sense and spirit of a text than of following the original word for word. It is a pardonable exaggeration to say that, in these terms, the great bulk of the *Roman* is an earlier version of Jean's *Boèce*. Boethius' hero was a sick man made whole by Philosophy; Jean's, a fool whom Philosophy cannot make wise. Boethius wrote, in an abstract sense, of his hero's involvement with things; Jean took the same theme but exemplified it with outrageous and comically explicit sexuality. C. S. Lewis has rightly remarked that Guillaume's part of the poem gives a

[10] Dedeck-Héry, p. 170.

111

tolerably convincing picture of "falling in love." For Jean such a process, with its sentimentality, its hypocrisy, its irrational passion —all of which are clearly present in Guillaume's beginning as well as in the continuation—provided the example par excellence of man's typical submission to the goods of Fortune. The *Roman* is not the first poem to link passionate love with the folly of Fortune, but it can be counted among the most important; and it is probably to the *Roman*, if a particular source is to be adduced, that the widespread popularity of the Love-Fortune *topos* in late medieval and Renaissance literature is to be traced.

The one character in the *Roman* who consistently preaches the Boethian doctrine to the uncomprehending Lover is Lady Reason, Jean de Meun's own Lady Philosophy and the real heroine of his poem. She talks, decorously, like Reason; but she also talks like Jean de Meun in the preface to the *Boèce*. There is, accordingly, substantial reason to believe that the store of traditional Christian wisdom which she opens for the Lover is that which Jean himself cherished; and to this proposition critical intuition must surely yield its consent. This does not mean that Reason is Jean's mouthpiece; for while Jean undoubtedly sought to reflect holy wisdom, it is unlikely that he confused it with himself. Reason's ideas are not his own in the sense that they are his original formulations; they are rather those of the Bible and Boethius, of St. Augustine and Alain de Lille, and of the great classical poets whose moral vision had been shared by medieval monastic culture. It is no accident that the margins of the manuscripts reveal that Reason's speeches were mined for their *sententiae*, and that it is her definition and characterization of "love," the first expanded from Andreas, the other borrowed from Alain, which are anthologized in the digests of the poem.

From the modern point of view, of course, Lady Reason does not make a particularly appealing heroine. She is not even a thing like the rose, but an abstraction, a walking idea, and her coldly intellectual charms lack fragrance or sensual titillation of any kind. Furthermore, while she is given prominence in the moral dialogue which is the backbone of Jean's poem, she does lose her argument with the Lover and, afterwards, disappears entirely from the poem, save for occasional and unfavorable allusion, for its concluding several thousand lines. Many writers in the psychomachic tradition, from Prudentius himself to John Milton, found it easier to draw captivating portraits of lively grotesques, demons, and vices than attractive exemplifications of God and his abstract graces; and Jean de Meun is no exception. His truly memorable characters—like Chaucer's—are the outrageously vicious and corrupt, the worldly-wise and the foolish. Nonetheless, to the medieval illustrators of the *Roman*, Lady Reason was a very popular subject; and hardly an illustrated copy of the poem exists without at least one picture of her to adorn it. Typically she is thought of simply as a queen: "Une roine qui parle a un clerc" is the brief instruction left for one fourteenth-century illustrator.[11] Usually she has a crown and is shown standing by or descending from her tower. The tower, a symbol of Lady Reason's exalted station and a reminder that she, like Lady Philosophy, descends to aid man, often leaps out of the confines of the miniature to climb up one of the margins, as in Fig. 28. Occasionally she has no crown, but wears instead the scarf which is a common attribute of fourteenth-century Gothic Virgins.[12]

The description of Lady Reason by Guillaume de Lorris is, as critics have been right to point out, conventional. That is to say, the particular physical attributes he gives her—her medium height, her shining eyes, her crown, and so forth—are meant to remind the reader of moral and philosophical qualities associated with such iconography rather than to construct a convincing verisimilar portrait. Guillaume thereby qualifies Lady Reason, very much as the young Geoffrey Chaucer was to qualify Lady Blanche, Duchess of Lancaster, in terms which immediately link her with Lady Philosophy and the Blessed Virgin. Such portraits, which are of course quite common in medieval literature and painting, are often described as conventional essays in "idealized feminine beauty"; and so they are, though in a different sense than that usually meant. The beautiful qualities suggested by such iconography are moral qualities, even when, as in the case of the Virgin, the details of the physical description become lush and emotive. Lady Reason's eyes, for example, do not characterize her as a woman, but affiliate her with a tradition of wisdom. As the *Echecs*

[11] Paris, Bibliothèque nationale MS fr. 25523, fol. 37ʳ.
[12] See S. Sawicka, *Les principaux manuscrits à peintures de la Bibliothèque nationale de Varsovie* (Paris, 1938), p. 72.

gloss puts it, "Likewise this is what Boethius means when he pretends that Lady Philosophy came to him to comfort him of his pains; so does the *Roman de la Rose* when it says that Reason came out of her tower to comfort the Lover and scold him for his folly. This is why Boethius says that Lady Philosophy has bright and shining eyes, as does the author of the aforementioned romance say of Reason. There can be no doubt that when the ancients spoke of Reason they always said that she had shining eyes like two stars and that it is for the same cause that poets so describe Pallas."[13] To say that Lady Reason shares the iconographical attributes of Lady Philosophy is also to suggest her kinship with Divine Sapience, or the Second Person of the Trinity, a kinship clearly established in the texts of both Guillaume and Jean.[14] More must be said on this matter when we come to examine Lady Nature and her iconographic qualifications, so that for the time being it is perhaps sufficient to note that the pictorial gloss staunchly supports the textual claim that Reason is sprung from the highest lineage.

Manuscripts of the *Roman de la Rose* are often much more than copies of a text which may be good or corrupt, reveal Picard or Norman forms, and fall into one of a number of groupings indicated by Greek letters. Frequently they are tiny but rich historical depositories which reveal the intimate connections which have existed between them and their readers during many centuries. One such copy, Additional MS 42133 in the British Museum, is a particularly lucid witness to the history of the poem's progress through different epochs of stylistic history and, in passing, a witness to the affection with which at least one late medieval reader of the poem regarded its heroine, Lady Reason. The manuscript dates from the end of the fourteenth century, and in its original state it was adorned with an iconographic cycle typical in most respects of the common French atelier work of its period. At some point before the eighteenth century, however, the book lost a number of its initial folia. In the eighteenth century the missing pages were replaced, copied on parchment from

---

[13] Bibliothèque nationale MS fr. 9197, fols. 148ᵛ-149ʳ.

[14] For an illuminating iconographic analysis see M. T. d'Alverny, "Le symbolisme de la Sagesse et le Christ de Saint Dunstan," *The Bodleian Library Record*, v (1956), especially 237-38.

another manuscript of the poem, together with an amusing series of pseudomedieval illustrations apparently done "after" those in some fifteenth-century exemplar which I have not identified. The composite manuscript thus presents an illumination schedule in both the Gothic and the Gothick styles and provides a curious footnote for an account of the poem's iconography.

The original fourteenth-century cycle of illustrations, at least that part of it which has survived, was itself unusual in one respect; for although the *exempla* in Lady Reason's long interview with Amant were amply illustrated, there was no picture of Reason herself. This was a most unusual deficiency for any manuscript with pretensions beyond those of Kuhn's *Kitschhandschriften*, and an early fifteenth-century amateur set out to make it good with a graffito in yet a third style, a kind of English perpendicular (Fig. 29).[15] With some care he has drawn into the appropriate margin at the beginning of Reason's discourse a picture of the lady as she leaves her tower. While marginal illustrations are by no means rare in the manuscripts, and indeed provide, as we shall see, important iconographic evidence for the interpretation of the poem, this would seem to be a unique example of a marginal illustration clearly intended to supplement the original cycle in the glossing of a specific text. Whatever Amant may have thought about Lady Reason, the amateur draughtsman of Additional 42133 apparently thought her too important not to be seen in the poem *par peinture* as well as *par parole*.

Before moving from Reason's iconography to an examination of the conventional wisdom of her long dialogue with Amant, there is one further matter which must be discussed, at least briefly: the matter of Jean's theological style. Gontier Col called him a "profound theologian." By this I presume that he meant Jean was a *poeta theologus* whose greatest work deals in a richly satisfying way with significant theological problems, including the central problem of human sin and redemption, of nature and grace; he can hardly have meant to suggest that Jean was a great

---

[15] E. G. Millar dated the drawing of Lady Reason as "more or less contemporary with the MS" in "A New Manuscript of the *Roman de la Rose*," *British Museum Quarterly*, v (1930), 88. See the *British Museum Catalogue of Additions to the Manuscripts 1926-1930*, p. 209, where, however, the subject of the illustration is mistaken.

original formulator of theological schema. As a matter of fact, from a medieval point of view Jean's theology is thoroughly unoriginal and commonplace. It is neither the bizarre "naturalism" or "Christian phallicism" which some critics have claimed, nor the avant garde Aristotelian Christianity of the thirteenth century. Indeed, Jean's theology is distinctly old-fashioned.

Since the important work of two Dominican scholars on the intellectual milieu of the *Roman*—M. Gorce and G. Paré—it has become accepted practice to talk of a distinctively "scholastic" cast to Jean de Meun's part of the poem. The stylistic influence of the *quodlibet*, and of scholastic *disputatio*, is of course discernible there, but the influence of systematic Thomism is not marked. This should hardly surprise us, since what little we know of Jean's Parisian career—mostly hypothesis drawn from the text of his poem—places him squarely in the camp of the secular enemies of St. Thomas. We have no right, without evidence, to assume that his philosophical politics were divorced from his philosophical practice. Furthermore, since there is "disputation" in the *Consolation of Philosophy*, and in *De planctu naturae*, Jean can be said to be working in a stylistic tradition which antedates Scholasticism even though it may not be unaffected by it.

Nor is the substance of the theological propositions in the *Roman* peculiarly scholastic. As far as the second long speech of Lady Reason is concerned, the speech in which the really fundamental questions of sexual ethics are discussed, the argument is more clearly Augustinian than Thomist; and despite the fact that Langlois concluded in his book on the *Sources et origines* that the direct influence of St. Augustine on Jean was limited to a phrase or two from the *Opera monachorum*, it seems clear that the broad outlines of Reason's speech follow the Augustinian *loci classici* of sexual ethics in *De Genesi ad litteram* and the fourteenth book of *De civitate Dei*. Indeed, while it would be an exaggeration to say that all significant thirteenth-century discussion of sexual morality and of the connection between concupiscence and sin is thoroughly Augustinian, it is no exaggeration to say that practically all such discussion centered on Augustine's remarks in the two books mentioned above.[16]

[16] This Augustinian influence is the subject of the important study by Michael Müller, *Die Lehre des hl. Augustinus von der Paradiesesehe* (Regensburg, 1954),

The richness of Reason's discourse on love is the richness of the *Roman* itself. She insists from the start that the word "love" is equivocal. It contains within one word those widely divergent meanings which St. Augustine discovered in it throughout the Bible and its appearance requires the same careful act of exegetical judgment to which St. Augustine subjected the scriptural occurrences of *dilectio*. In this there was nothing new to Jean de Meun or, for that matter, to St. Augustine himself, and it is not new to readers of the *Roman* today. A very great deal has been said and written, after all, about the ambiguities of love—the ambiguities of love itself and the ambiguities of the word. There are the twin loves, the four loves, *agape* and *eros*, *caritas* and *cupiditas*, and so on.

Yet much recent criticism of the poem has largely ignored Jean's interest in any kind of love other than that which his hero pursues. Lewis' chapter on the *Roman*, still highly regarded and influential, is chiefly devoted to a discussion of one of the few kinds of love which is not in the poem—"courtly love," its delicate delineation by Guillaume de Lorris and its crude rejection by Jean, who "had no final word on love or anything else." Under these circumstances it is perhaps permissible to admonish the reader to see in the word "love," wherever it appears in the text, ambiguous possibilities: the god of Love, the love of God; the Lover; the *Mirroir aux Amoureux*; the commandments of Love. Guillaume had promised, after all, "tout l'art d'amours"—*all* the art of love—and that is exactly what his admirer, Jean de Meun, set out to deliver. It will, accordingly, be useful to examine the long speech of Reason, with which Jean begins his continuation of the poem, with an open mind about love, sensitive to its many varieties, ambiguities, and uncertainties. Reason's speech is, in essence, a digest of the received opinion of the thirteenth century about some of the various kinds of love which lie camouflaged in the single vocable *amor*: "natural" love, carnal love, friendship, charity. In spite of what has been written about Jean de Meun's supposedly advanced views on love, there is nothing in Lady Reason's speech which is not thoroughly familiar, and there are no

which discusses a wealth of unpublished material relevant to the intellectual background of the *Roman*.

views of love expressed elsewhere in the poem, in howsoever bizarre a context, which she does not here touch upon and qualify.

Guillaume de Lorris, we may recall, left his Lover in agony, suffering that exquisite pain with which the god of Love had threatened him or, as the Lover puts it, promised him. Jean de Meun, picking up the story at this point, chose to begin again, so to speak, with the introduction of Reason; and her speech starts with a reference to this pain which she calls the product of "youth and folly." Such paradoxical torments, the fruits of carefully nurtured sexual frustration and self-pity, are typical of Amant's brand of love, which reveals an instability and uncertainty mirroring Amant's own vicissitudes. From the outset God's daughter is highly critical of the Lover's state, which would seem to reflect no subtle and sentimental mysteries with which she is not familiar or whose delicacy and ambiguity are beyond her competency to judge. What follows is not so much a simple discourse, let alone the beginnings of a "symposium on love," as a kind of quarrel or petulant catechism. Reason does indeed set out to make a précis of love, but she is constantly challenged by Amant to clarify her definitions and restate her positions in response to his obdurate sophistries.

She begins with a long, zeugmatic definition of love displaying a wit now unhappily dated, which Jean took from *De planctu naturae*. Love is a troubled peace, an amicable war, a light burden, a sickly health, a mighty feebleness. The burden of her definition is that love—at least the love which motivates Amant—is confused, inconstant, unreliable. It is also, of course, paradoxical, though that in itself would not make it unworthy. There is more than one apparent paradox at the heart of Reason's own creed, including the "light burden" itself. The principal quality of love, in this sense, is not its paradox but its sterility. What seems to promise happiness and freedom offers only unhappiness and enslavement. Love of this sort is clearly one of the *chosez* talked about by Boethius in the *Consolation of Philosophy*. Perhaps understandably, Amant is not satisfied with a definition which seems mainly the vehicle for some stale conceits, however well they may serve as rhetorical correlatives for his condition, and he presses Reason to give a more comprehensible account of love. This she does, yet once again in terms of the familiar, for the

118

definition she now succinctly gives is that of Andreas at the beginning of his book *De amore*. Love is a *passio*, a mental illness (*maladie de pensée*), engendered in members of opposite sexes by disordered sight. Such love incites its sufferers to a mutual lust (l. 4384), a desire to hug and kiss, to enjoy to the hilt the physical solace of sexual relations as an end in itself. We may note in passing that Lady Reason's appropriation of Andreas should raise a disturbing question for the criticism of both these central books about love, since Andreas' is commonly regarded as a handbook for the gentle (and secular) art of "courtly love," or "polite adultery" as Lewis calls it, while Jean's *Roman* is supposed to be a reaction against "courtly love" in favor of "naturalism." There is no question that, in Jean's poem, the daughter of God not only cites Andreas' definition with approval but uses it as the focal point of a brief discussion of love in an overtly religious context.

She goes on to explain that Amant's love is in fact unnatural since its end is not the regeneration of the race, which Nature urges upon men, but the pleasure of sexual intercourse. Reason argues, following the traces of St. Augustine, that Nature has put concupiscence into sexual relations in order to make the quite serious business of generation a pleasurable activity. With typical abuse, however, man pursues a secondary aspect of his sexuality, its physical pleasure, and ignores its primary end. According to Reason, who here introduces one of the recurrent themes of the *Roman*, such love as this is in fact a kind of subjection, and she finds it incomprehensible that men so willingly enslave themselves, becoming, in her words, "sers e chaitis e nices / Au prince de trestouz les vices" (ll. 4427-28). The prince in question is, of course, Satan; for Reason clearly believes that love, like everything else in the world, is to be analyzed according to immutable moral principles and a divinely revealed religion, and that it is not exempt from Christian morality nor on "a different level" from it.

For the Lover, fresh from his formal act of vassalage to another prince, that quaint and courtly *jeu d'esprit* which is supposed to reveal both the exquisite artificiality of the poetry of the "courtly code" and part of a "profound, full rendition of human psychology," the implications of Lady Reason's analysis of love should be painfully clear. There runs throughout the poem a chain of images and insinuations which links the sylvan archer, who is the god of Love, with Satan. Cupid is not Satan, for that is not how Jean's iconographic allegory works; but he has a very great deal in common with the charming and affable demons, like the one in Chaucer's Friar's Tale, who regularly appear in medieval literature. For Amant, for whom the nature of things resides in the superficial implications of words rather than in their substantial realities, the question never arises; but for the careful reader of Jean's poem, who must explore the many divergent ways which meet at the crossroads of "love," a more penetrating linguistic analysis is required.

Reason goes on to maintain that pathological love is particularly characteristic of youth. Such love is, she says, the root of all evils, "de touz maus la racine" as Cicero defines it in his book *De senectute* (1. 4429). Now Cicero does, in fact, write at some length about the folly of youthful *voluptas* and its debilitating effects, and the French text, interestingly enough, renders the Latin word as *deduit*. His sentence is "all one" with Lady Reason's, but he nowhere says that *voluptas* is the root of all evils. It becomes apparent that Reason, while citing Cicero as an authority, found her principal text in the Scriptures where, in a passage very familiar to medieval preachers, it is said that love (*cupiditas*) is the root of all evils (I Timothy 6:10).

The love which Reason has at such great length defined, at first playfully, then carefully and schematically, is sexual cupidity. The typical but not exclusive vice of youth, such love, both a disease and a prison, can rightly be called *fole amour* (1. 4593); Reason herself contrasts it with *bone amour*, love "born of a good heart." That it is this love, and no other, which has hypnotized Amant she is unequivocal:

> Mai l'amour que te tient ou laz
> Charneus deliz te represente,
> Si que tu n'as ailleurs t'entente. (ll. 4600-602)

What Amant calls simply love appears identical, under Lady Reason's analysis, with the *passio* of Andreas, the *voluptas* of Cicero, and the *cupiditas* of St. Augustine. For medieval readers familiar with such technical terminology, with the works from which they are taken and the contexts which amplify their meanings, the Lover's "complaint"—which actually was recognized by leading medieval medical authorities as a physical disease—was probably not mysterious. It is not really naturalism.

The Lover's response to Lady Reason's characterization of the first kind of love is difficult to account for. As one reads the poem through it becomes increasingly difficult to deny that the Lover is both an obdurate if engaging fool, an *ygnorans*, and yet "wiser than the sons of light," a sophist of some accomplishments. After admitting that everything she has so far said went in one ear and out the other, "tossed out by Amours," as he puts it, he makes a quite preposterous charge against her, rooted in a quibble over the very word whose breadth she has been at pains to teach. Since Reason preaches against love, she must be counselling hate.[17] Therefore, if he follows her advice he is a deadly sinner, in both Reason's theological schema and that of his god, who has prescribed that Hate be ever banished from the Garden of Deduit. That this line of argument is patently ludicrous is apparent perhaps even to Amant, for he ends lamely by saying that she has given him good advice and that "he who would not believe you is a fool"—an admission it may be well to remember when reading the concluding section of the *Roman*. He claims at least, to want to learn the nature of that kind of love (*bone amour*) which Reason does not condemn, and Reason, as always eager for her divine mission, sets out to explain another kind of love, *amicitia*.

Jean's interest in *amicitia* was probably extensive; he broaches the subject several times in the course of the *Roman*—its definition here by Lady Reason is merely its most formal and extensive treatment—and, perhaps more significantly, he translated the greatest of all Christian treatises on friendship, *De amicitia spirituali* by St. Ailred of Rievaulx. Curiously enough, Langlois, in his study of the sources of the *Roman*, does not draw attention to the influence of Ailred's book on Reason's treatment of friendship; perhaps the fact that she specifically cites Cicero's *Laelius* led him

---

[17] Amant's remark is even funnier than his blunder in logic, since hateful wrath was not considered as antithetical to "love," but the opposite side of the same coin. William of Conches finds them both disastrous *passiones* which overthrow Reason: "Ecce miseria humana quia anima prius passione turbatur, sensus detrahitur quam ratione vel intellectu illuminetur," *Glossae super Platonem*, ed. E. Jeaneau (Paris, 1965), p. 217.

to think that it was Jean's immediate and sole source; but since Ailred's work is, in effect, an extended Christian paraphrase and commentary on Cicero's, there is no good reason for supposing this to have been the case. In fact, Lionel Friedman has recently demonstrated the very clear influence of *De amicitia spirituali* on the *Roman* and offered a number of fruitful suggestions about the artistic uses Jean makes of Ailred's ideas.[18]

In general it may be said that Lady Reason's brief teachings on friendship have two major purposes in the *Roman*: they prepare the ground for the reader's judgment of Amis, and they provide ideas about a kind of love which closely parallels Amant's own *passio*, so that, in speaking of friendship, Reason not only invites him to an alternative "love" but also is able, with poetic ambiguity, to talk about his condition at one remove. Furthermore, a number of Ailred's central teachings about friendship, hinted at in her speech, clearly inform several of the principal themes of the *Roman*—the Golden Age, for example, or the rule of Reason, and nature and grace—enriching the reading of the poem in a way which is most satisfying, though difficult to demonstrate without protracted analysis. The following brief remarks are superficial and are not presented as a substitute for the careful reading of Ailred which will reward any student of the *Roman*.[19] Friendship, for Ailred, is both the gift of God and a reflection of Him, an aspect of man's perfect nature in Paradise. The Fall of man, however, "denatured" friendship along with man's other natural proclivities so that, since the Fall, friendship is no longer a spontaneous natural effusion but must be governed by laws. This at first appears cryptic, since it seems clear that Ailred does not refer to positive law; but as Fiske points out the laws of friendship are undoubtedly those established by Cicero.[20] This, in turn, means that friendship must be founded on virtue and dictated by Reason. But just as there is a kind of love ungoverned by laws,

---

[18] "Jean de Meun and Ethelred of Rievaulx," *L'Esprit Créateur*, II (1962), 135-41.

[19] The text of *De amicitia spirituali* is accessible in *Pat. lat.* 195, cols. 659-702, and in *L'amitié spirituelle*, ed. J. Dubois (Bruges and Paris, 1947); there is an illuminating discussion by A. Fiske, "Aelred's of Rievaulx Idea of Friendship and Love," *Cîteaux*, XIII (1962), 5-17; 97-132.

[20] "Aelred's Idea of Friendship," pp. 98-99.

so is there a kind of friendship which binds evil men together. Just as men cannot choose whether or not they are to love, but only what and in what manner they will love, the desire for friendship, of whatever species, is one of man's universal characteristics. Even the lecher cannot enjoy his lechery, according to Ailred, without a friend with whom he may discuss it.

Such are some of the ideas that lie in the background of Reason's discourse on friendship. Friendship is founded on virtue, tested by Fortune, confirmed by stability. It may be broken in five ways—*orgueil, ire, reprouche, reveler les secrez,* and *la plaie doulereuse de detraccion venimeuse*—according to Lady Reason citing, with Ailred, as Friedman has demonstrated, Ecclesiastes 22:25-30. All this prepares the reader's delayed reaction to Amis, whose attempts to hark back to the natural love and friendship of the Golden Age are much illuminated by the Ailredian doctrines implicit in Reason's speech. For the orderly *déroulement* of Jean's argument, the discussion of friendship also serves as the occasion for introducing the other principal theme of her discourse, the concept of Fortune.

One of the tests of friendship, according to Cicero and all medieval authorities, is the operation of Fortune, and Reason's discussion of friendship perhaps inevitably leads to a discussion of the fickle goddess. Although the concept of Fortune, her workings and her relationship to men, was very widely discussed in medieval philosophical, moral, and historical writings, it is not a simple concept to grasp. St. Augustine found that he was being so badly misunderstood on the meaning of *fortuna* that he was obliged to begin his *Retractions* by repenting that he had ever used the word. Fortune cannot properly be thought of as either the equivalent of, or the alternative to, Providence. Rather—as is explained by Boethius in the *Consolation of Philosophy,* clearly Jean's chief source for the relevant passage—Fortune is the phenomenon of unstable fluctuation which is characteristic of contingent creation. This is to say that the operations of Fortune are always material; they always involve *things:* the human body in sickness and health, material prosperity or depression, the success or failure of crops, the rise and fall of princes. Since Boethius denies the existence of chance, it is clear that the idea of Fortune as a real force is illusory. Yet the concept remains, for Boethius

and for Jean de Meun, a useful way to categorize the externaliza-
tions of fleshly human attitudes.

As we have seen, Jean regarded the *Consolation of Philosophy*
as an essay in the proper relationship between men and the created
order, which is to say the relationship between men and the
peculiar sphere of Fortune's operations. He went on, in the pref-
ace to his *Boèce*, to talk about the proper use of things by which
the mind moves from the visible and the contingent to the invisible
and the immanent. Such a process, which is, incidentally, the
method of medieval allegory, provides the only solution for the
problem of Fortune—whether good or bad fortune is immaterial
—since the vicissitudes of the fleshly world are of contingent
rather than immanent importance. With Boethius, Jean thought
of the transcendence of Fortune, with the material goods of the
world, as liberty; conversely, an engagement with Fortune could
lead to a kind of slavery or subjection.

In the rich body of Boethian literature of the high Middle Ages
the goddess Fortuna evolved a standard iconographical repre-
sentation which suggests the manner in which she enslaves her
subjects.[21] She is a crowned queen, as one who reigns in this world.
She is blindfolded, because indifferent in her ministrations, and
turns a large wheel, the Wheel of Fortune. Often, as in Fig. 30,
there are four men at the wheel's quadrants; their names are
Regno, Regnabo, Regnavi, and Sine-Regno-Sum. Regno sits
smugly for his moment's glory at the top, his crowned head jut-
ting out most immoderately over the confines of the border at the
top of the miniature. Regnavi slides head over heels on the same
road to misery represented by the wretched Sine-Regno-Sum, now
crushed below the wheel which once elevated him to his tawdry
glory. Finally Regnabo, slowly being raised toward his brief day
of wordly prosperity, proves the existence of a frantic kind of
good fortune.

Such illustrations are very common in fourteenth-century manu-
scripts of the *Roman*; indeed, hardly an illustrated copy is with-
out one. Kuhn thought that the frequent appearance of illustra-
tions like Fig. 30 testified to the artists' habit of violating the text,

[21] The iconography of Fortuna is well surveyed in the new book of Pierre
Courcelle, *La Consolation de Philosophie dans la tradition littéraire* (Paris,
1967); on the *Roman*, see p. 138.

since all that Lady Reason actually says by way of iconographic qualification is that Fortune "has a wheel which turns." Such a criticism is of course naïve, since what the illustrators attempt to convey is an idea rather than a literal statement in paint to match a literal verbal statement. But what has the concept of Fortune which an audience with a shared reverence for the *Consolation of Philosophy* would find in such an icon have to do with a poem about love?

The answer to this question will perhaps emerge from an examination of another illustration of the text in question (Fig. 31). Here the artist has been faithful to the letter, but at the same time he has reorganized his iconographic materials to indicate the precise relationship between Fortune and Amant's love. Considering the difficulty of the task, the Valencia artist's visualization of the ambiguous isle of Fortune may be regarded as a small triumph of the pictorial imagination. The goddess is shown blindfolded, holding a small portable wheel, in three different suggestive postures: standing, falling, and sitting. She acts out, as if in a charade, the very instability of which she is conventionally thought to be the source. The wheel is an unusual one, small and winged, suggesting its flighty uncertainty. While Fortune is upright, she is in the good side of her house, which is splendidly and beautifully constructed on that part of her island which looks rather like the Garden of Deduit. The goddess tumbles, however, just at the center of her house—half in a palace, half in a hovel—into the squalid shack of "bad fortune." The corresponding side of the island is bleak; and owls, birds of ill omen, have replaced the happier singing birds of "good fortune."

As an exemplary illustration of the mutability of Fortune, the picture is an ingenious and telling gloss; but its principal interest for the question under discussion lies elsewhere. The Valencia artist has quite clearly and unequivocally filled out his composition with icons of sexual love. Furthermore, he has done so in such a fashion as to leave no doubt that he considered such love as one of the goods of Fortune, one of the contingent created things which present to man the option of reasonable use or irrational and idolatrous abuse. Bathing in the two streams of Fortune are several of the goddess' chubby pre-Renaissance devotees. In the clear water at the left, obviously a pleasant spot to "swimmen in possession" or bask in idleness with a single foot lolling in the stream, are a number of men enjoying good fortune. At the right, wallowing in the brackish water, are the less fortunate. The implication of the two figures at the center of the stream, one recoiling in disgust as his head reaches the filthy current, the other swimming for all his might as he breaks into the clear water, is the same as that of the kings on Fortune's Wheel: life in Fortune's realm is unstable. Furthermore, so is the life of love because, in fact, the life of love is merely one species of subjection to Fortune. On the shore by the happy swimmers rides a quite unusual Cupid. Mounted on a winged horse, with a claw-foot like the Cupid of the Barberino codex, he rallies his lovers, encourages them, promises them, as he has promised Amant, a pleasant swim and a romp. On the other side, armed with a mighty Saracen sword instead of his wonted club, stalks Danger among the jagged rocks and weeds of darkest woe. The Valencia artist knows what Alain de Lille knew.

In the light of Reason's discourse, and the visual gloss which it elicited in Fig. 31, the connection between Fortune and Amant's kind of love emerges quite clearly. Jean de Meun's Amant regards love as a carnal *thing*, and however he may try to deny or to conceal this essential fact from himself and others, the meaning of the rosebud must become obvious to even the casual reader. Similarly, at the end of the poem, the Lover's rhetoric in describing its plucking leaves small doubt that he has been pursuing not a sentiment or an ideal but a thing. Inordinate, unreasonable love of a gift of Fortune is an idolatrous passion. Its vicissitudes, which are the same vicissitudes so exquisitely codified and sentimentalized in the sermon given by the god of Love on the mysteries of the joys and of the sorrows of love, are the familiar but illusory operations of Fortune.

Modern psychologists tell us that to regard the "love object" as a "thing" is typically infantile behavior. Evidence from the Middle Ages suggests that many medieval men, at least those who are subjects of medieval story, were guilty of such behavior, though it was not an attitude approved, let alone counseled, except by dubious teachers like Cupid. A substantial number of medieval poems, in fact, are Boethian meditations meant to cure such an attitude, and to lead the reader to a philosophical acceptance of the loss of someone greatly loved. One of the most beautiful of these, Chaucer's famous *Book of the Duchess*, is an elegy which rather ruthlessly exposes the attitude of regarding Duchess Blanche of Lancaster as a "thing," the loss of which is capable of engendering a desperate *passio*, as both foolish and unworthy. The poem strongly implies that such an attitude, one which may at first seem only human and natural, is in fact both superficial and immature, reflecting small honor on its ostensibly venerated object.

Amours has taught, rather commanded, Amant to think constantly of the rosebud and the promise of its physical joys. This counsel immediately places his love in the context of Lady Reason's zeugmatic definition, as he is moved by hope, fear, joyful anticipation, despair, and so forth, with regard to the "lady." He fills his cup from both of Fortune's tuns, now enjoying the rich Madeira, now spewing out the vinegar. For the Lover, happiness is not something within his own power; it is the capricious, whimsical gift of Fortune, and as his *passio* for what he cannot certainly attain grows fiercer, so does his madness. He cries out that what the rosebud offers him is more valuable by a thousand times than all the gifts of Lady Reason. In Chaucer's poem, to be sure, such an extreme form of the carnal view of the "lady" would hardly be appropriate, even as a straw-man's position. Nonetheless, while Blanche is not merely a sexual object to the Black Knight— though that would seem to be how he regarded her at his first approach—the riddling interior catechism at the heart of the *Book of the Duchess* reveals an attitude which views her chiefly as a good of Fortune. The strategy of the poem, which begins with a stylized description of physical beauty associating Blanche with specific abstract virtues, is to move the reader to understand that the true gifts which she displays are not physical, corruptible, or carnal, and hence not fortuitous. The true lover of Blanche, in short, cannot be inconsolable at her loss like Sum-Sine-Regno, for he views her not upside down from the base of a wheel which has become for him a rack, but rather in consoled Boethian detachment.

In the *Book of the Duchess* the occasion for sorrow is "of a certain magnitude"; it is nothing less than the death of one of the greatest ladies of European chivalry. The terrors which strike at Amant's heart in the *Roman* can only be considered mock-heroic by contrast. Nevertheless, Geoffrey Chaucer, who was never very far away from the *Roman* and here borrows freely from it as well as from another French poem written largely in imitation of it, is clearly addressing the same question raised by Lady Reason, and his answer to it is likewise her answer. It has become commonplace to write about Jean's poem as, in part, a conflict of "this-worldly values" with "other-worldly values." Such a characterization of the poem, though not the exoticisms of interpretation it has led to, seems to me essentially correct, provided that we view the matter from the perspective of all of Jean's medieval *conflictus*. It is the same conflict which is at the heart of the *Consolation of Philosophy* and medieval theology; not a Manicheanism of brittle polarities, but two contrasting ways of life: the old and the new, the carnal and the spiritual, the lower and the higher; in which the new redeems the old, the spiritual explains the carnal, and the higher perfects the lower. For an age which has little truck with any kind of systematic theological and moral formulations, and whose philosophical systems typically deny the validity of the kinds of philosophical questions asked by medieval philosophers, such a scheme may well seem flabby and incomprehensible. Our world cannot, I suspect, "understand" such matters in Dilthey's sense; we can only explain them. As the late poet laureate, a fond and sympathetic lover of medieval poetry, once remarked, "Boethius does not console me."[22] History, however, demands not merely judgments but the imagination to respond to ideas which often are very foreign to our natures; the historian must regard the objects of his thought, as Collingwood says, not as "spectacles to be watched, but experiences to be lived through in his own mind." Surely it is very wrong to reverse the process and merely to reflect into this great poem, which is also a major historical document, some prevailing characteristics of our own intellectual world, to glorify what is meant to be condemned in the poem as a triumphant emergence of "this-worldly values." Surely this is a sad mental laziness?

What is chiefly remarkable about the *Roman* is not that it reveals a number of ideas about love with which we are all

[22] John Masefield, *Recent Prose*, 2nd ed. (London, 1932), p. 217.

familiar, but that it advances some which may be unfamiliar. Lady Reason's discourse on the goddess Fortuna expands the central metaphor of the poem, the love story, to include a whole range of human experience with which modern literature is largely unfamiliar. It suggests why, according to the *Echecs* gloss, men value love stories for their philosophical and moral meanings, and gives a clue as to what Laurent de Premierfait meant when he called the *Roman* a "vraie mappemonde." The love of sublunary lovers is typical of the ambiguous goods of Fortune, because, unlike some other kinds of love which Reason praises, it is directed towards things created as worthy and necessary objects of love. It is a kind of idolatry. There is a rather moving *explicit*, dated 1352, in one of the French copies of the poem; it deserves to be printed and perhaps reproduced as part of the text's critical apparatus: "Anima magistri Johannis Medunensis per misericordiam Dei requiescat in pace, quia ad laudem, circumspectionem, et honorem tocius gentis hunc libellum gallicis verbis intellective et proficue composuit. Et nos cum ipso requiescamus et vivamus in pace, et feliciter transeamus per bona temporalia."[23] The poem which the anonymous but knowing scribe praises, a poem both richly comic and profoundly serious, is a discussion of love as a species of *bona temporalia*.

All lovers of course wish to be happy, to pluck their roses, to swim in the clear stream of Cupid and always to sit on the seat of Regno in their amorous kingdoms; thus Reason finds it apposite to define true happiness. She cites specifically the *Consolation of Philosophy*—with a playful aside to the effect that whoever might translate it would do a great service to men—to prove that happiness has nothing to do with material wealth. Like much of the wisdom of the *Roman*, a good deal of which echoes the sapiential books of the Bible, this idea was an old saw even in Jean's day, but he lovingly repeats it, introducing, in turn, a discussion of wealth, one of several in the poem, which is full of aphorisms gleaned from the popular literature of Christian asceticism. According to one of the more fantastic accounts of the *Roman* to be offered by a serious-minded book, Jean de Meun believed that "Poverty, whether secular or spiritual, was something evil and

[23] Paris, Bibliothèque nationale MS fr. 1556, fol. 129ʳ.

pedantic."[24] It is true that poverty is one of the vices banished from the Garden of Deduit, and in the mercenary sexual ethic of Lady Wealth or the Vekke to be poor is to be a pariah. But even Amant ends by cursing Wealth, without whose help he manages to pick his rose, and much of the satire against the friars in the Faussemblant chapter is based on the assumption that their failure to observe poverty is a serious vice. If Jean de Meun found the counsels of perfection and the aspirations of the Sermon on the Mount either evil or pedantic, he kept it a well-guarded secret. Certainly there is no such indication in his text of Reason's discourse, which is laced with apothegms on the contempt of the world.[25]

Amant, from time to time, seems not altogether unimpressed by the cogency of Reason's arguments; but he continues to plead the extenuating circumstances of the "human condition." Since the overthrow of the gods—as reported in the *Metamorphoses* and the *Fasti* of Ovid—true love, or absolute charity, has been impossible, he says. Lady Reason admits that for some absolutely disinterested individuals love is impossible, but that another form of love closely allied to it, a love founded on the golden rule, is possible for all. Laws must impel man to do what natural charity once commanded. In this sense, human legal and judicial institutions are testimonies to the failure of man's love and its fatal misdirections. (This bland Augustinian orthodoxy, incidentally, has turned the protean poet Jean de Meun into yet another modern character, the rabid anarchist.)

Reason then demonstrates, in proper academical fashion, the superiority of love to justice, using a mythological *exemplum* which is to have recurrence in the syllabus of the teachers of love: the story of the castration of Saturn by his son Jupiter, and of the end of the Golden Age. This *topos* must be considered in some detail when it reappears in the advice of Amant's Friend, for it

[24] Friedrich Heer, *The Intellectual History of Europe*, trans. J. Steinberg (Cleveland and New York, 1966), p. 146.

[25] For example, the lines on the futility of riches (ll. 5127ff.), cited with warm approval by Jean de Montreuil (*Epistolario*, p. 301), closely follow one of the most famous works of popular asceticism of the entire Middle Ages, the so-called *De contemptu mundi* of Innocent III. See *De miseria humane conditionis*, ed. M. Maccarone, p. 21.

is of central importance to an understanding of the shimmering and ambiguous paradises which haunt the poem. Suffice it to say for the moment that, as it is used here by Lady Reason, this *exemplum* underscores the point that fallen and imperfect human nature requires law to order actions once dictated by love. That law itself, in its human administration, is subject to all the imperfections of fallen human nature which made it necessary is demonstrated by the *exemplum* of Appius and Virginia (Chaucer's Physician's Tale).

Amant repeats his comic charge, revealing an elementary fault in logic which could hardly be missed by an attentive reader, let alone the clerks in Jean's audience, that in counseling him against love, Reason must be in fact enjoining him to hate. As Reason remarks to the Lover, "Tu n'ies pas bons logiciens." Reason says that she has been counselling a kind of love which represents a mean (*meien*). Such love is, according to Reason, the proper use of what she calls natural love (*amour naturel*), that is, sexual love which has as its end procreation. Natural love is the movement impelled by concupiscence which, according to St. Augustine, was injected into sexual relations after the Fall of man, when the sexual members no longer responded simply to the rational will but required the impetus of delight to fulfill their designated labors. This kind of love, this "naturalism," thus represents not man's original nature, but his fallen nature; in the latter part of Jean's poem it is closely linked with Lady Nature and with her chaplain Genius, who is a personification of post-lapsarian natural concupiscence. Natural love is common to men and beasts, and— a most important point to emphasize for the understanding of Jean's sexual morality—it is neither good nor bad in itself:

> Cete amour, bien qu'el profite,
> Nia los ne blasme ne merite,
> N'en font n'a blasmer n'a loer. . . . (ll. 5777-79)

It is the use to which this love is put which determines its moral characteristics. A man can follow natural love, guided by Reason, and be a man; alternatively, he can follow it against the dictates of Reason, and be a beast. There is nothing in the slightest degree "mystical" about the force of natural love, which is neither more nor less than a divinely willed biological propensity; it is not the music of the spheres nor does it make the earth move. Jean de Meun does not conceive of it as a substitute for any religious revelation more profound than Amant's patently ludicrous idolatry which, as Pierre Col pointed out five hundred years ago, treats the *bouton* as though it were a god.

At this point in her argument, Lady Reason does something poetically startling. She offers herself, in unmistakable if muted sexual terms, to Amant; she herself will be his *amie*. Lady Reason, the very daughter of God (*Fille Deu le souverain père*), will love Amant with an abandon never before seen in a *pucele de parage*; and she ends her libertine proposition with a playful reminder that *puceles* rarely make such offers more than once, alluding to the wrath of Echo and thus, by implication, to the well of self-love at the center of Love's garden. Can anything promised by the so-called god of Love compare with such passion as this? The poor Lover is amazed, nonplussed, for he believes according to the "courtly code" (i.e., the blasphemous parody of the Ten Commandments which Amours has taught him), that love is bondage, severe pain, servitude, chains and aigues, *friçons e autres dolors maintes*. Reason must be speaking Latin to him! "De quei voulez vous que je serve?" he asks. The lady answers rather that it is she who will serve him, faithfully and constantly. Her love alone, she claims, is exempt from the fickleness of Fortune. Thus her argument comes full circle, homing in again on her central position that carnal love is merely the commonest form of subjection to Fortune; and it is at this point in her speech that she speaks of that goddess at some length, using the *exempla* so beloved of the illustrators—the histories of Seneca and of Nero, of Croesus and Phanie, Charles of Anjou and Manfred—to show that all of human history is an eloquent plea to despise Fortune.

Lady Reason concludes her account of the workings of Fortune, her falseness and her deceit, with another simple appeal to Amant. She asks that he fulfill three wishes: that he love her, that he abandon the god of Love, and that he utterly reject and despise Fortune. In fact, she says, if he will only do the first—love Reason and follow her commands—the other two requests will also be fulfilled as a matter of course. She nicely turns the end of her discourse back to her principal matter, the identification of the service of the god of Love as subjection to Fortune. No one in the poem, neither Amours nor the Lover himself, nor any of their friends and relations, ever denies that this central position taken by Lady Reason is true; yet criticism of the *Roman* has insistently repeated that Jean de Meun is actively advancing the ideas, the attitudes, the system, which Reason exposes as hollow, illogical, carnal, and immoral. To maintain this is to say that Jean de Meun, translator of "the greatest book ever written for the persuading of men to despise the vile goods of this world," is seriously advancing as a respectable philosophical view and a way of life the necessity of subjection to Fortune. The suggestion is preposterous.

Just before Reason abandons the Lover, never to return because she is never invited back again, Jean accomplishes one of the great comic *coups* of his poem. Amant, having already hinted that he wished to call Reason to task for smutty talk, begins the attack in earnest. He says that he cannot but follow Amours, a master who can make him a hundred thousand times richer than she ever could (suggesting, presumably, that he is madder by a factor of a hundred than he was some lines previously when the odds were a simple thousand to one), if only he grants him the enjoyment of the rose. Since the only identity the rose has in Jean's poem is that of an entirely unsentimentalized and anonymous pudendum, Amant's inflated view of its value in comparison to the gifts of *Sapientia Dei Patris* can be regarded as ludicrous. What Amant wants, it is perfectly clear, is not a rose by any other name; yet having reiterated, politely and indirectly, his own carnal goal, he attacks Lady Reason for using language unbecoming to a nice girl (*preudefame*) in referring to the male sexual organs by their quite proper vernacular name of *coilles*.

Now in taking this preposterous line of argument, Amant is merely obeying, as he says himself, one of the commandments of his master, Cupid—the "clean speech" commandment. Before the poem ends Amant will, still under the god's protection and with his blessings, come to use the most blasphemous euphemistic language about his own genital equipment and that represented by the rose, speaking of the latter as "relics," and the former as the paraphernalia of the pilgrim; but as Reason points out, calling *coilles reliques*, or *reliques coilles*, does not change the thing nominated. From the point of view of the god of Love and his

133

votaries, of course, "courteous" (i.e., hypocritical) speech is a necessary accomplishment for a master player in the game of Love, since, if Amant's real intentions were known from the start, there would be no end of trouble with Shame, Fear, Danger, Bel Accueil, and Lord knows who else. Things are bad enough as it is.

The answer of the daughter of God, strangely neglected by critics seeking to find in the camp of Amant and his friends a gushing fountain of medieval naturalism, is devastating. She says that God created genitalia in Paradise where they were expected to be used, that what God has created is not evil, and that it cannot be evil to refer to it by its proper name. Sin does not reside in things, but in the use men make of them. It is almost certain that Jean is here appropriating for the argument of Reason St. Augustine's disclaimer of obscenity in his discussion of the difficult problem of sexual relations in Paradise.[26] St. Augustine there argues that in Paradise the sexual organs were responsive to the rational will rather than excited by concupiscence and that the penis "inseminated the field of generation even as now the hand throws seed into the earth." Even as the doctrine of plenitude is first enunciated by Lady Reason, it is also she who qualifies it with the Augustinian idea of the proper uses and improper abuses of things—including genitalia. The two concepts, plenitude and use, are of course related intimately in the context of Jean's poem, the last several thousand lines of which are given over to the wild and often richly comic misappropriation of the doctrine of plenitude by Love's captains. It should perhaps be mentioned here that while Lady Reason does not find genitalia unmentionable, neither does she recommend them as objects of religious veneration. There was not, in the School of Chartres or anywhere else, to my knowledge, a tradition of "Christian phallicism" such as Alan Gunn seeks to adduce. Bernard Sylvestris ends his famous description of the microcosmic man with the inferior members because, as Lewis pointed out, they were considered inferior; and Gunn's rejection of this easily documented fact as "certainly unacceptable" is particularly vivid testimony to the general enervation of his argument.[27]

[26] *De civitate Dei*, xiv, 23.

[27] *The Allegory of Love*, p. 97, and *The Mirror of Love*, p. 221n. Chartrian teachings in this respect seem explicitly clear in the light of Alain's remarks in

There is one final irony before Reason leaves the poem for the last time. Having defended her use of the word *coilles*, she goes on to explain that in its context—that is, in the story of the castration of Saturn—the word has an allegorical sense beyond its literal meaning.[28] She goes on to say a word or two about mythography and moral truths hidden beneath the fables of poets. Amant's decisive response to this kind of literary criticism should by this time be predictable:

> Mais des poetes les sentences,
> Les fables e les metaphors
> Ne be je pas a gloser ores. . . . (ll. 7190ff.)

Just as his linguistic interests are superficial, dealing with surface rather than substance, so also are his critical concerns in reading poetry. He sees no cause to go beyond the text itself or, that is, to move from the chaff to the grain; like his indispensable ally Faussemblant, Amant would "take the chaff and let the grain alone." He is an enemy of allegory, and Jean de Meun, a great allegorical poet, playfully maneuvers himself into the position of being abandoned—albeit in good company—by his Lover.

The squeamish attitude of the Lover toward the nomination of the dishonest member was obviously meant to be comic; and Pierre Col could treat Christine de Pisan's qualms about such "dirty talk" as laughable still in 1400.[29] There is substantial evidence to suggest, however, that there was a widespread reaction against "obscenity" in many European circles in the late Middle Ages and Renaissance, which probably helps account for the naughty reputation of the *Roman* by the sixteenth century. Certainly the large number of mutilated copies of the poem, and they are not a few, are apparently the victims of post-Reformation zeal rather than the outraged sensibilities of Jean's contemporaries and near contemporaries. An amusing analogue to Amant's linguistic prudery is to be found in a manuscript of one of Jean's other

---

De planctu naturae, *Pat. lat.* 210, col. 444, and William of Conches' in *Glossae super Platonem*, ed. Jeaneau, pp. 233ff.

[28] The allegorical significance of the *coilles* in mythographic tradition is remarked upon by the *Echecs* exegete, Bibliothèque nationale MS fr. 9197, fols. 41ʳ-41ᵛ.

[29] Ward, *The Epistles on the Romance*, pp. 57ff.

works, his translation of Abélard's *Historia calamitatum*, where, in the account of Abélard's castration, the vernacular equivalent of the Latin *testibus* has been violently scratched out.[30] What had happened to Abélard became, at one moment in European intellectual history, simply unspeakable to a large number of conventional people.

One further example, this time concerning a manuscript of the *Roman*, may further demonstrate the lubricity which the vision of later ages put into Jean's poem. A mediocre copy of the poem was executed at Arras in 1370 (now MS 897 in the Bibliothèque Municipale at Arras). Its early history is not known, but it came into the library of Saint-Vaast in the early seventeenth century. The book was, clearly enough, made up as a kind of popular religious anthology; in addition to the *Roman* and the *Testament*, it contains the *Vision de l'eremite Fulbert*, *St. Patrick's Purgatory*, an *Histoire de St. Jean Baptiste*, *L'Amoureuse prise*, a life of Chrysostom, and various prayers.[31] The illustrations of the *Roman*, while of undistinguished quality, are in some ways unusual for a northern French manuscript of its date. The iconography of the *incipit* illustration, for example, is unique, showing the rosetree growing out of the Dreamer's mouth; and the sheer bulk of the cycle, forty-five miniatures, is ample for its period. Its peculiar interest for the present discussion, however, arises from the fact that its illustrations have been carefully, not wantonly, expurgated, probably by a pious post-Reformation monastic librarian. The deletions are both amusing and instructive. On folio 87^r, a commonplace picture of Nature perpetuating the species has been completely destroyed, except for the upper right-hand corner where God appears in an attitude of benediction. The erasure is neat and total, but there is no doubt that the cancelled illustration showed a couple in bed, as do numerous other illustrations of this passage in fourteenth-century manuscripts. What was good enough for God in 1370 had become shocking to His servants two centuries later. It would of course be ridiculous to deduce from such testimony that there had been a profound and substantive change in monastic theology during

---

[30] *La traduction de la première épître de Pierre Abélard de Jean de Meun*, ed. Charlotte Charrier (Paris, 1934), p. 181*n*.

[31] See Langlois, *Les manuscrits*, p. 110.

this period, but it does eloquently attest to the kinds of changes in mental attitudes and taste, particularly with regard to responses to verbal and pictorial *littera*, which made the *Roman* increasingly incomprehensible to the very heirs of those who had cherished it for more than a century. On folio 119ʳ of Arras 897 there had originally been a picture of the Lover approaching a sanctuary in which there was either an actual woman or a sexual idol, as in Fig. 27. What was in the context of the poem, and had been for fourteenth-century illustrators, a clever and telling exposure of Amant's cupidity, was no longer palatable; so the picture was destroyed, along with the final illustration in the sequence (folio 120ᵛ), which showed the plucking of the rose, with the allegorical veil removed.

The illustrations in medieval books must often represent, at the very least, some hours of close and thoughtful work; yet their destruction is the work of a moment. The sixteenth-century iconoclasts who rushed about splintering fonts, roods, windows, and "images" acted from passion and policy. Their work required some planning, as well as a certain amount of heavy equipment, and it involved working up a sweat. To blot out a miniature takes merely an offended consciousness and a ready thumb, so that it is probably remarkable that there are so few, rather than so many, examples of vandalized manuscripts of the *Roman*.

Amant's rejection of Lady Reason, the first major dramatic moment in Jean's part of the poem, is the clearest possible indication of his poetic strategy, of his estimation of Amant's love, and of his expectations for his audience. In the context in which Jean lived and wrote, Reason was not generally despised. The long dialogue between Lady Reason and Amant, furthermore, is no romance convention such as the walk-on appearances of that lady found in Chrétien, but a schematic catechism which presents, in a convenient and appealing way, some of the most cherished, and therefore conventional, teachings of Christian theology, including those most crucial to an understanding of the poem's drama. That the Lover should spurn the advances of Reason, as less worthy of his attention than the shining crystals, the rosebud, or the sophistries of Amis and the polite blasphemies of Amours, is indeed a kind of triumph for love—but for that species of love which Jean and his audience habitually spoke of as sin. This is a point which cannot be too forcefully made. The rejection of Reason, is, indeed, the heart of all sin, and the first part of the *Roman de la Rose* is its emblematic delineation.

A question hotly disputed in the schools of the twelfth and thirteenth centuries concerned the operation and the culpability of the sensuality, and, as with so much else in Scholasticism, the debate centered squarely on certain statements of St. Augustine, in this case on the teaching advanced in his tropological interpretation of the Fall of man.[32] Augustine viewed reason as consisting of two parts, the higher (represented in the fable by Adam) and the lower (Eve). Sensuality, or the sensible appetite (the Serpent), tempts the lower reason, which shows a natural inclination toward it. A sin, which is invariably an echo of the Fall, takes place when Eve corrupts Adam, when the lower reason, beguiled by the sensuality, gains ascendence over the higher reason.

In the academic discussions of the high Middle Ages, the Augustinian categories were not always strictly kept. Some theologians, for example, dropped the distinction between the higher and lower reason, or failed to understand it correctly. Typically, sin was thought to consist simply of the corruption of reason by sensuality. A point of particular interest concerned the natural (referring to *natura vitiata*) inclination of the lower reason toward pleasure. The technical term for this inclination, as it manifested itself in particular instances, was the *primus motus*, or spontaneous first movement toward pleasurable satisfaction before the higher reason has asserted its mastery or yielded its consent. Though St. Augustine's teaching on this difficult matter is not unequivocal, he considered the concupiscence of the flesh as invariably polluted, and was generally held to maintain that the *primus motus* was venially sinful.[33] In the theological movements of the twelfth century, there was a growing insistence on a casuistry which takes some account of intention. Since the *primus motus* is natural and

[32] See the illuminating discussion by Robertson, *Preface to Chaucer*, pp. 69ff.

[33] A synoptic treatment of the question as it appears in leading thirteenth-century theologians is O. Lottin's "Les mouvements premiers de l'appétit sensitif de Pierre Lombard à Saint Thomas d'Aquin," in *Psychologie et morale au XIIe et XIIIe siècles*," II, i, 2, pp. 493-589; however, Lottin's summary statement of Augustine's position, p. 495, is an oversimplification. The complex history of Augustine's thoughts on the matter is traced by M. Müller in *Die Lehre von Paradiesesehe*, Chapter I.

spontaneous, involuntary and outside man's control, its operations may not, perhaps, be regarded as sinful. A thinker of the greatest importance in this respect and Jean de Meun's most weighty authority, Alain de Lille, attempted to mitigate the Augustinian doctrine of concupiscence by discovering a kind of *Ur*-form of the *primus motus* which he held to be without sin.[34] The broad outlines of Lady Reason's teachings about *concupiscentia* are, as we have seen, Augustinian; but since, so far as sexual behavior is concerned, the *primus motus* is identifiable with the natural inclination rightly ordered by Genius, it may be that Reason's insistence that *amour naturel* is amoral reflects Alainian doctrine. Yet the meaning of the iconographic action in the first part of the *Roman* is unmistakable, since both for St. Augustine and for those who maintained his teachings on concupiscence and those who modified them alike, the heart of mortal sin was in the denial, or corruption, of reason. In the psychological terminology which became almost universal in the later Middle Ages, the final of the three stages of sin is the "consent of the reason." Such a term does not, of course, imply a natural defect in the reason itself, but underscores the reason's vulnerability to willful desire. Lady Reason cannot force Amant to follow her directions, since he has free will; nor does she consent actively to his folly in the sense of agreeing with his preposterous arguments or conniving in his campaign against the rose. But she does leave him, in effect dismissed by his obstinacy, to the sadly insufficient guidance of his aesthetic faculties and his wounded nature.

The lady whom the Lover here rejects is the same Reason who, according to a fourteenth-century French allegory which borrows most of its ideas from the *Roman*, "is so beloved of God that no one can please Him except through her, who governs the friends of God."[35] But Amant has no intention of pleasing God or God's daughter; he has a god of his own, and friends of his own—one in particular, Amis, is a miserable comforter and cynical advisor whose sophistries and alternating worldly wisdom and sentimen-

[34] P. Delhaye, "Le Péché dans la théologie d'Alain de Lille," *Sciences Ecclésiastiques*, xvii (1963), 7-27.

[35] *Les Livres du Roy Modus et de la Royne Ratio*, ed. G. Tilander (Paris, 1932), I, 269. Cf. Wisdom 7:27.

tality parody the rational process of dialectic demonstrated by Lady Reason.

The structure of the *Roman,* as we have seen, has much in common with that of a morality play. A *persona* who in some ways represents "everyman" retraces the steps of Hercules toward the crossroads; on one side he has good counsel, on the other, bad. One of the places where the flesh of the *Roman* is leanest, where its skeletal structure is seen articulate, is the dialectical matrix where the Friend replaces Reason as the Lover's advisor. Reason, who has recently offered herself as an *amie,* is rejected for Amis; that is, Divine Sapience is rejected and worldly wisdom embraced. Iconographically, the action is no less meaningful than the crucial psychomachic confrontations in a number of other set pieces of the literature of the "two ways": the Judgment of Paris, Hercules at the crossroads, the strait way and the wide way.

Thus it is that the illustrators quite naturally conceived this central episode in love's progress in terms of the cliché configuration of the Pythagorean Y. Amis and Reason stand on opposite sides of Amant, each vying for his attention, his heart, his love; each, too, offering a different kind of love. In some illustrations the battle is already done; and defeated Reason walks away with downcast visage as a sprightly Amis hastens to take her place. Such illustrations are very common. One particularly interesting picture in this genre (Fig. 32), involving not Amis but Amours himself, glosses the passage early in Reason's interview with Amant when he says "Ainsinc Raison me preeschait; Mais Amours tout empeeschait" (ll. 4629-30). Figure 32 reveals a miniature drama, a psychomachic tug-of-war; and its iconographic characteristics, which have little to do with the literal text of the *Roman* (Amours is not, after all, present at the time), are obviously closely related to other pictorial emblems of the "two ways."[36] Such an illustration, incidentally, seriously undermines the metaphysics of allegory insisted on by C. S. Lewis: "You cannot really have the lady, and, say, the lady's Pride, walking about on the same stage as if they were entities on the same plane." Both Amours and Reason are "abstractions"; yet so far as the action of

[36] The iconography of the "two ways" is treated by Erwin Panofsky, *Hercules am Scheidewege und andere antike Bildstoffe in der neueren Kunst* (Berlin, 1930).

the plot is concerned, they are aspects of the Lover, his *cupido* and his *ratio*. It is only the fact that they all, in fact, do act on the same stage which makes Fig. 32 coherent.

In any case, the iconographic context in which we first see Amis, whether in Guillaume's text or Jean's, is in psychomachic confrontation with Lady Reason, and this immediately raises an important question of interpretation. Friendship has just been praised by Reason as one of the good kinds of love. How is it, then, that friendship can be as starkly contrasted with reason as the context of the poem unequivocally suggests? The answer must begin with the reminder of Ailred's view that there is, necessarily, friendship among the wicked as well as among the just. Like "love," the word "friendship" bears a double lesson, since it must also be defined in terms of its ends. Thomas Aquinas can talk about the friendship of married partners being enriched by properly governed sexual intercourse; and Chaucer can talk of the collusion between a quack doctor and a dishonest apothecary as friendship. The defining characteristic of friendship, its "control," so to speak, is its end. The ends of the friendship of marriage in Thomist theology are the familiar three "goods." The end of the friendship of Chaucer's Physician and his accomplice is some quick cash in their pockets.

Now it is patently obvious that the end of the friendship which unites Amant and Amis is the capture of the rose. It is likewise clear, by this point in the poem, that the rose quest, however euphemized by Amours and Amant, is a very common kind of carnal pilgrimage, to use one of the Lover's own images. On the allegorical level (*quid agas*) it is a well-planned seduction, not the pursuit of ideal love or some other ineffable flower. On the tropological level—or according to what the *Echecs* gloss calls the "moral meaning," corresponding to the *quo tendas* of the exegetical distich—Lady Reason has patiently taught the Lover that his pursuit of the rose is a typically youthful manifestation of subjection to Fortune, a pathological infection, and downright foolishness. It should be clear that such an end of friendship would hardly be sanctioned by the author of the *Laelius* or its greater Christian version by St. Ailred; therefore, there is absolutely no good reason to believe it would be approved by Jean de Meun. Nevertheless, predictably enough, the Lover's Amis has more than once been described as an ideal friend, one who exemplifies the ideals of medieval friendship. What truth there is in such judgments—and that is practically none—depends upon a somewhat peculiar use of the word "ideal." In medieval iconography Pharaoh, Haman, and Herod frequently appear as ideal figures exemplifying kingship and the administration of justice; Jezebel is an ideal of pleasure. In a similar sense, perhaps, Amis is an ideal of friendship in the *Roman de la Rose*. He provides a nice antithesis for the friendly offices outlined in Reason's account of *amistie*.

Yet while Amis' essential iconographic functions in the poem are, or should be, easily identifiable, he is one of the most complex of Jean's characters, constantly shifting his ground, speaking now out of one side of his mouth as the hard-headed cynic, now out of the other as a romantic and sad spectator of human degeneracy. The discrepancies are more apparent than real, but they provide a pleasurable richness to his emblematic garb. Our initial glimpse of Amis in Guillaume's part of the poem was hardly edifying: he there counseled Amant, quite wisely according to the wisdom of this world, that he could speed his case with Danger and Bel Accueil with a little flattering prevarication. He arrives on the scene in Jean's text not so much to counsel lying—though he gets around to that soon enough—as to remind the Lover of his pact with the god of Love. He does not chide Amant for talking to Reason; rather he encourages him to remember the service he owes Amours. In particular, one of Amis' chief purposes is to reinforce the desire for the *bouton* by constructing fantasies of pleasurable thought. This expression, *douce pensée*, is the French equivalent of *delectatio cogitationis*, which is the second stage of sin, making it, in its context, a dubious counsel of love. Amis then repeats the burden of advice offered earlier in the poem: the Lover should flatter, make himself nice, deceive the guardians of the rose about his true motivations. While he may talk of love, he should never let them know that his principal, if not sole, object is carnal satisfaction; he should instead pretend that he is moved by honorable love (*amour leial e fine*). In effect this means that while the Lover must not follow Reason, he should pretend to.

Amant, who from time to time seems to suggest that he has for a moment come to believe in the resounding but hollow courtliness of the code of Cupid, is revolted by advice that seems to be absolutely "diabolic," advice which would make him seem a "false hypocrite." Amis' somewhat curious reply, which Amant immediately accepts as convincing, amounts to a statement that the ends justify the means. Malebouche, who is ever on the lookout for scandal and who, in a society which provides few convenient opportunities for private and undetected sexual liaisons, usually finds it, will expose the Lover if given the slightest chance. The Lover, a man of high honor, suggests that Malebouche be hanged; but Amis thinks the better method of taking care of the problem is simple deceit (*traïson*). All honor spent, Amant agrees that such must be the case and promises never to disagree with his friend's counsel again.

To speak as one must of the Lover, to call him a cad and a fool, will perhaps be thought to betoken an insensitivity to the mysteries of love; yet what else is one to say of him? A simple paraphrase of the surface action of the allegory, a straightforward rehearsal of the plot which strips the religion of Amours of some of its grandiose rhetoric, reveals Amant and Amis as carnal, base, dishonest, and unworthy. Their friendship, in the categories of Ailred, is that which unites evil men for evil purposes. Amis seriously presents to the Lover under the guise of good counsel what is absurd and immoral. The love of which he speaks so knowingly is at best sordid stuff, shoddy goods connived for and bought with gifts; such love is the pleasure of the rich, and no poor man can aspire to it. Amis has the manner of a *doctor amoris*, to be sure, but the mind of a pimp. He rails at whores, true enough, but he still counsels a fat pocketbook as the quickest way to love.

Such is the character of this strange friend; yet despite the fact that Jean de Meun exposes that character, layer by layer, during the nearly three thousand lines of Amis' speech in the *Roman*, its most salient features have until recently hardly been commented upon by critics, who have instead been typically preoccupied with two other aspects of it. These are Amis' sage advice about the incompatibility of *amour* and *seigneurie* and Jean's use of the passage to express "bourgeois," "realistic," and "antifeminist" ideas. Furthermore, these topics have been examined not for what they tell us about Amis, but rather as the views of

Jean de Meun himself. For example, Dunn claims that "Flying in the face of contemporary assumptions, he eloquently insists on the necessity of equality between husband and wife."[37] It will, I think, be necessary to re-examine the pertinent passages in another light.

The constant attitude behind Amis' many faces is one of worldliness. Like Lady Reason he is an abstraction who advises, counsels, and teaches the Lover; but, in direct and carefully controlled contrast to Divine Sapience, Amis represents worldly wisdom. Indeed, he is not so much wise as he is knowledgeable about the ways of the world. He is entirely a carnal creature, yet he yearns after man's lost innocence. He is at once a Mr. Worldly Wiseman and a Minever Cheevy; he can talk like a whoremaster and yet echo Bernard of Cluny. What at first may seem paradoxical and unresolved in Amis is explained, as his speech carefully develops, by a consistent and frightening mental attitude. Amis represents, in the *Roman de la Rose*, the worldly attitude toward innocence; and it is this attitude, subtly and comically delineated by Jean de Meun, which controls his discourse on the incompatibility of *seigneurie* and *amour*.

Midway through Amis' long, one-sided conversation with the Lover, he tells of the glorious Golden Age of yore, the fabled pious times ere priestcraft did begin; he recites the moving legend of unfallen human nature and the peaceable kingdom, held safe for the Middle Ages in the rich coffers of Vergil and Ovid, and enshrined in one of the finest meters of Boethius. The Golden Age knew not brutality, lust, or mercantile competition—neither the "acquisitive ethic" nor "gracious living."

> Unkorven and ungrobbed lay the vyne;
> No man yit in the morter spyces grond
> To clarre, ne to sause of galantyne.

The illustrators of the *Roman* are often rather playful in their visualizations of Golden Age life. The most common illustration shows a couple embracing—or doing something even more "free" —leaving to the eye of the beholder the necessary injection of innocence.[38] Numerous artists, however, make playful attempts

---

[37] Dunn's Introduction to *The Romance of the Rose*, trans. Robbins, p. xxv.
[38] British Museum, MS Egerton 881, fol. 62ʳ.

at some sort of archeological detail. In Douce 195 in the Bodleian, "free lovers" in caveman costumes lounge in pastoral dalliance while the acorn harvest goes on about them in a world far, far away from that of Amant's practical and meretricious friend.[39] But the playfulness and fascination of such surface detail, as in the imagery of the text, actually conceal one of the more cunning traps Jean has prepared for the unwary; for, as Jean's more sophisticated readers would have known, the Golden Age was not a remote pastoral idyll taken unbaptised from the pagan poets, but a multifaceted emblem charged with theological significance.

It is probably unnecessary to rehearse at length the common medieval Christian exegesis of the fabled poetic Golden Age or to demonstrate the numerous parallels by which Christian writers recognized it as a type of pre-lapsarian Paradise. Lactantius, a politely educated Christian writer for whom the poems of Ovid and Vergil were no distant classics but part of a tradition of living wisdom, had already, at the turn of the fourth century, seen the poets' "aureis temporibus . . . iam Saturno regnante" confirmed and explicated in the light of Christian revelation.[40] Nearer to Jean's own time, and more in tune with his own satirical spirit, Bernard of Cluny had written at great length of the theological and moral implications of the classical myth of the Golden Age in his mordant *De contemptu mundi*, a poem which Jean de Meun almost certainly knew, and which is possibly part of the *letre*, or literary tradition, on which Amis explicitly relies for the details of the myth. The characteristics of the Golden Age extolled by Bernard and more briefly by Amis—justice, frugality, sexuality governed by reason rather than passion—echo the Augustinian doctrines of Lady Reason. As Robertson has pointed out, the "classical 'Golden Age' was taken to represent the state of nature before the Fall or the restoration of that condition in the Church of the Faithful."[41] That is, we shall find a Christian Golden Age and an earthly paradise at the beginning of the world and at the end of Purgatory. But those are the only places we shall find it, for

---

[39] Tuve, *Allegorical Imagery*, p. 254, Fig. 93.

[40] *Diviniarum Institutionum*, VII, 24; *CSEL*, XIX, 658ff. Cited by Pierre Courcelle, "Les Exégèses chrétiennes de la Quatrième Eglogue," *Revue des Etudes Anciennes*, LIX (1957), 295.

[41] *Preface to Chaucer*, p. 202n.

man's sin—like that of "Jupiter the likerous"—has excluded the earthly pilgrims from their ancestral home.

Of the striking parallels between life in Eden, as expounded by the exegetes, and life in the Golden Age, extolled by the ancient poets and the medieval mythographers, one of the most telling is that of the "reign of Justice." It is in the context of a broad discussion of justice that Matelda tells Dante of the earthly paradise:

> Quelli ch'anticament poetaro
> l'eta dell' oro e suo stato felice,
> forse in Parnaso esto loco sognaro.[42]

We have already seen that Lady Reason, in her second long discourse with Amant, likewise brought up the matter of the Golden Age and its violent end with the castration of Saturn in the course of a discussion of justice: "When Saturn was king, justice reigned supreme." In frenzied and aberrant revolt, Jupiter emasculated his own sire and threw the *coilles* into the tumid sea, whence sprang, in marvellous and grotesque birth, Venus, goddess of lechery. The Age of God was at an end; and man's sad progress toward the Age of Iron had begun.

For the brilliant and mythographically sophisticated illustrator of the Valencia ms the disorders of nature inherent in the first fall from the Golden Age could be emblematically suggested by a late Gothic grotesque, a mermaid Venus, half queen and half penis (Fig. 33). Drawing upon the same mythographic sources which inspired the *Echecs* gloss, the illustrator captures, in a dramatic conflation of temporalities, the tableau of violent and willful rebellion against order and justice which enthroned Venus in the hearts of men, not least of all in the heart of Amant, vassal to her son and captain in his wars. The *coilles*, the unruly members which Amant is loath for courtesy to name but happy enough to worship, become, fittingly enough, Venus' "lower parts." The goddess here so marvellously born of the spume, so obscenely stripped of the grace, softness, and majesty we may, looking back through Botticelli, wish to bring to the myth, is the same great force around whom rally Amant and Amis and Faussemblant and

---

[42] Purgatorio, xxviii, 139-41; cited by Charles Singleton in his valuable discussion in *Journey to Beatrice (Dante Studies, II)* (Cambridge, 1958), p. 188.

Amours and La Vieille and the whole sordid and disreputable gang who would banish Reason to make war on chastity—and all in the name of Love. It was her birth, in the eyes of the ancients, which witnessed the loss of primal justice from the world. Similarly, the Christian theologians held that the Fall of man in Eden was to be understood in terms of the privation of original justice.

Few *questiones disputatae* of Gothic theology found authorities more widely divided than that of original sin, and the raging debate, which in the first quarter of the fourteenth century produced such a rich dossier of Augustinian and Thomist positions and counter-positions, clearly has its roots in the Parisian academy of the 1270's and, consequently, in Jean de Meun's immediate intellectual milieu.[43] As interesting as the complexities of this debate are, however, they cannot command our present attention, for on the question of the relation of original justice to original sin there is wide agreement, indeed virtual unanimity of opinion. Perhaps the most common definition of original sin in the theological vocabulary of the late scholastic period is Thomas' own definition, "carencia justitiae originalis," the "privation of original justice." The term "original justice" itself is a slippery one, used as it is by medieval theologians in varying senses: the natural rectitude of the will, the supernaturally imposed dominion of reason over sensuality, and so forth.[44] But the sin of Adam, the stain on man's post-lapsarian nature and the rent in Nature's garment, whether it be considered a "morbid quality" linked to the concupiscence of the flesh or a disorientation of the relationship between the rational and sensible faculties, is the *carencia justitiae naturalis*.

Reason, with her Augustinianism, insists that the essence of sin is irrationality. The thirteenth-century theologians, while agreeing with her, generalized the definition of sin, viewed from the affective point of view, as the denial of justice. The great myth to

[43] Specifically, the focus of the argument is the Augustinian position of the secular master Henry of Ghent, who maintained that original sin is an actual "morbid quality" of post-lapsarian nature, intimately connected with the concupiscence. For the documents in the debate see Raymond M. Martin, *La controverse sur le péché originel au début du XIVe siècle* (Louvain, 1930).

[44] See the lucid discussion by Cyril Vollert, "The Two Senses of Original Justice in Medieval Theology," *Theological Studies*, v (1944), 3-23.

which both Reason and Amis turn—and to which La Vieille implicitly and Genius explicitly also turn—presents, enshrined in a reliquary of Egyptian gold, a Christian truth concerning the irrational privation of justice.

There is a fine irony in the fact that it is with reference to this very fable that Amant announces his contemptuous ignorance of allegorical significances; for the truth which the fable conceals speaks directly to his own case. The "lover" of the *Echecs*, called L'aucteur, has an encounter with Diana, who is said to be the opposite of Venus in every way, and the chaste goddess uses the story of the Golden Age as a telling argument against the young man for wanting "to go into the Garden of Deduit to follow the insane and dangerous life they lead there."[45] She attributes his folly to the perverse and pervasive influence of Venus, the goddess who has been in the ascendant since the end of the age when virtue and chastity flourished, and she compares the lover's example with some of the better-known disorderings and denaturings of literary history: Ulysses and Circe, Jason and the Golden Fleece, Paris and Helen. But Amant is not alone in his ignorance of what the story of the Golden Age may mean, and one of the happy poetic indirections of the *Roman* is the way in which Amis' carnal misconception of primal innocence undercuts all his own arguments.

For Amis' explication of the Golden Age, in the context in which it arises, is built upon a comic but fatal sophistry; he seeks to justify the concupiscence of the Age of Iron (which is itself the direct result of the castration of Saturn or, in Christian terms, the *carencia justitiae naturalis*) by an appeal to the freedom of innocent and just sexuality of the age when justice reigned supreme. Amis here reveals himself as another character like the Lover, who thinks he can happily traipse through the terrestrial paradise clothed in his ill-fitting post-lapsarian human nature, plucking fruits and flowers with impunity. The cortex of the fable attracts him mightily; he would love to be able to play caveman, taking his pleasures freely without the intrusion of a busybody morality, like those antique shepherds in the illustrations, who seem to be having it so good. Of the fable's meaning for a Chris-

[45] Bibliothèque nationale MS fr. 9197, fol. 203ʳ.

148

tian society, Amis is as much in the dark as his friend Amant, for whom he wistfully recounts this little history of a paradise on earth. According to St. Ailred, love (*caritas*) could in a sense recapture the Golden Age; and "charity attains its full measure only in friendship, which therefore renews God's original plan and restores Paradise and is also a foretaste of the fulfillment of the full redemptive restoration in heaven."[46] That Jean's ironic exemplar of friendship would likewise wish to "restore Paradise" —carnally, of course, not spiritually—is a nice touch.

Unfortunately, love cannot be "free" in a world in which man has destroyed his own freedom. Furthermore, it never was "free" in the sense envisaged by Amis' carnal imagination. Rosemond Tuve has commented on the humorous effect of the Friend's sentimental *Sehnsucht* for a Golden Age misconstrued by him as a Bower of Bliss. It is the sentimentality of a cad and a cynic, a man capable of promoting the base and the commonplace as though they were sublime and extraordinary. In a moral allegory more obvious in its techniques and less dependent upon the sophistication and iconographic sensitivity of its readers, the Lover's Friend would be a Mr. Worldly Wiseman or Wicked Counsel. In the *Roman*, at any rate, Jean did not conceive of satire, as so many of his contemporaries did, primarily in terms of polished and hyperbolic *sententiae* on the wickedness of man; he chose another, perhaps higher, road which led to extended ironic and dramatic formulations requiring the reader's engagement and arbitration, indeed his complicity, rather than his passive acquiescence in unexceptionable commonplaces grandly stated. Bernard of Cluny, writing of the decay of the Golden Age and man's viciousness resulting from it, is careful to make his satirical intent obvious: "Pardon, modesty, there is much that is not nice in the following ... but it is my care to forbid the sinful and urge the right ... I indulge in satire here. Spurn the evil. Clothe thy heart with wisdom. I speak in a right spirit; do thou look upon it in the right spirit."[47] Only once in his own poem, when he turns his barbed pen against dishonest religious, does Jean de Meun apparently consider his subject so sensitive, so vulnerable to misunderstand-

[46] A. Fiske, "Aelred's Idea of Friendship," p. 15.

[47] Trans. Henry Preble, in Samuel M. Jackson, *The Source of "Jerusalem the Golden"* (Chicago, 1911), p. 132.

ing, that he must remove for a moment the satirist's ironic mask. Even then he does it mockingly, and even then his disclaimer did not save him from misunderstanding. He has paid the price of his audacity and, perhaps, of his poetic failure. Since Gerson's day to our own critics have more or less consistently failed to make even the most elementary of overtures—such as paying some attention to speaker and context in his poem—which Jean thought he could expect from his readers. Turning Amis, apparently on the basis of his name alone, into an ideal friend who expresses ideal medieval attitudes is a typical if extreme example of the inevitable distortions fathered by such abuse.

The Golden Age theme introduces Amis' formal discussion of marriage, but it also qualifies that discussion in a richly comic way. Amis maintains that men and women in the Golden Age recognized the sagacity and truth of the saying that *"amour* and *seigneurie* cannot keep company."* Annotators of the *Roman* are agreed that the source of this *sententia* is Ovidian ("Non bene conveniunt . . . Majestas et amor"); but in its context in the *Metamorphoses* the sentiment has nothing to do with marriage at all—it merely explains why the mighty king of the gods saw fit to become a bull when he wanted to rape Europa. On the other hand the term *seigneurie* is the technical word for the "lordship" or hierarchical authority which the husband was supposed to have over his wife, according to medieval teachings on marriage, and it is clearly this sense in which Amis uses it. As the sentence of what the story of the age of original justice has to teach fallen human nature, the advice that *seigneurie* and *amour* cannot exist together is peculiarly perverse. The institution of Christian marriage founded on the husband's *seigneurie* was specifically intended to provide some remedy for the frantic sexual disorders occasioned by the privation of original justice. In fact, the only way that sexual love could be lawfully pursued was in the strict governance of the marital hierarchy. From the point of view of Christian teaching, that is, *amour* could exist only in close company with *seigneurie*. The sophistry of Amis' argument is thus total and hilarious.

In saying this I am not unaware that a Dominican scholar has recently maintained that Amis' doctrine is no joke; indeed, he asserts that it is the expression of an *"ideal"* view of marriage held by the mature Middle Ages. According to him this same *ideal* teaching, the fruit of a "mellow Christianity," is found in Chrétien's *Cligès* and Chaucer's Franklin's Tale, as well as in Nicole Oresme's late fourteenth-century glosses to the pseudo-Aristotelian *Economics*.[48] This claim merits brief examination and swift rejection. The doctrines of marriage advanced by *Cligès* and the Franklin's Tale are, from the point of view of scholarly discussion, very much *sub judice*; both poems are complex works of art written by poets who are widely believed to exhibit a number of sophisticated literary techniques, including irony, which make it difficult to offer convincing definitive interpretations of them. It seems to me most unlikely that Chrétien de Troyes in the twelfth century and Geoffrey Chaucer in the fourteenth should without further comment reject as dead letters the explicit teachings about marriage found in St. Paul, St. Augustine, and virtually every formal discussion of marriage for a thousand years, as well as the words of the marriage rite itself, to seriously maintain the view that the husband's *seigneurie* is inimical to love in marriage; but it may be considered possible. It would, however, hardly make such an opinion an *"ideal"* view; nor would it mean that it was sanctioned by responsible authority. Certainly Oresme, who was a responsible if minor theologian, never held it for a moment; and to represent that he did, especially in an attempt to demonstrate the alleged ignorance of another scholar, is extraordinary. The closest that Oresme comes to an "original" view of the marriage hierarchy is in his gloss to "Aristotle's" citation of the words of Ulysses to Nausicaa: "Domine . . . tu mihi terribilis est." From this, Oresme concludes that "it appears that the husband should fear his wife."[49] Such fear as there is, however, is based on the apprehension of the moral virtues which the wife is counseled to have. Each partner is to consider the other better than himself in a moral sense, but this says nothing about their positions in a social hierarchy. It would have been extremely awkward for Oresme to believe in Amis' view of marriage, since "Aristotle" himself, strangely echoing St. Paul, calls the husband the "head" of the wife. Elsewhere he is clearly her governor and preceptor. In

---

[48] F. Parmisano, in *Medium Ævum*, xxv (1966), 278.

[49] *Le Livre de Yconomique d'Aristote*, ed. Albert D. Menut in *Transactions of the American Philosophical Society*, n.s., XLVII, 5 (1957), 840.

domestic decisions she is expected to agree to the will of her husband. As a matter of fact, the introduction of Aristotelian ideas into Christian discussion did nothing to weaken the doctrine of the marital hierarchy; on the contrary, Aristotle bolstered the doctrine. Giles of Rome, whose famous *De regimine principum* actually *can* be regarded as a repository of the *"ideal"* views of the fourteenth century, cites Aristotle to prove that the man's *seigneurie* is a fundamental law of nature.[50]

Men were of many minds about marriage in the Middle Ages, so that I should hesitate to express the *"ideal"* medieval view of the subject in a few lines. It was a topic widely debated from a number of different points of view, and it is easy enough to produce conflicting ideas about the sacrament and the institution drawn from the wide literature of antifeminism, from commentaries on the *Sentences*, from formal theological tracts dealing with the sacraments, and the like. However, I know of absolutely no authority who denies the Pauline (or Augustinian, or Thomist) principle of the marital hierarchy—that is, that the husband in Christian marriage must have *seigneurie* over the wife. That Jean should deny it would be most remarkable; that he should use Amis as his mouthpiece even more so; and that Amis himself should pause in the midst of his campaign to further Amant's irrational passion by teaching him the arts of false flattery, lies, and gifts in order to enunciate the ideal Christian view of marriage would present an artistic problem of some difficulty.

Jean's handling of the matter of *seigneurie* is witty, to be sure, but he clearly accepts and plays against a set of traditional ideas; and since the whole *Roman* is an extended sexual metaphor, technicalities of medieval teachings about sex are a legitimate if not indispensable matter of concern to its student. It is well known, for example, that the austere justification for marriage made by St. Paul and expounded by St. Augustine was a commonplace of moral theology throughout the thirteenth century. According to this teaching, one of the *principales causae* for the marriage insti-

---

[50] *De regimine principum*, ii, i, 6; citing Aristotle's *Politics*, i, iii: "Nam nunquam est dare communitatem aliquam bene ordinatam, nisi aliquid sit ibi dirigens, et aliquid directum: vel nisi aliquid principans, et aliquid obsequens. Quare cum in communitate maris et foeminae, mas debit esse principans et foemina obsequens."

tution is the *remedium*—that is, the suppression of fornication and the proper direction of concupiscence. In the common schema of the three so-called goods of marriage the *remedium* is of course connected with the first good, the *bonum fidei*.[51]

Such a position was neither cynical nor puritanical, merely realistic; nor did it obviate any of the beautiful (and perhaps mellow) teachings by which the penitential *summae* reveal a moral theology sensitive to the complexities of human sexuality and convincing in their teachings concerning the non-physical ends of human marriage. The husband's *seigneurie*, which according to William of Auvergne perfects the "chains of society," brought with it seignorial duties as well as seignorial rights. Since, according to medieval theories of physiology, the sexual desire of the wife, as also her pleasure in sexual intercourse, was considerably greater than that of the husband, his duty to serve his wife in the payment of the marriage debt was correspondingly increased. It is typical of Amis' dubious dialectic that the *exemplum* of the Jaloux, ostensibly illustrating the evils of marital *seigneurie*, really has little to do with it. The Jaloux is by his literary definition not a reasonable "lord" of his wife but rather a ridiculous tyrant and, in fact, does not have *seigneurie* in any case.

There is, in short, nothing in the historical background to Jean's poem nor in the immediate poetic context of Amis' speech to lend any intellectual respectability to the fantastic idea that the Friend's views on the incompatibility of love and *seigneurie* express the ideal of Chaucer's society or any other Christian society before the twentieth century. It simply means that the husband's *maistrie* was not to be a tyranny, nor to be abused for selfishness of any kind. This should be apparent in the implications of the analogy so frequently drawn between human marriage and the marriage of Christ and His Church. Christ is indeed "one who serves" the weaknesses of his beloved as far as Calvary and beyond. This hardly means that He is not Lord, king, ruler, head, husband to the Church; or that the cosmic bonds of love which unite Him and His Church are cruelly severed by the blade of His lordship.

There is a further irony, for, in one important sense, what Amis says is perfectly true—provided that by "love" we understand

---

[51] See Josef Georg Ziegler, *Die Ehelehre der Pönitentialsummen von 1200-1350* (Regensburg, 1956), p. 39, *et passim*.

"irrational passion." In fact, the defining characteristic of irrational as opposed to rational love is that it is not subject to any governance; as one of Chaucer's characters, suffering from an advanced case of it, says: "Who shal yeve a lover any lawe?" Chaucer's French contemporary and admirer, the poet Eustache Deschamps, wrote a *ballade* entitled "La loy souvent contraire à la nature" which plays with this conflict, briefly developing two of the ideas about the end of the Golden Age which are also found in the *Roman*.[52] Deschamps first argues the natural superiority of love to justice, as proved by Lady Reason, and then points out that, since the end of the Golden Age, law often runs counter to nature. The *seigneurie* of marriage in effect destroys love. What he is saying, rather elegantly and indirectly, is exactly what Saint Paul said: marriage was instituted to put down concupiscence. The point once again is that it is sophistical to apply the categories of Golden Age nature to man's condition after the *carencia justitiae naturalis*. The insufficiency of human nature, attested to by the necessity for the constraining institutions of justice, is thus the real subject of Deschamps' lament.

Amis, having thus introduced and seemingly disposed of the question of *seigneurie*, takes up another subject which was destined to be regarded by the poem's critics in subsequent centuries as one of the principal themes of the *Roman*: the vices of women. As the dustjacket blurb of a modern English version puts it, "It was finished by Jean de Meun, who radically changed the original intent of the poem and made it a satire on many aspects of medieval life, but especially on women and marriage." The process by which this is done is somewhat delicate. The Friend uses an imaginary *persona*, the Jealous Husband, well-known to medieval comedy, to speak against women and marriage. The Jaloux in turn cites a good number of authorities to bolster his case, Valerius, Juvenal, Ovid, and others, so that the antifeminist point of view is in no way very obviously Jean's own. Nonetheless, the conventional interpretation of the *Roman* maintains that these views were indeed Jean's, that furthermore they are "bourgeois" in character, and that from a literary point of view the entire intermezzo of

[52] *Œuvres complètes de Eustache Deschamps*, ed. Queux de Saint-Hilaire, 1 (Paris, 1878), 225-26; cited by L. Friedman, " 'Jean de Meung,' Antifeminism, and 'Bourgeois Realism,' " *Modern Philology*, LVII (1959), 18.

the Jaloux is an important moment in the history of medieval "realism."

The weaknesses of these recurrent assumptions about Jean de Meun, and their debilitating influence on criticism of his poem as *a priori* critical principles, are ruthlessly exposed in a felicitous and learned article by Lionel Friedman entitled " 'Jean de Meung,' Antifeminism, and 'Bourgeois Realism.' " Friedman shows that the Jaloux, along with several other characters in the *Roman*, including Amant himself, reflects a stock figure in Latin comedy who can be expected to represent a certain stock point of view. Furthermore, his antifeminism reflects to a marked degree neither realism nor a bourgeois sensibility; rather, it is conventional and learned. "Just as he is clerical in his sources, our Jaloux is clerical in his expression and knows the colors of rhetoric and how to compose an invective in the approved manner; in all respects, he shows a far greater reflection of the medieval schools than of an observation of contemporary life. Any measure of 'realism' which may be found in the diatribe is of precisely that amount and kind to be found in any satirical work of a literary moralist."[53]

Friedman's article should clear the path of some of the more entangling underbrush (realism, subspecies bourgeois) so that it may be possible to suggest what the episode is actually doing in Jean's poem. While it is very probable that such Jankyn clerkes as were in Jean's audience would have enjoyed the echoes and citations from the various books of wicked wyves to which the Jaloux turns, it seems likely that the principal force of the satire is directed not at women and not at the institution of marriage in itself, but at certain attitudes represented by the Jaloux, a stock foil of medieval comedy. Amis introduces the whole episode of the Jaloux with the implication that it will further illustrate the rightness of his views on the marital hierarchy; but as we have just seen his *exempla* by no means invariably prove the points he thinks they do, so it is necessary to examine this assumption. Specifically, Amis claims that the history of the Jaloux shows that men cannot expect to have the "maistrise . . . dou corpse sa fame." In the recent Robbins translation this expression is rendered, in its context, as follows (italics added): "True love cannot for long

[53] Friedman, " 'Jean de Meung' and 'Bourgeois Realism,' " p. 23.

endure when . . . men treat *their own wives like property*." It is
this sentiment, so translated, which led Professor Dunn to com-
ment upon Jean de Meun's striking modernity and freedom from
"contemporary assumptions."

But Jean de Meun has said nothing, and Amis, who has spoken,
has said nothing about men treating "their own wives like prop-
erty." He says instead that *bone amour* cannot exist when the man
has "power over the body of his wife"; this is almost certainly a
scriptural joke rather than sage advice. Since "power over the
body of his wife" is precisely what the Jaloux does *not* have, in
one crucial sense, it is initially unclear how the sentiment charac-
terizes his situation at all. "Maistrise dou corpse sa fame," on the
other hand, renders closely enough the phrase "Mulier sui corpo-
ris potestatem" (I Corinthians 7:4) in a scriptural passage in
which St. Paul is discussing precisely the same question of marital
relations as Amis. "The wife hath not the power of her own body,
but the husband: and likewise also the husband hath not the power
of his own body, but the wife." It is thus true that someone is
flying in the face of contemporary (Pauline) assumptions, but it
is Amis, not Jean.

The episode of the Jaloux, like most of the major episodes of
Jean's *Roman*, serves a number of complex and complementary
purposes; but it quite cunningly grows out of the dictum on *amour*
and *seigneurie*, which it amplifies and, in effect, explains. Like so
much of what Amis says, his account of the Jaloux from the Punch
and Judy literature of the thirteenth century illuminates a half-
truth—which is also, of course, a half-lie. The Golden Age pre-
sents an ideal of natural charity and natural justice which Amis
himself can see but faintly if at all; looking back at Eden from
far beyond its gates, he can but reconstruct its history as though
it were a flattering mirror which transforms the image of his own
fallen nature. He sees neither true innocence, which he cannot
understand, nor justice, which he cannot afford to recognize, but
rather a fantasy paradise like the Garden of Deduit itself. Where
the poets and theologians had seen original justice, Amis sees free
love in a nudist camp. The image of the Jaloux, brutal, self-pitying,
venal, deceived by himself and by others, is perhaps the per-
fect "objective correlative" for the kinds of carnal attitudes meant
by the theologians in the expression *carencia justitiae naturalis*;

156

and it is therefore very telling that Amis should hold it up before our eyes while the vanishing form of the *aestas aureis* seems still fixed for one split second against our retinas. But neither the images nor Amis' skillful manipulation of them should be allowed to deceive us. The Jaloux does not exemplify the rightness of Amis' doctrine of the marital hierarchy; rather, he exemplifies evils which arise from its breakdown or inversion as its chains snap with the forces of passion and avarice.

Though Jean did not say that love cannot exist when "men treat their own wives like property," he well could have. The attitude exemplified by the Jaloux, in the *Roman* as elsewhere in the diverse topology of the literary type, is acquisitive, mercantile, carnal. The Jaloux's wife, wherever she appears in medieval literature, is defined almost entirely in terms of his attitude toward her. She herself is a species of goods, and the goods of marriage, so sacred to the medieval concept of matrimony, become a kind of easy lubricity. The wife, in short, is a *thing* and is so regarded by her husband and by the entourage of lovers, students, friars, or priests who (invariably with success) seek to pinch, fondle, kiss, or tup her. When the Jaloux is at last made a cuckold, the raucous laughter which ensues is not directed at a commonplace adultery, but at a sharp business deal in which a skinflint is beaten at his own game. "Thus swyved was the carpenteres wyf," says Chaucer's Miller, "for al his keping and his jalousye."

It is furthermore perfectly clear that the Jaloux in Amis' *exemplum* does not have the "maistrise . . . dou corpse sa fame" in anything like the Pauline sense; it is, in fact, the very lack of such *maistrise* which makes him a Jaloux. He may revile her, kick her, beat her, but he cannot own her even in terms of his proprietary ethic, let alone in terms of the kind of possession in mutual love which St. Paul speaks of. It is in his attitude toward his wife that the coarse and brutal Jaloux, in so many superficial ways unlike the Lover, who is refined in speech and, to a point, diplomatic in his behavior, actually reveals their essential and close kinship. Amant, who stands to the rose throughout the romance as a plucker, ravisher, possessor—whose very love was proven by Lady Reason, perhaps at excessive length, to be a typical kind of subjection to Fortune—has essentially the same attitude toward the *bouton* as the Jaloux has toward his wife. It, or she, is something which can be had, enjoyed, lost, or stolen. Indeed the Jaloux, as Amis himself maintains, is a kind of slave; but his slavery does not result from the vices of women nor from the institution of marriage established to control the passions born at the end of the Golden Age with Venus. His slavery is the slavery talked about by Reason, the slavery of Fortune's wheel; it is implied in the attitude of the worldly Amis, and it is typical of the worldly Lover. Yet the Jaloux speaks neither for one nor the other, let alone for Jean de Meun, but for himself. The Jaloux, as Pierre Col insisted long ago, talks like a Jaloux. The *Roman de la Rose*, properly understood, does not advance an antifeminist position. "Qui bien entend la glose, de femmes il ne mesdit point." It does attack what medieval writers called "effeminacy," but that is a moral concept which has no more logical connections with women than abstract nouns in the feminine gender do.

Claude Fauchet reported, or invented, a joke about Jean de Meun which has something to say about his supposed antifeminism, not to mention his bourgeois vision. According to the legend, a group of irate ladies of the court captured Jean in one of the chambers of the palace and prepared to punish him with a sound thrashing. To this ignominious chastisement he was willing, reluctantly, to submit himself, provided that the beating was administered, in his words, by "la plus forte putain de toutes celles que i'ay blasmées."[54] Like his anticlericalism, which extends no further than hypocritical religious, his antifeminism is very selective, directed as it is to the various kinds of *putains* who symbolized for him the meretricious wedding of avarice and carnality. Fauchet goes on to remark that Martin le Franc answered Jean as if he had attacked women indiscriminately, but that Martin wrote long after the event.

Much of the advice with which Amis concludes his dialogue with Amant reveals the same kind of double lesson of love as do the disquisition on the Golden Age and the episode of the Jaloux. Love must be carefully nourished, tended, cultivated; but time and again Amis peremptorily shatters the image of love's tenderness and dignity which his words so seductively create by abruptly announcing the Lover's venal motives. The Lover, for example, should be particularly solicitous for his beloved when she is ill,

[54] *Les Oeuvres de feu M. Claude Fauchet* (Paris, 1610), p. 590ᵛ.

hover about her bed, make extravagant vows of pilgrimage against her recovery, tell *plaisanz mençonges* about the sleep he is losing worrying about her and the auto-erotic fantasies he spins thinking of her. The purpose of all this humanitarianism and love, it turns out, is to deceive her so that she will "estre empres plus agreables" (l. 9872). He must lie to her, flatter her outrageously, pay her lavish and undeserved compliments. Amis' final bit of advice, his last *brief mot*, is to the effect that the aspiring lover must declare himself totally conquered by the lady's beauty. No woman, he claims, neither "vieille, jenne, mondaine out none, / Ne si religieuse dame," is unresponsive to flattering remarks about her physical charms. Thus it is that Amis ends, very much as he began, with an open appeal to fraud. His long disquisitions on the splendors of the Golden Age and the perversities of his own, on the tenderness of love and its fragility, in short, all of the sentimentality which is the opposite side of the coin to his pragmatism and efficiency, neither are meant to, nor do, conceal his essential carnality, his oldness, and venality.

When he leaves, as abruptly as he first came, he encourages Amant with a prediction of his likely success with the *bouton*; he tells him further that, when his joy is complete, he should then "keep" (*garder*) her as a priceless possession. The fact that his advice runs precisely counter to that which he has previously given about the freedom of the lady, and that he counsels Amant to follow the policy of keeping which he criticized so severely in the Jaloux, is hardly noticeable in a context so rich in contradictions. Certainly Amant shows no sign of noticing it, dazzled as he is with Amis' profound wisdom:

> Ainsinc Amis m'a conforte
> En cui conseil grant confort ai
> E m'est avis, au meins de fait,
> Qu'il set plus que Raison ne fait.

Like so many of the outrageous judgments and opinions which Jean de Meun puts into the mouths of Love's soldiers, Amant's adjudication of the comparative wisdom of Reason and Amis is shocking not so much because it is wrong as because it states one perverse kind of truth. Amis possesses expert knowledge, in all its technical minutiae, of a realm of experience which Lady Reason would choose totally to reject. The children of this world are in their generation wiser than the children of light, and Amis is exceptionally wise even for a child of this world. When he encourages Amant with all his experienced wisdom, he truly performs a kind of grotesque parody of the office of a friend. Amant, buoyant, spirits high with renewed hope and the anticipation of sweet success, sets off to free Bel Accueil from Jalousie's castle, win another kiss, and after that, he hopes, "there cometh more."

The road leading to amorous conquest is called the way of Trop Doner, and in a little *locus amoenus* by its side (*un beau leu trop delitable*), the Lover encounters its guardian and toll-taker, Dame Richece. This allegorical abstraction expounds some of the chief worldly impediments to the Lover's progress, even as Reason outlined the philosophical and moral one; and Richece shares with Reason the Lover's supercilious rejection. In the iconography of the miniatures, this elegant lady and her spiffish but dubious boyfriend appear gorgeously attired, dallying by their *fontenele* in an attitude which could perhaps be described as lubricious affluence. There are in the illuminations frequent iconographic indications of courtly lechery, small furry animals, or an indelicate caress of the lap. What the illustrators suggest explains the logic of the episode in the poem. Richece lectures the Lover that, to be admitted free passage on the road he has chosen, he must sell all that he has and give it, not to the poor, but in the gifts and bribes of love—expend it, in short, in that courteous liberality commanded by Amours. What this means in effect is that the Lover must make friends of the mammon of unrighteousness, but the operation is rather different from its scriptural analogue. Richece's description of the mad and spendthrift life required by the rules of the game of love—the dances, the games, the feasts, the flowered chaplets —is strikingly reminiscent of the amusements in the Garden of Deduit described by Guillaume de Lorris; and just as Lady Reason could counsel against such frantic joy, so can Richece, talking from the point of view of the big money. Reason explained to the Lover that to love *par amours* was to debase the gifts of nature; Richece now shows that the courteous manifestations of such love also require the squandering of the gifts of Fortune. It is Amant's great triumph, of which he is able to boast in the concluding lines of the poem, that he achieves his end without the help of either lady.

Up to the point at which Amis leaves the Lover, Jean has developed his poem along the somewhat schematic lines which he inherited from Guillaume de Lorris. The structural mould of the poem is simply that of Amant's tandem experiences, as he moves from one more or less formal lecture on life and love, to another —as he moves from the god of Love, to Reason, to Amis, back to Reason, and so on. At this point, however, Jean alters the rhythm of his narrative flow by introducing a lengthy intermezzo in the form of a long soliloquy of Faussemblant, O.P. Unlike the other teachers of love, Faussemblant is not ostensibly concerned with instructing the Lover or Bel Accueil, though in fact his doctrines add a new and rich dimension to Love's theology; his apparent motive is rather self-expression and explanation, a compulsion to describe his moral nature and to recount the deeds it fathers. That this long speech, or "confession" as it is often called on account of its principal subject matter, is a major achievement of thirteenth-century narrative there can be no doubt. Charles Muscatine, in his study of *Chaucer and the French Tradition*, rightly considers it a crucial and formative influence on Chaucer's own verisimilar dramatic dialogue, and the stamp it has left on such a little masterpiece as the Pardoner's Prologue is readily apparent. Yet while the importance and originality of the narrative techniques of the Faussemblant episode have not gone entirely unnoticed, the specific targets of Jean's satire have frequently been misunderstood in a way which is particularly damaging to a sound reading of the *Roman*, and which has inevitably given rise to totally unwarranted suppositions about Jean de Meun's own attitudes toward formal religion.

In the long section of his poem dealing with Faussemblant Jean de Meun narrows to a fine point the focus of his literary verisimilitude. Reason is eternal, lovers like Amant perennial, and there will always be fellows like the Friend, full of worldly wisdom and wicked counsel. But the external manifestations of that great evil which Jean embodies in Faussemblant reveal to a marked degree the kind of artistic exemplification of abstract principle through concrete image which I briefly discussed in my first chapter. That is, while the thematic implications of Faussemblant are as universal as any in Jean's poem, the specific materials from which the portrait is composed come from a specifically identifiable context: that of the strife between the secular masters and their regular antagonists at the University of Paris in the 1250's. With this apprehension comes a new series of critical problems, since a really proper understanding of Faussemblant and his role in Jean's poem would require a far more detailed and careful analysis of the documents in the university dispute than has so far been made or indeed can be made on the basis of published texts. Many of the scriptural citations and echoes with which the *Roman* reverberates are charged with exegetical implications defined by academic polemics, and some knowledge of the antifraternal hermeneutics of William of Saint-Amour greatly aids one's reading of Jean's poem.

Yet once again specialized iconographic study must await a foundation; a preliminary understanding of the broad outlines of the *Roman* requires not so much an expert's knowledge of the technical aspects of Faussemblant's historical lineage, but a clear view of the poet's strategy and his line of attack. Jean knew that his treatment of "religion," in its technical sense, was highly sensitive and easily susceptible to misunderstanding, and he explicitly makes the point that he attacks not true religion, but rather the hypocrisy which uses the external manifestations of religion to disguise carnal attitudes (ll. 15243ff.). That his fear of misunderstanding was amply justified is evidenced by continuing references to his "anticlericalism," his "antireligious spirit," "antiaceticism," and the like. Thus according to Alan Gunn, Jean's principal purpose in the Faussemblant intermezzo is to attack Chastity. His argument runs as follows: Jean de Meun was philosophically opposed to the religious aspiration of chastity, since it runs counter to the natural prerogatives of sexual generation, the "sacredness" of which Jean stoutly maintained. Since Faussemblant is a religious under a vow of chastity, in attacking him Jean attacks the sterile aspirations he represents.[55] But even granting that Jean de Meun despised the counsel of chastity—a proposition which strikes

[55] *Mirror of Love*, p. 126. Part of Gunn's argument is based on a dubious interpretation of Deguilleville, which I have discussed in *Romance Philology*, XVIII (1965), 431ff.

me as approaching the incredible, and which arises from a "rein-
terpretation" of the *Roman* I find unusually perverse—he could
hardly attack Chastity by attacking Faussemblant, for if there was
ever one who *did* heartily despise the counsels of perfection it is
the wicked friar. He vaunts the fact that while he preaches absti-
nence he practices luxurious self-indulgence; that he should be
traipsing around the countryside not with the *socius* stipulated
by Dominican legislation but with the very dubious Beguine,
Constrained Abstinence, could have been nothing else than a lewd
joke to Jean's audience.[56] The carnality at which Jean is content
merely to hint is revealed in full biological detail in the Faus-
semblant episodes of the marginalia in Bibliothèque nationale MS
fr. 25526. Insofar as Jean is at all interested in Faussemblant's
sex life, in short, it is to condemn him for pretending to a chastity
which he does not practice.

Coarse charges of immorality against the friars, after all, are
typical of antifraternal literature from William de Saint-Amour
to seventeenth-century drama. Yet not only has Jean de Meun
been painted as a despiser of Chastity, but the whole tradition of
antifraternalism on which he draws has been labelled "anti-
ascetic"! Thus, in one of the most ambitious analyses of Jean's
thought in recent years, Helmut Hatzfeld argues to the effect
that Jean "continue les livres anti-ascétiques tels que celui de
Guillaume de Saint Amour . . . et celui de Gérard d'Abbeville."[57]
It is not to pick a quarrel with a distinguished scholar, but to
attack a debilitating presupposition typical of even the most seri-
ous scholarship on the *Roman*, to say that this statement is little
short of preposterous.

---

[56] The Beguines, who had a reputation of lasciviousness in popular literature,
were in particular accused of liaisons with friars:

> Nam populo quanto reddunt se simpliciores,
> In ludo tanto, Veneris sunt fervidiores . . .
> Queque sibi patrem cordatum vel jacobitam
> Querit. . . .

Les Lamentations de Matheolus et le Livre de Leesce, ed. A. G. van Hamel
(Paris, 1892), I, 91-92. The French translator of the *Lamentations* hesitated
to translate the frankest parts of his Latin sources, especially since Jean de Meun
had amply treated the subject "Ou chapitre de Faulx Semblant," p. 92.

[57] Helmut Hatzfeld, "La mystique naturiste de Jean de Meung," *Wissen-
schaftliche Zeitschrift der Friedrich-Schiller-Universität Jena*, V (1955/56), 259.

While there is no doubt whatever of Jean's heavy debt to Guillaume's *De periculis novissimorum temporum*, and while it is possible that Jean actually thought of himself as carrying on, in a formal sense, the task begun by Guillaume a generation before him, the characterization of the work of either man as "anti-ascetic" seriously mistakes the nature of the Parisian quarrel of the 1250's. A chief charge of *De periculis*, a markedly stern and dour work, is that the friars have abandoned the entirely admirable ascetic principles of St. Francis for a soft life of hypocrisy.[58] The *Contra adversarium perfectionis*, Gérard's antifraternal diatribe, presents an ideal of the secular Christ life much influenced by the concept of monastic perfection, that is, the traditional aspirations of Benedictine asceticism which the author claims the friars have abandoned.[59] Both works condemn libertinism vigorously. The *De periculis* in particular enjoyed a very long run as a reformatory tract; Nicolas of Clamanges is full of echoes of it, and it was, of course, clandestinely printed after the Reformation.

De periculis novissimorum temporum is no meat for babes, but it is not untypical of the strident *odium theologicum* of the thirteenth century. Heresy, according to one cynical definition, is being on the side that loses. Guillaume de Saint-Amour, whose works are neither readily available nor widely known to literary scholars, is often spoken of as if he were a heretic. In fact he was at worst an unsuccessful polemicist. He crossed swords with the giant Aquinas, and he was deemed an inflammatory enthusiast by the pope, just as the young visionary, Francesco Bernardone, was judged by another pope some decades earlier. In his debate with the Angelic Doctor, who was forced into an unusual defensive posture, Guillaume acquitted himself better than historians have recorded.[60] Though his motives in attacking the friars no doubt smack of a conservative's special interests, he was an honest man, a moving preacher, and a studious exegete. To characterize his

[58] Although Guillaume de Saint-Amour's principal adversaries were Dominicans, he frequently cites the general principles of the Franciscan *Regula bullata* against them; see his *Opera*, pp. 300 *et passim*.

[59] *Contra Adversarium Perfectionis Christianae*, ed. Sophronius Clasen, *Archivum franciscanum historicum*, xxi (1938), especially 285-86.

[60] Guillaume was not "silenced" by the Thomist polemic *Contra repugnates* as is frequently maintained; see *RTAM*, xxxii (1965), 132ff.

works, or Jean de Meun's borrowing of them, as "antiascetic" is ludicrous. We might as well call "antiascetic" the whole mighty stream of literary antifraternalism which flows, ultimately, from the spring of *De periculis*; by this criterion the *Roman de Fauvel*, *Piers Plowman*, and the Summoner's Tale, not to mention the homilies of such theological heavyweights as Fitzralph and Wyclif, are all "antiascetic."

Hatzfeld's further contention, that Jean "n'attaque pas seulement les ordres mendiants . . . mais toute la spiritualité chrétienne, dont ils étaient les représentatives les plus radicaux,"[61] is totally misconceived. In the first place, it is most doubtful that the spirituality of the Parisian friars in the 1250's was generally acknowledged to be more radical than that, say, of the monastic chapters or the secular masters. The Dominicans, it is true, had with the help of large armies proved successful in the South of France where the Cistercians had failed. Furthermore, both major fraternal orders, but especially the Franciscans, had excited throughout Western Europe a new kind of lay piety. But to refract these academic disputes through the prism of quite modern historical judgments, to suggest that in Jean de Meun's world the friars were the unquestioned vanguard of Christian spirituality, seems cavalier. To suggest that Jean de Meun attacked the friars for their advanced spirituality seems flatly perverse. The monastic authors who turned with reverence to the *Roman* in the fourteenth century no doubt had their axes to grind, just as had the Parisian secular masters whose view Rutebeuf advanced in the 'fifties. It seems to me inconceivable, however, that Gilles li Muisis, whose popular ascetic theology fills two large volumes, found in Jean's poem an attack on spirituality.[62]

Jean apparently shared Guillaume de Saint-Amour's reverence for the fraternal founders and their idealism as it shone through the lives of saintly men. He did hate the Phariseeism, the oldness of spirit, self-righteousness, and hypocrisy which, in literary convention established by Guillaume, Rutebeuf, and others, he found associated with the formal pretensions of the friars and the pronouncements of their more radical spokesmen, like Gerard of

---

[61] "La mystique naturiste de Jean de Meung," pp. 259-60.

[62] *Poésies de Gilles li Muisis*, ed. Kervyn de Lettenhove (Louvain, 1882), I, 94.

Borgo San Donnino. Faussemblant does not "represent the friars"; he represents certain attitudes to which Jean was able to give a local habitation and a name by reference to a peculiar local historical experience. As Rosemond Tuve has forcefully reminded us, while in speaking of Guillaume de Saint-Amour and academic antifraternalism we have undoubtedly identified the sources of Jean's iconography, we have only begun to suggest the richness of Faussemblant's meaning as an allegorical exemplification. Only in one respect is the *De periculis* on which Jean so heavily leans an ephemeral political tract. It is also an essay in eschatology, an attempt to come to terms with the spiritual implications of the disorders of the "last days" (II Timothy 3:1). Guillaume presented a vision of unspeakable evil borrowed wholesale by Jean, and we are invited to regard it seriously. While it is true that the kind of blasphemous hypocrisy which is Faussemblant's being may have characterized one or more particular friars known to Guillaume, just as it may have characterized the pitch of one or more young men on the make whom Jean knew, we must not demean Jean's design by making the facile equations of a *roman à clef*. As a friar, Faussemblant is an effective and amusing satiric device, but his evil is limited to the finitude of friars. As an idea in Jean's poem, he shares the apocalyptic plenitude of the *seipsos amantes* of St. Paul and Guillaume de Saint-Amour.

But if we maintain that only part, indeed the smallest part, of Jean's purpose in creating Faussemblant and shaping his magnificent soliloquy is to "attack the friars," what is the binding relation of this episode to the central metaphor of his poem, the love quest? The answer is that Faussemblant exemplifies a major aspect of love, one which he vigorously advances in his preaching and to which his whole being is a living sacrifice. It is, furthermore, the generic manifestation of the same love of which a subspecies, "civilized" sexuality, animates the Lover and his trivial conspiracy. The great scriptural text of antifraternalism from II Timothy, begins as follows: "Hoc autem scito, quod in novissimis diebus instabunt tempora periculosa: erunt homines seipsos amantes, cupidi, elati, superbi, blasphemi. . . ." The phrase *seipsos amantes* to which the antifraternal exegetes returned time and again has obvious relevance to the vile Jacobin who readily confesses, indeed boasts, that his single-minded goal is self-gratification; it should now be no less obvious that its application to Amant, and to his single-minded quest, is equally appropriate. The reader who has followed with some care the course of love's dance as it has been controlled by Guillaume de Lorris and Jean de Meun, and who is prepared to believe that Jean's ideas about sex and love may turn out after all to be predictably medieval rather than surprisingly modern, will see that the ultimate object of Amant's love is not the "lady," not "love itself," not even some fragile and immeasurable mystery of the human heart known only to poets and a few lovers—but himself. Amant's object is *seipsum*. It is difficult to see how the poets could have made this more clear without abandoning all the techniques of sophisticated allegory and simply penning another rather elaborate sermon *contra luxuriam*.

The textual evidence remains very convincing. Amant, like Faussemblant, is a "lover of himself," one of those *seipsos amantes* who operate by fraud, hypocrisy, and the false front; but of course this is not to say that the two are true peers. The area of Amant's operations of *fol amour* are circumscribed and finite, however they may typify much broader categories; the hypocrisy which he learns studying under Amours and Amis is limited in its techniques and comparatively modest in its goals. The evil of Faussemblant, on the other hand, is total, indeed cosmic; he is one of "Antichrist's men," and his characterization by Jean de Meun reverberates with terrifying echoes of Guillaume de Saint-Amour's *De Antichristo*. If Amis represented the worldly attitude toward innocence, in all its cynicism and sentimentality, Faussemblant pre-eminently represents the conscious worldly perversion of the channels of supernatural grace which alone offered remedy, in medieval theology, for man's fall from innocence.

For Milton, hypocrisy is "the only evil that walks invisible, except to God alone"; but Milton enjoyed the technical advantage of the omniscient author to be able to tell us so. Jean's problem, in a poem which maintains a surface of more or less consistent dramatic decorum, is rather trickier. The decorous speech of a hypocritical speaker is, after all, probably going to be hypocritical and deceitful, and though Jean is able to exemplify some of Faussemblant's falseness in concrete detail, as in the shrift scene, his chief device for exposing the friar is the long and self-revealing

167

monologue which is notably deficient, from the point of view of psychological motivation, in literary "realism." This deficiency, however, need raise no insuperable artistic problem; Faussemblant is a walking idea, a moral abstraction in a medieval allegory, and for Jean his iconographic truth is more important than his truth of literal verisimilitude.

Thus it is that from a superficial point of view Faussemblant is one of the poem's *dramatis personae* most easily understood. His outrageous boasting to Amours, flaunting the moral qualities which will make him a fitting warrior in the god's army, is clear and precise. Yet there are implications in his description of himself which are not overt, and which make demands upon the reader's ability to trace intricate metaphoric relationships.

If there is one single statement which in its medieval implications neatly generalizes the qualities which Faussemblant represents, it is the friar's boast that he follows the externals of religion only, despising its substance: "De religion . . . j'en les le grain et pregn la paille." Faussemblant here uses the word *religion* in the technical sense of "the state of living under vows and a rule"; he wears the habit and the tonsure, not the invisible imprint of charity on his heart. His religious profession is carnal and external, not spiritual and internal; a dead letter, exposing only its outward form to the eyes of the world, tokening no hidden and spiritual reality. The figure of the wheat and the chaff which Jean employs is pre-eminently one of literary criticism and, in particular, of scriptural exegesis. Faussemblant's religion is that of the "text itself," the letter, not the spirit; it is old, cold, carnal, and it "slayeth."

Thus the friar's metaphor of the *grain* and the *paille* immediately links him with the unregenerate literalism of the Old Law and the hollow formalism of the Pharisees, two familiar strains from the sermons of Guillaume de Saint-Amour. Furthermore, it provides a comic yet serious link with the poetic theory outlined early in Jean's part of the poem by Lady Reason, who attempted without success to convince Amant of the necessity of the allegorical interpretation of poetry. What we might call Jean de Meun's own aesthetic theory, expressed under his name in the introduction to the *Boèce*, held with St. Augustine that the human process of intellection ideally moves from the corporeal apprehension of *visibilia* to the spiritual contemplation and comprehension of *invisibilia*. Such is, in the sphere of literature, the process of exegesis and the *accesus ad auctores* which consciously shaped allegory assumes and which Lady Reason explains. It will be recalled that the Lover proved himself a determined literalist who saw no necessity to move beyond the "text itself," that is, to move from the chaff of the letter to the grain of spiritual understanding. The whole point of Amant's squabble with Lady Reason about allegory seemed at the time to be a clever maneuver to juxtapose the poet to his creation; here Jean once again picks up the specialized vocabulary of literary criticism to reveal yet another fraternal bond between Amant and the forces of Antichrist. The brotherhood between Amant and Faussemblant, incidentally, is quite real from a medieval point of view. Several of the illustrators show the friar, crowned as *roi des ribauds* at Cupid's court, making homage to the same "lord" whose brother-vassal Amant has earlier become.[63]

Though the illustrators can hardly do as much to expose Faussemblant as the friar himself does, iconographic suggestions of his moral postures constantly appear in the manuscripts. Like the Lover, he is a plucker of rosebuds (Fig. 34), and he carries the glove which in the iconography of the *Roman* is clearly associated with lechery (Fig. 35). For her part, Constrained Abstinence knows the *olde daunce*. There is also in the illuminations a certain amount of more conventional, but still playful antifraternalism. One manuscript in the British Museum, for example, shows two finely attired friars of the major orders very sniffily regarding their "ideal," Poverty, huddled in rags on his *fumier*.[64] Such wit is gentle, compared with what antifraternal illustrators could do elsewhere. In the unique manuscript of the wild fourteenth-century eschatological mystery about the Schism, a manuscript which also contains Jean de Meun's *Testament*, Antichrist is dressed as a Cordelier in the spirit of Guillaume de Saint-Amour's *De Antichristo* sermon.[65]

[63] Princeton, MS Garrett 126, fol. 77ᵛ, gives the type.

[64] British Museum, Royal MS XIX B 13, fol. 8ʳ. A similar illustration (with an additional layer of humor) appears in the technically exquisite Brussels MS 9574/5, fol. 14ʳ, where a female *Povreté* beckons to a Jacobin, who recoils in horror.

[65] Besançon, Bibliothèque municipale MS 597, fol. 10ᵛ; see *Le Jour de Jugement*, ed. Emile Roy (Paris, 1902), p. 257.

Faussemblant not only gives his own game away, but that of the whole *Roman* as well. It requires truly blatant modernism to maintain that Love's new man, who plays an indispensable role in advancing Amant's cause, is being put forward by Jean as an admirable representative of the side he backs in the lists of this psychomachia. The comedy of the scene in which Amours first meets Faussemblant (" 'Qu'est ce?' dist il, 'ai je songie?' ") springs from the same source as that in Amant's dialogue with Reason on smut: the ironic undercutting of hollow claims of moral superiority. That the god of Love should perhaps find Faussemblant's sombre Preacher's garb dowdy and uncouth is not surprising; the god is, in the illustrations of the poem (Fig. 16), rather a dandy, like Chaucer's young Squire: "Embrouded was he, as it were a mede / Al ful of fresshe floures, whyte and rede." Yet for Amours to view his new-found ally from beneath an arched eyebrow as a bounder, "not a gentleman," can only be well-wrought comedy, since Faussemblant merely distils those characteristics of self-serving hypocrisy at the heart of Love's Commandments. When the god accepts the friar's services according to a principle which they clearly share—that the ends justify the means—their essential kinship lies clearly revealed for all to see. Papelardie, the trivial hypocrisy of lovers who change their minds—presumably like Absalom in the Miller's Tale—is banished from the garden of Deduit. Faussemblant, the far superior fiend, lives in clover there.

Faussemblant is to be the secret weapon in Amours' arsenal, the creeper-into-houses who can dispose of the troublesome Malebouche; with his enlistment the roster is complete and the army ready to march. Disguised as pilgrims, Faussemblant and Constrained Abstinence go to Malebouche, accuse him of slandering the Lover, and recommend speedy confession for the good of his soul; but like the fox in the Middle English lyric, this one hears the goose's confession only to wring its neck. Faussemblant's sacrilegious abuse of the confessional and his explicit claims of superiority as a confessor to Malebouche's own parish priest gain particular topicality and comedy from the dispute over the administration of penance arising from the publication of *Omnis utriusque sexus*; but it is also a telling exemplification of the works of Antichrist, through which evil is made good and good, evil. In the allegory

170

of the *Roman*, in its "love story" that is, Malebouche seems to represent public scandal or the kind of gossip which was no doubt very well-informed in a society of tightly-knit social groups without motels. Far from having told "lies" about the Lover, Malebouche has obviously been spreading the truth; so Faussemblant strangles him, cuts out his tongue, and tosses the corpse into a ditch. For Love to have silenced scandal through hypocrisy and homicide is a stunning victory for the Lover's cause, and one which the warriors immediately move to consolidate. Murdering the Norman guards in their drunken slumber is child's play, and Faussemblant and his *amie*, now joined by Courtoisie and Largesse, burst into Jealousy's castle to confront the old whore who guards Bel Accueil, and who is the next of Jean de Meun's *doctores amoris*.

As a "stock character" the old lady (*vieille, vekke, vecchia, vetula*) was probably as familiar as her fellows Amant and Amis. She is at least as old as Ovid's Dipsas and appears in the Latin comedy of the twelfth century and the "antifeminist" literature of the thirteenth. We shall find her in Gautier d'Arras and Chrétien de Troyes. In the fourteenth century the most brilliant appearance of the *vetula* is probably Alisoun of Bath, but there is also a splendid if more conventional one in the *Libro de buen amor*. There is still something of her in the bawdy nurse of *Romeo and Juliet*. As a literary type, the *vetula* is a truly European phenomenon, appearing in all the major vernacular literatures of the West as well as in Latin poetry and exemplary fiction. Whether Jean de Meun could have known the thirteenth-century pseudo-Ovidian poem *De Vetula* or its French translation, apparently executed by his contemporary Richard de Fournival, is not certain. Insofar as Jean uses a specific single "source" for his portrait of La Vieille it is Ovid, but *De Vetula* nonetheless provides a convenient and amusing example of the well-developed type. The poem pretends to describe Ovid's last love affair, which ends in a total debacle convincing him once again of the fatuity and self-destruction of passion. Its lengthy final sections are given over to the extended development of *sententiae* and to prophecies of the advent of Christ through the Blessed Virgin. In the second book of the poem "Ovid," infatuated with a lovely young girl whose physical charms he describes sensuously and at length, bribes the *vetula* who guards her to make an assignation for him.[66] In the burlesque which follows, the *vetula* thoroughly mulcts "Ovid," demonstrating a wide variety of venal and worldly-wise ruses and eventually substituting herself in the supposed bed of the young girl. In the poems written under the influence of the *Roman* itself the *vetula* emerges more clearly as a formal authority and lecturer on love, the special tutor to youth in the old dance of cupidity: "Par ses dits et par sa parole / Les fait dancer a sa karole."[67]

Yet it is not merely, or perhaps even primarily, as a recurrent literary type in medieval comedy that the *vetula* makes her appearance. As Friedman puts it, "The classical origins of the Vieille, her use in medieval 'Latin comedy,' and her proliferation in European romance and courtly literature have been well elucidated. Her connections with moral literature must still be traced."[68] And indeed a systematic investigation of the moral tradition of the *vetula* would lead us to a wide spectrum of texts—homiletic, exemplary, exegetical, medical, penitential. Friedman adduces a most significant passage, from the *Summa de vitiis et virtutibus* of Peraldus, which lists among the seven incitements to lechery the "exhortatio vetularum vel aliarum personarum que sunt consiliatrices turpitudinis." The other incitements, incidentally, include "ocium" (Oiseuse), "pravum exemplum" (Amis), "auditus vel cantilenarum amatoriarum vel instrumentorum musicorum vel turpiloquiorum" (the carol of Deduit), as well as a number of the traditional "steps of love" by which the *Roman* progresses. That Jean de Meun knew this *Summa*, as Chaucer knew it and used it after him, is entirely likely; it was, after all, one of the most extraordinarily successful books of the later Middle Ages.[69] If Jean was measurably indebted at all to the theological encyclopedias of the blackfriars, he is much more likely to have been influenced by the *Summa* of Peraldus than by the

---

[66] *La Vieille, ou les derniers amours d'Ovide*, ed. Hippolyte Cocheris (Paris, 1861), pp. 137ff.

[67] *Les Lamentations de Matheolus*, ed. van Hamel, I, 95. In the *Canterbury Tales* it is the Wife of Bath who "coude of that art the olde daunce;" and the Pardoner begs her to "teche us yonge men of your praktike."

[68] " 'Jean de Meung' and 'Bourgeois Realism,' " p. 18n.

[69] A. Dondaine remarks, "Peu d'ouvrages, dans toute l'histoire littéraire, connurent un aussi brillant succès," in "Guillaume Peyrault," *Archivum fratrum praedicatorum*, xviii (1948), 162.

Summa of Aquinas; but this is speculation, and possibly idle. The *vetula* of Peraldus, no less than La Vieille herself, can be considered a commonplace of moral literature; they are both in large measure conventional figures from diverse but convergent traditions.

One tradition of the *vetula*, in which she is associated both with magical or superstitious rites and with the incitement to lechery, has real historical roots in the dim past of Roman religion. Caesarius of Arles, whose sermons had such extensive circulation, repeatedly warns against the *annicula* (a lexical variant of the *vetula*), and it seems certain that Caesarius' *anniculae* are to be associated with the obscenities of the Roman Saturnalia and their survival into the January revels of the early Christian period.[70] This *vetula*, both a whore and a witch, is capable of the most monstrous crimes, according to the best authorities of the thirteenth century. "What should be done," asks St. Raymond of Pennyfort, "if a *vetula*, pretending to be sick, thus comes into possession of a Host and sells it to Jews?"[71] Elsewhere in the *exempla* of the friars, in their "moralized stories" and sermons, it is the vanity and carnal-mindedness of the *vetula* which is the object of comic derision.[72] Vain, whorish, hypocritical, worldly-wise, she is as much a convention of the pulpit as of closet comedy. She makes further obscene appearances in the annals of medieval medicine. The *vetula* is a midwife of most dubious repute, privy to the vile secrets of abortion and contraceptive potions. The secret filthiness of her person is prescribed as a cure for the kind of love she incites.[73] That she could be called *medica*, as one sharing in the learning and honor of an esteemed profession, seemed remarkable to the moralists of the Middle Ages and a commentary on

[70] See Gerhard Rohlfs, "Die anniculae bei Caesarius von Arles," *Studia Neophilologica*, xxi (1948/9), 42-46, for further references.

[71] *Summula Raymundi* (Cologne, 1502), fol. xxviʳ. (She should be burnt.)

[72] See, for example, *Anecdotes historiques . . . d'Etienne de Bourbon*, ed. A. Lecoy de la Marche (Paris, 1877), pp. 228-29; for a story still in use by St. Bernardino a century later, *Opera Omnia*, ix (Florence, 1965), 401.

[73] See the citations from the *Lilium medicinae* of Bernard of Gordon adduced by Robertson, *Preface to Chaucer*, pp. 459-60. Alfonso Martinez de Toledo writes of the "ynormes pecados" of such women: *El Arcipresete de Talavera o sea El Corbacho*, ed. Lesley Byrd Simpson (Berkeley, 1939), p. 139.

the vanity of human wishes.[74] One final appearance of the *vetula* in moral literature can serve to bring us back to the *Roman* and, at the same time, show the impossibility of making a marked distinction between the "secular" and "religious" forms of the old whore as she appears in the monastic and casuistic tradition and as she appears in Ovidian comedy. It is to be found in the ascetic writings of one of Jean de Meun's great authorities, St. Ailred. In his rule for anchorites, Ailred warns that the solitary must beware of the *vetula* who, insinuating herself among the poor people seeking alms, will come as a procuress for some monk or cleric: a category of ascetical theology has taken on the flesh of Dipsas.[75] We may recall that Gérard of Liège could likewise speak of the religious life in the language of the *Roman*: "Dius nous a enfremes en son castiel de sainte religion par tres grant ialousie damour." It is impossible to confine what Guillaume and Jean are talking about to the narrow intrigue of the *allegoria* when their categories are those of a commonplace moral tradition.

The illustrators of Jean's poem usually thought of the Lover as a tonsured cleric; his allies Faussemblant and Constrained Abstinence are also religious. Between them they have small trouble in enlisting a *vetula*, for once La Vieille discovers which way the wind is blowing, she is entirely at their service, and only too glad to be able to take Amant's touching gift to Bel Accueil. The gift, incidentally, a *chapel* or rose-crown, is one appropriate to the nature of Amant's quest. It is almost certainly emblematically akin to the antique marriage crowns, or flower chaplets, which Tertullian associates both with idolatry and lechery.[76] In the iconography of the *Roman*, a similar chaplet of red roses is a fre-

---

[74] Albertus Magnus *Metaphysica*, iv, i, 6, in *Opera Omnia* (Cologne, 1951ff.), xvi, i, p. 169; and St. Bernardino in "Selecta ex autographo Budapestinensi," *Opera Omnia* (Florence, 1950ff.), ix, 369: "O medici, studuistis in grammatica, logica, philosophia, medicina, cum multis spensis, periculis, et laboribus; e la vechia rinchagnata n'a l'onore!"

[75] "The 'De Institutis Inclusarum' of Ailred of Rievaulx," ed. C. H. Talbot, *Analecta Sacri Ordinis Cisterciensis*, vii (1951), 179: "Nolo ut insidiatrix pudiciae vetula mixta pauperibus accedat propius, deferat ab aliquo monachorum vel clericorum eulogia, non blanda verba in aure susernet, ne pro accepta elemosina osculans manum, venenum insibilet."

[76] *De corona militis*, xv, in *Pat. lat.* 2, col. 98. See Karl Baus, *Der Kranz in Antike und Christentum* (Bonn, 1940), pp. 98ff.

quent attribute of Oiseuse (here following Guillaume's text), or of Venus herself; it also appears in numerous obscure "secular scenes," illustrative of "courtly love," in the ivory carvings of the fourteenth century.[77] According to the *Echecs* gloss, speaking of Venus' chaplet, the red rose "accurately signifies the amorous life . . . unreasonable love, or that which principally seeks carnal delight." It is "ardent" in color because

> concupiscence . . . when it first comes is ardent like fire, and it kindles love so that the body thus affected does not know what course to follow to relieve the pain it feels. . . . Avicenna says that heroic love—that is to say that love which makes the lover ill through loving madly—is a kind of melancholy which is engendered by too much attraction and continual thought about the beauty and the grace which are in the beloved, or are imagined to be. . . . The rose above all flowers is beautiful to look at and to smell, and it is therefore called the 'flower of flowers'. . . . However, roses taste bitter, and they grow among spiked thorns, and their beauty vanishes in a short time.[78]

La Vieille praises the rare beauty of Amant's *chapel*: "Les fleurs eulent mieuz que basme."

Nowhere in the scholarship devoted to the *Roman de la Rose* is there an adequate analysis of the literary techniques which Jean de Meun uses, often with great originality and always with brilliance, in constructing La Vieille's speech. Several useful points of departure, however, are provided by Robertson's brilliant analysis of the Wife of Bath's Prologue, for which Chaucer freely appropriated and adapted materials from the "chappitre de la Vieille." Chaucer's iconographic techniques are more sophisticated than Jean's, and the specifically theological groundwork for his old lady's monologue, more schematic; furthermore, the Wife's Prologue is qualified by a narrative context markedly different from the speech of La Vieille in the *Roman*. Nevertheless it remains true that Chaucer is here following Jean quite closely,

[77] In the iconography of the *Roman* the qualification of the *chapel* clearly associates it with *luxuria*; for example, in the marginalia of Bibliothèque nationale MS fr. 9345 (14th century), fol. 11ᵛ, there is a mermaid with withered breasts, holding a comb in her left hand and a mirror in her right, wearing a red chaplet. The illustration glosses the first appearance of Venus, in the text above it.

[78] Bibliothèque nationale MS fr. 9197, fol. 129ʳ.

and that the techniques to which Robertson draws attention are essentially those Chaucer found in Jean de Meun.

Jean builds his controlling images around La Vieille's ready-made oldness and its allegorical implications. He further puts into her mouth a number of doctrines which hilariously exemplify in vivid and convincing detail her carnality and her literalmindedness, as well as a number of patently sophistical arguments ironically undercut by the very literary sources she adduces in their support. Thus she begins her lecture to Bel Accueil by contrasting, ostensibly, her age with his youth, developing a *carpe diem* theme modelled on a similar development in the third book of the *Ars amatoria*. But in the *Roman* the episode has taken on new layers of suggestion through its connections with La Vieille's discussions of "natural" behavior and her mythographic allusions. In effect, the contrast is not simply between an old lady and a young man but between the spiritual antiquity which her career and counsels of love so comically exemplify and the "newness of spirit" which they deny. Young people, she says, are destined to "swim in Venus' stew" and be fired by her torch (ll. 12752ff.). This is a commonplace bit of medieval wisdom, of course, but iconographically significant in light of the associations which Venus' attributes have in mythographic tradition and in the later sections of the *Roman*. Furthermore, says La Vieille, there is great danger for young people in this natural proclivity—unless, that is, they are well counselled in the "jeus d'Amors." The danger, however, is not spiritual but carnal. Medieval morality worries for the loss of virtue, honor, or one's eternal soul; La Vieille is concerned with the cashbox. Jean's *vetula* is a moralist of great originality. The specific danger is that, without proper tutelage, young people may find that they cannot escape love without "selling their goods" (*beste vendre*). The sense of the expression is probably closer to "losing one's shirt," and it clearly fits in with La Vieille's mercantile gauge of love. It is also, perhaps, an ironic echo of that teaching of love which Christ gave to the rich man, and to all those who would be perfect.

It is generally maintained that in Jean's "grand symposium" on love the views of the Vekke provide a radical contrast with those of Amours. The gentle god teaches a sophisticated, urbane, "courtly," and noble code of amorous service; while the old lady, meretricious, bawdy, robust, teaches a kind of pragmatic sexuality which is far from ethereal. As she herself puts it, she knows the *practique* of love, not its *theoretique* (ll. 12803f.). Indeed, she flatly rejects two of the "commandments of Love," as they were given to Amant by Amours: that the lover should extend himself in largess, and that he should put his heart in a single place only. Yet upon closer inspection, the differences in doctrine of these two *doctores amoris* become superficial, and their basic agreement, or rather collusion, more marked.

What differences remain stem not only from their literary personalities but from the fact that Amours addresses himself to the male side in the love intrigue, and the old lady to the female. Amours instructs Amant, while the old woman lectures Bel Accueil. In the penitential *summae* of the later Middle Ages, under the section on *luxuria*, the questions put by the confessor to men differ somewhat from those put to women. Likewise, Amours teaches *luxuria* primarily from a masculine point of view, the old whore from a feminine point of view. Thus Amant, in order to be successful in his rose quest, should be single-minded in his devotion and a free spender. This will impress the lady with the worthiness of his love and, if he is lucky, get her to bed. From the lady's point of view, as La Vieille puts it, this is fine sauce for the gander but not for the goose. The lady should grasp every penny she can—but never spend a farthing. Likewise she has nothing to gain from single-minded devotion and can get a great deal more, both in *frissons* and in cold cash, the wider she throws her net. The teachings of Amours and La Vieille are not, then, in a dialectical contrast; they are complementary. The two teachers are on the opposite sides, true enough, but on the same see-saw. Amours teaches Amant that he must expect to be kept on tenterhooks, alternating between hope and despair; the *vetula* sets out to make sure that such expectations will not be disappointed (ll. 13663ff.). The illustrators of the *Roman* several times suggest the common cause of Amours and La Vieille. In one particularly careful composition from the beginning of the fifteenth century, the *incipit* marginalia presents a carefully balanced scene. At the right a man and woman clutch each other in passionate "courtly" embrace—in the manner typical of the iconography of *amour par amours.* At the right the old hag cackles instructions to Bel Accueil.[79]

It is true that through La Vieille's speech Jean de Meun makes the code of the god of Love seem ridiculous; but that, I should submit, is because it is ridiculous, as well as blasphemous and idolatrous. La Vieille, speaking from the woman's point of view, simply exposes some of its more ludicrous implications. The truth of the matter is that the code of "courtly love," or whatever we wish to call Cupid's doctrine, implies a view of women—insofar as they are considered as other than things—quite as misogynistic as any put forward by the Friend or the Jaloux. The woman whom the courtly code supposedly venerates must indeed be exceedingly vapid, a pushover for any lad with a good tenor voice or a suit of expensive clothes. La Vieille teaches Bel Accueil how to make the most of such expectations: she clearly regards lovers as fools to be used for pleasure and profit. The richly comic specifics of her doctrine—for example, that the lady should always insist that her lover sneak in through the window, rather than walk through the open and unguarded door—demonstrate once again the marked stylistic difference between Jean's tightly woven veri-similar, exemplary narrative and the more abstract and lapidary elegance of Guillaume de Lorris; but this difference does not argue a marked contrast between the teachings of Guillaume's god of Love and the Jean's *vetula.* The two teachers coach opposing teams, but the game is the same for both.

The exemplary richness of La Vieille's tutorial with Bel Accueil is one of Jean's finest comic moments; and this section of his poem, greatly admired by his contemporaries and near contemporaries to judge from allusions and imitations, is probably one of the parts of the *Roman* which seems most appealing to the modern reader. Many of the impediments to a harlot's progress in the thirteenth century—a flat chest, thick legs, "halitosis"—have become simple social embarrassments made venial by cosmeticians and drugstore chains in our own day, but they remain topical. Indeed, La Vieille's apparent modernity has lured conventional criticism into judging her an earthy, vivacious, bawdy, and vibrant "unforgettable character" with whom Jean himself "clearly sym-

[79] Bibliothèque nationale MS fr. 1572, fol. 1ʳ.

pathizes." That such a judgment is an honest tribute to an achievement in narrative style then quite new in Western vernacular literature perhaps mitigates its vulgarity and triviality; the judgment itself in no way suggests what Jean's achievement, which has little to do with the creation of a literary character who is the proper object of the reader's sympathetic, psychological identification, really is. The Vekke is a brilliantly realized literary type richly exemplified in convincing verisimilar detail, but she is still a vekke, not the poet's old grandmother drawn from "real life" on the drafting-board of "bourgeois realism."

If Faussemblant is Amours' *roi des ribauds*, La Vieille is certainly his *reine*. Her arsenal of meretricious stratagems is seemingly inexhaustible, her practical experience immense. Yet despite her academic diffidence, she is as much at home in Love's lecture hall as in his laboratory; she even develops a theory of love, indeed a rather more coherent one than the courtly code of the god himself. It may be well to consider her theory briefly since Jean uses it nicely to introduce the major themes with which he concludes his poem, and since it, too, has inevitably been regarded as the personal credo of Jean de Meun, the Averroist poet, here displaying for the world to see his "sensualism," "naturalism," and "sexual Communism."[80]

The language of radical politics and revolution is not in fact at all farfetched; yet surely the voice is that of Rousseau rather than Marx? "Women are born free," proclaims the *vetula*, yet everywhere they are in what William of Auvergne called the "chains of society"—in accordance with law, but contrary to Nature, woman has been subjected to marriage. La Vieille even has a revolutionary slogan not unlike that of the revolution which she anticipates by five hundred years:

> Toutes por touz et touz por toutes,
> chascune por chascun conmune
> et chascun conmun a chascune.

But this is to get ahead of our matter somewhat. Actually, her discourse on free love begins not with this manifesto but with a mythological *exemplum* illustrative of the jealousy which the

---

[80] Franz Walter Müller, *Der Rosenroman und das lateinische Averroismus des 13. Jahrhundert* (Frankfurt, 1947), pp. 12-13.

lady should keep her lover in: it should be as exquisite as that which Vulcan felt when he trapped his wife Venus in bed with Mars. Venus' indiscretion, says La Vieille, was excusable on two grounds: first, Vulcan was terribly ugly; but secondly, Vulcan's ugliness did not have anything to do with it—Venus would have cuckolded her husband even if he were Absalom or Paris. At this point she abandons her *exemplum*—leaving the guilty pair caught in Vulcan's trap—to go on to her principal *matière*, that of the "naturalness" of free love: women are born free, but their natural liberty is robbed from them by monogamy. Marriage was instituted to put down concupiscence and crimes of passion and facilitate the raising of children, according to the *vetula*, but nature urges women to seek their original freedom, however disastrous its consequences. In the good old days, men would rape whatever woman pleased them, kill each other, and abandon their children —so that marriage was instituted by the counsel of wise men. Read Horace, says La Vieille: "Before Helen of Troy there were many battles fought over the *con*." There will be many more wars among the *amoureux* through which men will lose body and soul. Nature is very powerful, as the following examples will show: a bird in a cage is unhappy, like a religious; a fish in a trap, like a monk, regrets succumbing to the bait. Horace says, "We cannot escape Nature"; La Vieille claims this excuses Venus. Nature is more powerful than upbringing. Horses, cows, and sheep mate indiscriminately; the females welcome all the males. People ought to behave the same way—'I always did.' Nature governs us, moving our hearts toward pleasure.

A bald paraphrase of La Vieille's argument totally fails to do justice to the poet who has so cunningly filled out its bare bones with a wealth of vivid and often hilarious detail, but it will, perhaps, demonstrate the quality of the old girl's dialectics. Such a manifesto is satire, not socialist realism. Her arguments are illogical and self-contradictory, founded on an obviously sophistical premise and encased in a classical *exemplum* which, in its medieval interpretation, cuts the ground from beneath her feet. The story of the love affair between Mars and Venus comes from the second book of Ovid's *Ars amatoria*. Ovid, however, points a rather different lesson than does La Vieille. He attributes the cause of this ludicrous affair, which ended so embarrassingly for all concerned, not to nature but to folly: "Mars pater, insano Veneris turbatus amore." Furthermore, the *praeceptor amoris* ends the episode by reminding his students that he celebrates only those pleasures which the law permits: "In nostris istita nulla jocis." La Vieille, on the whole admirably faithful to her literary source, is silent on these matters. To listen to her one would never know that unchecked irrational passion was not regarded as freedom in the Middle Ages, but as a kind of enslavement. That the *vetula* should break off her story of Mars and Venus leaving the guilty pair fettered, literally in the "chains of concupiscence," to praise the freedom which the *exemplum* illustrates, is a dialectical enormity intended, one presumes, to earn a hearty guffaw from Jean's readers.[81]

It is perhaps curious that Horace, no friend of whores, should be among La Vieille's favorite authors. An examination of the poems from which she takes her citations solves the mystery; Horace's *sententiae* about Nature are meant not so much to instruct readers in the laws of "naturalism" as to delight an audience with some awareness of literary contexts. For example, his somewhat indelicate lines on the wars of the *cunnus* explicitly condemn the "nature" of man which caused war, theft, and adultery during his animal stage before the establishment of law (*Sermones*, I, iii, 107ff.). The medieval scholia spell this out: the poet contends against the false notion that "natura est per se satis sufficiens ad omne bonum expetendum et a non bono separandum."[82] But *nature*, as we shall see in the next chapter if not before, can mean more than one thing, and the second Horatian *sententia* works the other way around. La Vieille cites the *Epistolae* (I, x, 24)— "Naturam expellas furca, tamen usque recurret"—as an imperative for venereal love. In its context, however—which is a contrast between the "natural," rural, abstemious life and the "unnatural," urban, luxurious life—the point is quite different. The natural things the poet here has in mind, according to the scholia, are "bread and water."[83] La Vieille on the other hand believes

---

[81] See Thomas D. Hill, "La Vieille's Digression on Free Love," *Romance Notes*, VIII (1966/7), 113-15.

[82] *Scholia in Horatium*, IV, ed. H. J. Botschuyver (Amsterdam, 1942), 209.

[83] *Scholia in Horatium*, IV, 364.

that the banquet of nature offers a more sumptuous spread than the modest, indeed ascetic, repast of the Golden Age.

The Golden Age itself is nowhere the specific subject of La Vieille's attention, but a distorted notion of the freedom associated with it permeates her argument. Like Amis, she would love to be living in the "state of nature." The trouble arises over the word "nature." We have just seen that Horace could talk of nature in markedly contrasting senses. So did the medieval theologians, as it will be necessary to remember when considering the personification of the goddess Natura in the next chapter. It is possible, however, to characterize without defining this nature which excuses both Venus' and La Vieille's indiscretions and will, hopefully, make Bel Accueil see the light too. Natural behavior gives rise to rape and murder; it caused the Trojan War and innumerable other wars of the *con*. Nature is antithetical to law and marriage and the advice of wise men. It is very powerful, indeed irrepressible. Finally, natural behavior is observable in all kinds of beasts.

Indeed, La Vieille's long suit would seem to be animal analogy. A bird in a cage and a fish in a trap can very well illustrate the sorry plight of the young man constrained by religious or marital vows; and the sexual behavior of the barnyard is full of convincing lessons for us all. In fact, the only arguments the *vetula* marshals to support her contention that the indiscriminate mating of men and women is proper and desirable is the now familiar idea that such behavior is natural. Horses do it, cows do it, sheep do it—let's do it. The argument makes a good popular song but raises certain problems. As a logical statement, it takes the form of an elliptical syllogism built around the premise that a man is an animal; but in the scholastic literature which is frequently said to leave its indelible stamp on the "disputations" in the *Roman*, the statement that a man is an animal is a copybook example of a *sophisma*.[84]

A *sophisma* was a patently false statement which was "literally" true by virtue of an equivocation, usually blatant. For example, the sentence which in its context means "The donkeys belong to the bishop" (*Asini episcopi sunt*) sophistically means that "Don-

[84] See, for example, the *Introductiones in logicam* of William of Shyreswood (d. post 1267), ed. Martin Grabmann in *Sitzungsberichte des Bayerischen Akademie des Wissenschaften*, 1937, No. 10, pp. 100-101.

keys are bishops," by taking *episcopi* to be a nominative plural rather than a genitive singular. Sophism is thus a peculiarly slovenly kind of literalism, or victory of the "text itself" over common sense and discursive argument. Just as figurative or allegorical language depends upon a distinction of figurative or allegorical meaning from literal meaning, all logical discourse, according to medieval philosophy, depends upon the proper distinction of literal meanings. Amant, in his confrontation with Divine Sapience, bluntly rejected Reason's brief formulation of the allegorical method as a lot of rot; likewise, he failed to grasp essential distinctions of literal meaning in the word "love." In propounding a number of patently sophistical arguments, La Vieille is merely following the path made by Amours, Amant, Amis, and Faussemblant.

In this particular instance the *vetula*'s ambition extends beyond the comparatively simple trick of making a jackass of the bishop; she wants to make jackasses of the whole human race. For men to behave like beasts was not generally considered natural in the Middle Ages; in particular, bestial lechery was said to be particularly inappropriate to men and even "against human nature." As William of Auvergne puts it, lechery is fine for pigs, but vicious in men.[85] Indeed, indiscriminate abandon to the works of Venus, excused by La Vieille on natural grounds, was frequently said to denature (*denaturare*) man. A little poem which has been entitled "Contra amorem Veneris" makes the point rather wittily; its ascription to Alain de Lille is dubious, but it is frequently found appended to the *De planctu naturae*, the single chief source of the *Roman de la Rose*:

> Vix nodosum valeo nodum denodare
> Et indemonstrabile monstrum demonstrare,
> Unde volens Veneris vultum denodare
> Quae naturas hominum vult denaturare.[86]

The *Echecs* gloss, as we have already seen, uses this same term, "denature," to describe Amant's subjection to Oiseuse.

This discussion is not intended merely to rehearse rather elab-

---

[85] Cited by Robertson, *Preface to Chaucer*, p. 24; see also pp. 397ff.

[86] Polycarp Leyser, ed., *Historia poetarum et poematum Medii Aevi* (Halle, 1721), p. 1092. The lines echo the prologue of *De planctu naturae*.

orately what everybody must know already—namely, that La Vieille's ideas about sex differ radically from those of medieval casuists. My point is that the structure of her arguments, as well as the network of allusions and associations which bind them together, is demonstrably and comically faulty. As is generally true in Jean's poem, the comedy here is multi-faceted and intellectual. As one of the most vociferous "naturalists" in the *Roman*, La Vieille nicely exemplifies the simple absurdities implied in a carnal and faulty understanding of Nature. Her speech, therefore, is a fitting prologue for that long *chapitre*, usually taken to be the real heart of *Roman de la Rose*, in which Nature herself speaks.

CHAPTER FOUR

Natural and Unnatural Nature

N THE Preface to the *Boèce* Jean characterized his part in the composition of the *Roman* as instruction in the means of storming the castle and winning the rose. This description is, perhaps, rather coy, for it leaves unmentioned the vast bulk of his work; but it does draw attention to the part of his poem which is most notorious and which, his critics suggest, contains his true *sententia*.[1] His final "chapter," the delineation of the final step of love (*factum*), is particularly rich in apparently exotic "doctrines," and even its surface action moves along at a comparatively sprightly pace. The intervention of the *vetula* with Bel Accueil is successful, but before the Lover can get what he wants Bel Accueil is reincarcerated. There ensues an indecisive battle between the forces of Amours and Jealousy, and Cupid takes advantage of the uneasy truce which follows to send for his mother, Venus. Meanwhile Lady Nature appears on the scene, and talks for a few thousand lines in a confession to her priest, Genius; Genius then preaches a sermon to Love's soldiers and offers them plenary pardons. Venus shoots an arrow at the castle, which falls apart in flames, and Amant picks the rose.

What we shall make of all this depends, in large measure, upon what we make of the four major characters who take up Amant's cause: Cupid, Venus, Nature, and Genius. The judgments required are pre-eminently iconographic—that is, they involve the correct identification of the significant content of icons. Such iconographic judgments will, in turn, guide the direction of literary analysis of the concluding speeches of the poem. Yet before we can address ourselves to the examination of Love's final and "definitive" teachings, and to his final and successful assault on the castle, we must take some account of the comparatively minor skirmishes which serve as its prelude.

Just before the inconclusive psychomachia begins, Jean de Meun intrudes himself into his poem for one final personal word.

---

[1] See, for example, Gunn, *Mirror of Love*, pp. 396ff, and Friedman, " 'Jean de Meung' and 'Bourgeois Realism,' " p. 19.

185

Addressing himself to all "loyal lovers," he prays that Cupid will grant them their desires. He promises that he has almost reached the end of his matter, that his "rabbit hunt" is nearly done: one can hear the baying of the hounds. He then playfully yet patiently explains that he is neither antifeminist nor antireligious: his remarks about female behavior are all taken from distinguished authorities, and the Faussemblant chapter attacks hypocrisy, not the religious life. He ends his little digression by offering up the *Roman* for the correction of *Sainte Iglise*.

Jean's "rabbit hunt" is an alternative metaphor for the "pilgrimage" which Amant makes to his pudendal "sanctuary." The illustrators of the *Roman*, who were not unaware that its principal literal theme was a certain kind of cony-catching, frequently play with a visual scene from the chase. In the Stuttgart manuscript, for example, the *chace du connin* takes up half of the sumptuous initial diptych.[2] In another careful fourteenth-century manuscript an elaborate rabbit hunt appears among the marginalia of the initial folio.[3] In part, the image derives from the general iconographic associations of the rabbit with natural sexuality (as in Fig. 36) and lechery, and from the specific pun in Old French between *connin* and *con*, the literal signification of the rose. But the image also has a specific mythographic source in the story of Venus and Adonis which Jean introduces into his poem within a few pages of his apologetic digression, and for which the image in the digression is clearly a carefully baited literary trap. It comes about as follows: the psychomachia is indecisive, and Amours arranges a treacherous armistice so that his messengers will have time to fetch Venus from Mount Citheron. Jean then recites the story, from the tenth book of the *Metamorphoses*, of Venus' infatuation with Adonis. She taught him to hunt only timid animals (*fugaces*) like the rabbit and the stag, never *audaces* like boars and lions, which fight back. One day, however, Adonis disobeyed Venus and went after a ferocious boar, which killed him. According to Jean, the moral of this tale is that lovers should always believe their mistresses, treat their promises like paternosters, and deny Reason even if she should swear by a crucifix.

[2] *Codex Poeticus* 6, fol. 1ʳ. See Kuhn, "Die Illustration des Rosenromans," Fig. 31.

[3] Chantilly, Musée Condé, MS 1480, fol. 1ʳ.

This *allegoresis* is not unlike Guillaume de Lorris' jolly interpretation of the Narcissus legend. Like Guillaume, Jean finds an ironic sentence in an Ovidian fable to draw his readers' attention more forcefully to its more conventional and logical meaning, while the extravagance of his blasphemous language (*paternostres, croicefis*) connects the whole episode with the Lover's idolatry and the paraphernalia of the religion of Love. As a matter of fact, there is a substantial moral tradition concerning the hunts of Venus which interprets the matter otherwise.[4] Arnulf of Orléans, for example, the most famous of the medieval Ovidian mythographers, commends the disobedience of Adonis in the "hard hunt" as the charity typical of those who flee Venus.[5] That is, to follow the works of Venus in the "soft hunt" of the *fugaces* is to give oneself over to carnal pursuits. Not merely rabbits, but also the *fugax* stag roams at will through the marginalia of the manuscripts of the *Roman*. There is a fine stag hunt on the initial folio of Fitzwilliam Museum (Cambridge) MS 168; and one of the textual illustrations in Egerton 881 in the British Museum contrasts the "hard" and "soft" hunts.[6] When Jean promises the loyal lovers in his audience that his rabbit hunt will soon be over, he is not merely making a bawdy pun appropriate to the longest *fabliau* ever written, but making witty and elegant reference to traditional moral ideas which qualify his poem. Specifically, he gives the initiated reader some idea of what the psychomachia is really about.

It is not, I think, an abuse to call the battle before the castle gates a "psychomachia." Certainly in this episode Jean is, stylistically, never very far from Prudentius or from Alain in the *Anticlaudianus*. Furthermore, the psychological events represented are typical moral operations analyzed according to commonplace moral categories. Indeed, it is generally true in the *Roman* that psychological analysis is moral analysis; the description of Amant's rejection of Reason, for example, though it deals with a battle within the mind, defines the action in terms of schematic moral

---

[4] See D. C. Allen, "On *Venus and Adonis*," in *Elizabethan and Jacobean Studies Presented to Frank Percy Wilson* (Oxford, 1959), pp. 100-11.

[5] F. Ghisalberti, "Arnolfo d'Orléans, un coltore di Ovidio nel sec. XII," *Memorie del R. Istituto Lombardo di Scienze e Lettere*, XXXIV (1932), 223.

[6] See Robertson, *Preface to Chaucer*, p. 263 and Fig. 109.

categories. Similarly, the duel of Danger and Franchise is, above all, a confrontation of moral alternatives as they are exemplified in a specific instance; and it is insufficient, in my view, to explain the personifications involved simply as objectifications of abstract psychological processes. What, after all, are we to make of this character Danger, who plays such a major role in the *Roman* and causes the Lover so much grief? Amant calls him a churl (*vilain*), and so he appears in the iconography, a very large and often oafish man with a club to rival Cuchulain's. Etymologically, "danger" is connected with the Latin word *dominium* meaning "power" or "control," and Danger does, up to a point, exercise control over the rose. He thus used to be taken to personify the external forces which keep the Lady under lock and key—her husband or other guardians. This interpretation, however, would appear to be no older than the sixteenth century,[7] and C. S. Lewis was certainly right to discard it as an unnecessary reduction which strips the poem of allegorical richness and too severely limits allegorical implications.[8] Lewis insists instead that Danger is a psychological aspect of the Lady's personality, the opposite side of the coin to her Bel Accueil, her disdain, aloofness, and caution. Such an emendation seems very promising, for it offers convincing explanations of the poetic action at the *quid agas* level; but when pressed it likewise reveals itself as an unsatisfactory reduction since Danger, thus interpreted, is limited to the whimsical operations of a particular female psyche. If Danger is simply the obverse, as it were, of Bel Accueil, surely we should expect that these two would fight it out. But Danger does not fight Bel Accueil; he fights Franchise. And Franchise is not a personality trait but an abstract moral category. Franchise means "liberty," and its great exponent in the *Roman* is La Vieille, who claims that it is what women most desire in the whole world. However, her speech specifically qualifies *franchise* to mean the lawlessness of the bestial state of vitiated nature before the institutions of positive justice had been established. It is *franchise* which is the cause of murders, wars, and other serious social disturbances, and it was to control *franchise* that marriage was instituted. Thus, the identification of Danger

[7] See Benoit Court's note in the *Aresta amorum* of Martial d'Auvergne (Paris, 1544), p. 23[v].

[8] *Allegory of Love*, pp. 123-24.

with the "Lady's husband," while unsatisfactory in itself as narrow and reductionist, is not altogether beside the point. The force which can overcome Franchise is clearly something more than the particular haughtiness of a particular lady or even the haughtiness of ladies considered generically. It is a moral category which manifests itself in psychological restraint: the power of the rational will which exercises in specific instances—tropologically—the same control of passion which, in society at large, is exercised by positive justice based on reason. This is why the *Roman* says that Danger, like Fear and Shame, is "of the lineage of Lady Reason born." He can be Amant's enemy only if Amant maneuvers himself into a false dilemma by loving irrationally. In Figure 31, an allegory of love considered as one of the goods of Fortune, the issue seems clear enough. On one side Cupid's votaries swim at their ease, urged on by the god of passion; by the muddy waters of bad fortune, Danger stands guard against such lovers. Danger is Amant's enemy only insofar as Amant has become Cupid's man; Danger's real enemy is the god himself (see Fig. 11).

It is of some interest that even with Reason banished the forces who are of Reason's lineage—Danger, Fear, Shame—are sufficient to withstand the assault of Cupid's army against the castle. Danger is a formidable foe. Amant can get around him temporarily through duplicity and deceit, but not for long, and it becomes evident that if he is finally to pluck his *bouton* it must be with the aid of a more powerful divine intervention than he has so far enjoyed. Such aid is not denied him; Venus herself hastens in her dove-cart from Mount Citheron to the plain where the barons have pitched their tents. Having great power and sagacity, she knows that what has been denied in the name of Love may be won in the name of Nature. Her arrival marks the beginning of the last act in Jean's tragi-comedy, at once the most daring and the least understood section of the *Roman de la Rose*.

It must be granted from the outset that much of the considerable confusion which has characterized discussions of the closing sections of the *Roman* simply reflects, at one remove, similar confusions about Jean's sources. The last chapter of the *Roman* reveals the full flowering of Jean's poetic genius in the richness of its ironic techniques and the brilliance of its iconographic devices, but it is at the same time the most derivative of the longer sections of his poem. Here his particular source, from which he lifts a good quarter of his work, is Alain de Lille's *De planctu naturae*. It is no exaggeration to describe Alain, a polymath genius who combined the rhetorical gifts of a major poet with the brilliant mind of an original speculative theologian, as one of the major intellectual figures of the high Middle Ages. In his own time his reputation was enormous, and his most "sublime" poem, the *Anticlaudianus*, was considered worthy company for the *Sentences* of Lombard and the Bible itself as a set text for academic exegesis. Yet until very recently many of his most important works lay unedited, and several, including *De planctu naturae*, are now available only in deficient editions.

All of the major quartet of the final act of the *Roman*—Amours, Venus, Nature, and Genius—appear in *De planctu*, where they are sufficiently qualified to offer reliable guidance for their interpretations in the *Roman*. The close and informed reading of Alain's poem, accordingly, would seem an indispensable introduction to Jean's. Yet apart from the most mechanical and unthinking rites of source hunting, students of the *Roman* have virtually ignored Alain, thereby demonstrating the peculiarly debilitating tendency of literary scholarship to avoid difficult intellectual confrontations with essential primary sources and to rely instead on secondhand and usually inadequate descriptions of them. Mighty edifices are thus built on sandy soil. For every word which has been written about Jean de Meun, there are a hundred devoted to Chaucer; yet much of Chaucer is uphill work without a sound understanding of the *Roman*. And as Geoffrey Chaucer is to Jean de Meun, Jean is to Alain: a bibliography of critical studies of *De planctu* takes up three lines of type.

The following analysis does not pretend to remedy this chronic philological deficiency, or to offer the kind of collation between the *Roman* and *De planctu* which remains so urgently needed. It will be useful, however, to adduce the testimony of Alain de Lille to aid in the iconographic identification of the *Roman*'s chief actors. To this end, one objection must be anticipated. Since Jean uses Alain's ideas and allegorical abstractions in a very different context from that of *De planctu*—it can generally be characterized as disordered as opposed to ordered—it has seemed to some that he uses them in name only. Thus G. Reynaud de Lage writes of the *Roman* that "Il faut affirmer que Genius, comme Nature, est là surtout pour porter la parole au nom de Jean de Meung . . . il leur fait apporter sa propre pensée comme il la souffle aussi à La Vieille et à la Raison."[9] Such a judgment seems to me misconceived, for even if we deny elementary literary decorum to Jean's *personae*, the intellectual confusion of the mind which manifests its "own thought" in the lengthy and contradictory discourses of Genius, Nature, the Vekke, and Lady Reason must be very great. Jean does not use Alain's allegorical figures as mere window dressing, or appropriate five thousand lines of *De planctu naturae* only to substitute his own thought for Alain's carefully worked-out ideas. He does place Alain's characters—in particular Nature and Genius—into a context very different from that of *De planctu*, and for different poetic reasons; but that is another matter.

It is probably easiest to consider the four characters in pairs: Venus and her son on one hand, Nature and her chaplain on the other. The first pair is the more familiar and accessible. Both Venus and Cupid (called the god of Love or simply Love in the text of the *Roman*) are well-known inhabitants of the enchanted wood of medieval mythography. There is no particular reason to believe that Guillaume de Lorris was following Alain, as Jean certainly was, but from their early appearances in Guillaume's text the mythographic identities of Venus and Cupid are clearly established with the deities of *De planctu naturae* and a dozen other poems; together they preside over the rites of carnal love, or what is usually called *luxuria* in medieval texts. Although they are surrounded in the *Roman* by a certain aura of exoticism, they nonetheless constitute the same familiar moral categories of the mythographers of Orléans and the Platonists of Chartres. Bernardus Sylvestris, whose famous poem on the microcosm has frequently been misunderstood as "pantheistic" and thus abused to provide a sort of spurious precedent for some of the wilder notions about Jean de Meun's *Roman*, also wrote a spiritual commentary to the *Aeneid*. He there distinguishes between two Venuses: one, the mother of Jocus and Cupid, is a figure for the *voluptas carnis*;

[9] G. Raynaud de Lage, "*Natura* et *Genius*, chez Jean de Meung et chez Jean Lemaire de Belges," *Le Moyen Age*, LVIII (1952), 136.

while the other, the mother of Aeneas, represents the *mundana musica*.[10] Alain de Lille accounts for the matter somewhat differently, defining the good and bad ends of the carnality represented by Venus in terms of her lawful and unlawful unions.[11] The *Echecs* exegete goes into the matter in some detail.

> Venus had three sons by the god Bacchus. One of them is Jocus who is the god of games and worldly pleasures, and he is the one who is named Deduit in the *Romance of the Rose.* . . . Some authorities say that Jocus represents the delight found in hugging and kissing. And Cupid, taking it a step further, represents the pleasure enjoyed in the consummation of unreasonably desired joy. And the third [Hymen] represents that delight which is enjoyed in perfect accord with reason, that is, for the purpose of generation.[12]

The gloss talks at some length about the good Venus and Hymen, and gives some account of their iconography. For example, reasonable love, associated with the good Venus, is signified by the white rose, as opposed to the *vermeille* of the *Roman*.

More work remains to be done on the specific mythographic influences on the *Roman*, but so far as Venus and the god of Love are concerned, the general significance is clear enough: in the *Roman* they represent exactly the same ideas that Venus and Cupid represent in *De planctu naturae*. The marked differences of their roles in the two poems are dramatic rather than iconographic in function. In Alain's poem, Nature explains that she has established Venus in order to facilitate generation (col. 456); Nature, that is, is meant to be in charge of Venus. She goes on to explain, however, that Venus and Cupid rebel and become immoderate *passiones*. So they are in the *Roman*, where the rebellion has already taken place and they use Nature rather than are used by her.

It is a more difficult matter to identify Genius and Nature, though these two figures dominate the final section of the poem and are clearly crucial to its interpretation. Genius in particular may seem elusive, since outside his brief appearance in Alain he

[10] *Commentarium super sex libros Eneidos Virgilii*, ed. G. Riedel (Greifswald, 1924), p. 10.

[11] *De planctu naturae*, Pat. lat. 210, cols. 459-60.

[12] Bibliothèque nationale MS fr. 9197, fol. 197ʳ-197ᵛ.

has no clear iconographic tradition; yet such extravagant claims are made on his behalf—both within the poem by Love's barons and in scholarly print by Professor Gunn and others—that it appears vital to establish his identity. What we know about Genius before his appearance in the pages of *De planctu naturae* can be summarized in a few sentences. Lewis drew a distinction between the genius which is the tutelary spirit of an individual man and Genius, the universal god of generation, drawing attention to a promising text in St. Augustine (*De civitate Dei*, VII, 13).[13] One would hope that the learned Augustinian humanists of the later Middle Ages would provide an explanation of the classical *genius* in specifically Christian terms, but they are disappointing. Trivet and Raoul de Presles, following him, are content to associate Genius with the *anima mundi*.[14] There is perhaps a useful hint in the commentary written in 1333 by the Oxford Minorite, Ridewell, who associates Genius with antique phallic rites.[15] It seems, however, that only from the School of Chartres, the supposed cradle of Jean's amazingly modern "naturalism," do we learn the most theologically precise and appropriate definition of the abstraction, Genius, as he appears in *De planctu* and the *Roman*. It comes from William of Conches, one of the most profound Platonists of the Middle Ages, in his commentary on the *Consolation of Philosophy*. William explains the spiritual meaning of Eurydice as follows: "Hujus est conjux Euridice, id est naturalis concupiscentia que unicuique conjuncta est: nullus enim sine ea, nec etiam puer unius diei, in hac vita esse potest." He then cites Horace and continues: "Genius est naturalis concupiscentia; sed hec naturalis concupiscentia merito dicitur Euridice, id est boni judicatio; quia quum quisque judicat bonum sive ita sit, sive non, concupiscit."[16] Though offered merely as an exegetical aside, Wil-

---

[13] *Allegory of Love*, "Appendix I: Genius and Genius," pp. 361-63; cf. E. Curtius, "Zur Literarästhetik des Mittelalters, II," *Zeitschrift für romanische Philologie*, LVIII (1938), 193ff.

[14] *De civitate Dei . . . cum commentariis Thome Valois et Nicolai Triveth* (1515 ed.), sig. q. 4ᵛ; and *De la cité de dieu* (Abbeville, 1486), I, E. ii ʳ.

[15] Corpus Christi College, Oxon., MS 187, fols. 151ᵛ-152ʳ.

[16] "Des commentaires inédits de Guillaume de Conches et de Nicolas Triveth sur la Consolation de Philosophie de Boèce," ed. Charles Jourdain, *Excursions historiques et philosophiques à travers le Moyen Age* (Paris, 1888), p. 66. Cf. St. Augustine in *Pat. lat.* 44, col. 801: "Naturalem esse libidinem et ego dico quod quia cum illa nascitur omnis homo."

liam's remark gives the specific identification most useful for an understanding of Genius' role in *De planctu* and the *Roman*; he is natural concupiscence, the particular aspect of man's nature which incites "natural" sexual activity. In this capacity, Genius can be regarded simply as "nature," or "the god of nature," though not without further qualification.[17] While the allegorical meaning of *De planctu naturae* is not exhausted by an attack on buggery in the Burgundian monasteries, Alain does follow St. Paul (Romans 1:26) in taking homosexuality as the type of man's crimes *contra naturam*; and it is the function of Alain's Genius to castigate and "excommunicate" those who are guilty of such "sins against nature." The specific meaning of the *peccatum contra naturam*, in terms of which Genius' authority is defined, is, furthermore, very precise for Alain: "Peccatum contra naturam est quando extra locum ad hoc deputatum funditur semen."[18]

Thus William of Conches' commentary yields Genius' *significatio*, and Alain's definition of the *peccatum contra naturam* suggests his function. Yet since he is an aspect of Nature, it is not possible to understand how Genius operates in the *Roman* without first coming to terms with Nature herself, the most difficult and yet the most important of all the categories Jean borrowed from Alain. We have already seen, in the clever equivocations of Amis and La Vieille, the ambiguities present in the term "nature"; it will be necessary to proceed with caution, and Alain de Lille himself (or his glossator) will be the safest guide. In the prose *summarium* to Alain's *Anticlaudianus* there is a distinction made between two ways of using the term "nature," and this distinction is a crucial one for the interpretation of the *Roman de la Rose* as well. "Nature vero duo; unum in pura natura consideratum, ab omni corruptione alienum, quale opus Nature fuit ante Ade peccatum, aliud uero vario curruptione viciarum, quale fuit post peccatum Ade."[19] The Natura of the *Anticlaudianus*, a sublime figure intimately associated with Divine Sapience and the Nous, cannot be the subject of our attention here. But what of Natura

---

[17] "Genius enim natura vel Deus nature dicitur," Alain de Lille, *Textes inédites*, ed. M. T. d'Alverny (Paris, 1965), p. 228.

[18] *De virtutibus et de vitiis et de donis Spiritus Sancti*, ed. O. Lottin, in *Psychologie et morale aux XIIe et XIIIe siècles*, VI (Gembloux, 1960), 75.

[19] *Anticlaudianus*, ed. Bossuat, p. 199.

at her forge, the Natura of *De planctu* and the *Roman?* A brief analysis of the lines in which Lady Nature makes her appearance in Jean's poem provides the answer. She stands by her anvil thinking about "things which are beneath the stars"; her specific function, elaborated in poetic language in some detail, is to combat the work of Death by perpetuating the species. Since Death came into the world only through the sin of Adam (Romans 5:12), it cannot be possible that the noble lady in the *Roman* is *pura natura.* Her reproductive office clearly defines her as Nature considered *post peccatum Ade.*

The implications of the distinction of the two "natures" for Jean's allegory are very broad, for, like the distinctions necessary to understand the word "love," this one offers the poet a richness of superficial ambiguity which is the stuff of ironic formulation and equivocal argument; certainly it is this distinction which makes Jean's recurrent and playful use of the Golden Age *topos* so satisfying. Furthermore, such a distinction is central to the chief medieval discussions of grace and nature, particularly to the theology of the Doctor of Grace himself, St. Augustine. The concept of "fallen," "wounded," or "vitiated" Nature—Nature made defective by man's sin—is a Pauline category ("We were by nature the children of wrath"), which St. Augustine repeatedly expounds in his discussions of the theory and psychology of sin and the operations of nature and grace.[20] Indeed, the very cause for Nature's "complaint" is the "wound" of man's sin, his "unnatural" behavior.

Yet Lady Nature in the *Roman* is not precisely the same as Natura in *De planctu*; with regard to her alone can it convincingly be said that Jean has altered one of Alain's *personae.* The concept of Genius, as I have just suggested, is not altered, merely put into a radically different context for purposes of comedy. Lady Nature, on the other hand, while still representing the same concept of *natura post peccatum Ade* as in Alain's poem, has been poetically decreased. Alain's Natura, though wounded, represents a force working in conjunction with Reason; human rationality seems to

---

[20] The most important Augustinian texts devoted to this subject are conveniently anthologized with an illuminating commentary in Joannes Mehlmann, *Natura filii irae: Historia interpretationis Eph 2, 3 ejusque cum doctrina de Peccato Originali nexus* (Rome, 1957), pp. 169ff.

be within her gift (cols. 442ff.). In the context of the *Roman,* on the other hand, Nature is a force kept carefully distinct from Reason, and she speaks of man's rationality as a divine gift outside her capabilities (ll. 19146ff.). The first indications of her poetic diminishment in Jean's poem are iconographic. Whereas, in the opening lines of *De planctu,* Alain expended his mighty poetic energies at length describing Natura's glorious arrival, her visage, her brilliant and emblematic garments, Jean gives her a couple of lines. She stands at her forge, "thinking of things." The iconographic attributes which in Alain link Natura with such sublime concepts as Boethian Philosophia, or the Theologia of the *Anticlaudianus,* are given over to Lady Reason in the *Roman.*[21] Lady Nature's emblems, the rough tools of her smithy, her hammer and anvil, emphasize her role as goddess of generation and her function of renewing the race.

The great originality of the final chapter of the *Roman* is poetic rather than speculative. Jean formulates no significantly new intellectual concepts, but he exemplifies the operations of a number of traditional theological categories to brilliant comic effect; and the reader who brings to the *Roman* some awareness of the literary tradition of Jean's *dramatis personae* and can follow complex dramatic action with a certain amount of intellectual rigor will be richly rewarded. Venus and Cupid, regarded generically, are the deities of carnal love (*luxuria*), but in Jean's poem it is possible to make certain loose distinctions between them on the basis of dramatic function. Venus represents what Bernardus Silvestris calls *voluptas carnis* and the *Echecs* gloss, *charnel delict.* She is the general force of "concupiscence of the flesh," considered as a moral defect, which has been rampant in man since the end of the Golden Age. Her son, Amours, as used by Guillaume de Lorris and Jean de Meun, incites specific incidents of venereal love. Any lecher is a worshipper of Venus; but the man who has "pathologically fallen in love," that is, one who has cultivated a *passio,* has become Cupid's man. Indeed Cupid is simply a personification of a term, *cupido,* which is commonly used as a synonym for *passio.* Venus makes the lover burn with concupiscence, and Cupid counsels him to keep his heart set on a specified object. It has

[21] See M. T. d'Alverny, "Alain de Lille et la *Théologia,*" in *L'Homme devant Dieu (Mélanges Henri de Lubac)* (Paris, 1964), II, 111-28.

been said that in the *Roman* Amours represents a "civilized" sentiment, and this may be superficially true. An idolatrous passion, as defined by Andreas and Reason, perhaps implies a certain amount of free time, and hence social station. Any degree of "civilization" implied by Amours, however, is precisely that kind damned as degenerate by satirists from Horace to Bernard of Cluny. Venus and Amours are specific moral ideas; as iconographically qualified in the *Roman*, they are serious vices. An interpretation of the *Roman* which claims or implies that the poem counsels or condones the worship of Venus and subjection to Cupid must take on a crushing burden of proof since it maintains, in effect, that the most important vernacular poem of the Christian Middle Ages is a schematic rejection of specific Christian values and doctrines.

Nature and Genius are not moral categories (virtues or vices), though moral operations can be defined in terms of them. Nature in the *Roman* is *natura vitiata*, or nature wounded by man's propensity for vicious behavior such as that emblematically suggested in the cult of Venus and Cupid. Genius, on the other hand, is the *naturalis concupiscentia* which has characterized human nature since the Fall; he is the badge of vitiated nature. He is, so to speak, an amoral Venus, a natural inclination or appetite, like hunger and thirst, which man shares with the beasts; so far as man is concerned Genius is "good" or "bad" in relation to whether he is "used" or "abused." As Natura explains in *De planctu*, Venus (concupiscence) was established with generation of the species as her *raison d'être*, but through rebellion she became a vicious *passio*, subordinating her primary end to the incidental and contingent means of pleasurable incentive. The *Echecs* gloss maintained that there need be no conflict between Nature, Venus, and Reason, so long as man's principal allegiance lay with Reason: Reason is the indispensable control of natural concupiscence. Such a concept explains Jean's poetic strategy in diminishing Lady Nature to exclude man's rationality from her immediate domain. The action of the final chapter of the *Roman* runs its course without reference to Reason, and the necessary hierarchies are neatly inverted. Nature does not use Venus; Venus uses Nature. In effect, the final act of the *Roman* is a dramatic representation of the kind of human "unnaturalness" of which Alain's Natura complains.

Extravagant disorder offers rich opportunities for a medieval

comedian, and the concluding section of Jean's poem is character-
ized by a robust hilarity. In the deranged landscape of Amours'
camp, poor abused Nature becomes something of a comic figure,
and there may be a temptation to underrate her dignity in Jean's
theological vision. It seems to me that Rosemond Tuve has suc-
cumbed to this temptation, misconceiving Jean's exposure of
Nature's inadequacy as the sole guide of human behavior as a
slighting evaluation of the goddess herself, so that her often
brilliant analysis of the last few thousand lines of the poem suffers
from a noticeable imbalance. In view of the prevailing interpreta-
tions of the *Roman*, such an overemphasis on Nature's limitations
and vulnerability is understandable and perhaps inevitable; cer-
tainly the recurrent error has been to make too much rather than
too little of her. The concept of nature *post peccatum Ade* is a
seriously limited one; Nature thus conceived cannot offer salva-
tion but must be redeemed by sacramental grace, and with the
category of reason removed she is neither a sufficient nor a safe
guide to human conduct. Yet having said all this, one must still
conclude that for Jean de Meun, Lady Nature is an elevated and
indeed divine concept. Under God Himself, she rules over the
vast empire of the created order, and her lengthy discourses on
stars, mirrors, meteors, and meteorology are not mere garrulous
chatter, but a veritable encyclopedia of academic *scientia*.[22] Her
account of "things created" is clearly intended to move the reader
to the contemplation of the "invisible things of God," His maj-
esty, and His infinitely wise ordering of the universe. Both the
style and the content of her discourse, as has long been recognized,
reflect the profound influence of Alain's *Anticlaudianus*, the
explication of which was an established academic exercise in the
thirteenth century. It would appear that Nature's discourse in the
Roman is, in effect, Jean's own commentary to the *Anticlaudianus*;
certainly it is strikingly similar in tone and content to large sec-
tions of the commentary of Raoul de Longchamps (Oxford,
Balliol MS 146B).

That Jean should on one hand hold the goddess Natura in the
highest respect, making her the vehicle of much conventional
knowledge and wisdom concerning sublunary matters, and on the

---

[22] Paris, Bibliothèque Mazarine MS 3872 appends an encyclopedic alphabetical
index to the chief topics discussed by Lady Nature.

other expose her as a slightly ridiculous figure of fun reveals no confusion of poetic design or philosophic formulation. As always Jean depends upon his readers to bring to the poem a set of fairly rigorous if commonplace theological concepts against which his ironies can play. They will know that Lady Nature is in many matters authoritative: zoology, astronomy, the nature of true nobility—all this, and much more, is properly within her province. Such authority as she has over man, however, is strictly limited to his animal capacities. She herself knows that the characteristic which distinguishes man, and the angels, from creatures fully within her domain is his reason. It is his reason alone which establishes man's dominion over the beasts. In one of the most significant lines of her lengthy discourse, dropped almost as an aside, Nature says that man ought to follow Reason. All this is very wise.

There are, however, many things about which Nature can know nothing whatsoever, and the adduction of "natural" solutions to questions which demand supernatural ones gives rise to the comedy of the *Roman*. With specific regard to sexual behavior, Nature's advice to man is no different from that which she gives to animals. She urges heterosexual intercourse to the end that the species may be preserved. Her only concern in this matter is to combat the work of Death: she is not a casuist, and questions of sexual morality and moral intentionality are not within her sphere of influence. Since Venus and Cupid urge "natural" love, she considers them her allies. But human sexuality has much higher claims upon it that those of bestial nature. It is the specific subject of a commandment of the Old Law established by God Himself, and under the New Dispensation it has been sanctified by supernatural sacramental grace. Thus when characters in the *Roman* appeal to "nature" as an authority on human sexual behavior they are by implication denying the supernatural workings of God in the establishment of the Law and the grace of the Incarnation, turning back the clock of human history to the time when "Death reigned, from Adam to Moses" (Romans 5:14). The pseudo-theological mandates of the "doctrines" of plenitude and replenishment were several thousand years out of date by the time Jean de Meun wrote his poem, however "strikingly modern" they may seem now; and there is absolutely no reason at all to believe that Jean considered them more authoritative than the New Law. Lady Nature, it should be remarked, makes no such extravagant claims on her own behalf. She urges man to reproduction, but says that he ought to follow Reason. This, of course, is the solution to the pseudo-problem raised by the "demands of Nature." Nor is Nature guilty for considering Venus and Cupid as her well-beloved allies when Reason would reject them. It must be remembered that in Jean's poem Reason is supernatural; she is Divine Sapience, beyond the power of Nature to frame (ll. 19146ff.), and Nature cannot be expected to perform her functions. Furthermore, Nature's rather unflattering view of man as merely a peculiarly perverse species of *fauna* is simply the logical implication of man's own viciousness which has "changed the glory of the uncorruptible God into an image like to corruptible man, and to birds, and four-footed beasts and creeping things" (Romans 1:23).

Jean's theology of nature, which is not his own at all but rather a set of cherished ideas about the relation between nature and grace, is sketched quite lucidly in Nature's "complaint," with which she ends her discourse, that man alone of all creation is unnatural and ungrateful in his willful disobedience. It is man alone, the *chef d'oeuvre* of the works of Nature and a perfect microcosm of the universe itself, who disturbs the harmony of the spheres with his discordant music. All of this is, of course, borrowed more or less *verbatim* from Alain's *De planctu*, although the idea is a theological commonplace which Jean expresses in his own words in the preface to the *Boèce*. It will nonetheless perhaps be fruitful to review Nature's argument, not so much for its familiar substance as for the careful qualifications of the goddess' powers and authority which lie scattered on its periphery. She does not complain of the animals whose heads bend toward the earth; they all join in fruitful and unmercenary copulation. It is man alone, who enjoys all the finest gifts of Nature, whose face lifts up toward the sky, of whom she complains. Man has only one thing that Nature has not given him, and that is his understanding. Nature is not wise or powerful enough to make him that gift; everything she creates is mortal. Nature cites Plato at some length to her purpose, but even Plato, she says, could know nothing of the Incarnation. God Himself made man's reason. Nature knows that God is all-powerful, but she cannot understand the Incarnation, since according to her credo a virgin birth is impossible. She then goes on to indict man on twenty-six counts, so to speak, and to remind him of the stern justice which awaits him.

This summary, needless to say, is not intended to do justice to the dignity of Nature's rhetoric or to the wide-ranging knowledge with which Jean de Meun buttresses her arguments. I wish rather to draw attention to the very severe limitations of the goddess' authority. The unique characteristic of man, namely his reason, is not within Nature's gift or governance. Furthermore, Nature stands complacently helpless before the central fact of Christian history, the Incarnation of Jesus Christ. This means that, by her own testimony, she can guide man no further than the threshold of the Christian revelation—which includes everything of ultimate importance to him—and the feet of his true guide, Reason. For a Christian audience, these limitations must be considered at the very least quite substantial; and it seems likely that the poetic devices which characterize Nature's complaint, as opposed to the eloquence and authority of her preceding disquisitions on natural phenomena, are intended to draw attention to these limitations, and ruthlessly to expose her insufficiencies as a preceptor of love. For she ends her complaint to her lieutenant and confessor, Genius, by commissioning him to go to the camp of her allies, Amours and Venus, to carry the great good news of her weighty help toward a cause which Christian theology considered well lost —that is, the carnal combat against carnal death.

In my attempt to adduce some of the basic theological ideas which lie behind Jean de Meun's (and Alain's) concept of Nature, I have several times cited St. Paul's Epistle to the Romans. This has not been merely for the sake of convenience, for it seems likely that Jean de Meun is mining this specific text for his own ironic purposes. In the first chapter of Romans, in the passage which inspired *De planctu naturae*, Paul uses man's sodomy as the type of his vicious behavior and as an introduction to a long list of specific vices (Romans 1:29ff.) which is strikingly similar to the list of twenty-six charges which Nature brings against man in the *Roman* (ll. 19225ff.). Furthermore, Nature, like Paul, moves immediately from this lugubrious enumeration to hortative exclamations in the high style about the retributive justice of God which will punish such crimes. Various other similarities of phrasing, as well as the whole context of argument, make it appear certain that Jean is both inspired and guided by this Pauline text, using it with considerable sophistication as a control for the ideas and attitudes represented by Nature and Genius.

The Epistle to the Romans is of course one of the most fruitful scriptural sources of allegorical imagery for a wide spectrum of medieval poetry, for in it St. Paul introduces not only the exegetical method itself but also those contrasts of the "Old" and the "New," the "carnal" and the "spiritual," life under the Law and life under grace, which provided Christian poets like Alain and Dante and Chaucer and Petrarch with a good deal of their most cherished and versatile poetic vocabulary. The letter is a profound theological essay, and does not readily lend itself to summary, but reference to some of its central doctrines will perhaps make more easily accessible the ironic inadequacies of Lady Nature's attitudes. Like St. Paul, Nature holds that man's sins merit damnation, but man's judgment she quite properly leaves to God (ll. 19323ff.). The only sins which she herself can seek to redress are those of which the god of Love complains, and these, clearly enough, reduce themselves to one: man's refusal to use properly the "tools," or sexual members, which Nature has given him. Of the twenty-six charges Nature originally laid against man, only the last, that of the *peccatum contra naturam*, falls into this category.

If she went no further than this Lady Nature would probably not have confused the issues of the *Roman* so much as she has. But she is by herself as incapable of understanding the implications of grace as she is of creating Reason. Her solitary enemy, but a formidable one, is Death. Any force that combats Death by working for procreation is therefore necessarily good. Nature even stands ready to pardon Faussemblant and his dubious girl friend, the very forces of Antichrist, if they help the god of Love toward Nature's goals (ll. 19357ff.). By this point in her argument, if not long before, the careful reader must suspect that something has gone wrong and that Lady Nature is far exceeding the authority of her mandate. She can, after all, neither damn nor save any man; she can only give him a physical body which, like the carcasses of brute animals, is subject to death and putrefaction.

St. Paul, who *was* living under grace, discusses many of the same issues but with very different conclusions, for the great paradoxes of the Christian revelation greatly alter the case. Paul points out, in the first place, that it is not Death which is the enemy, but Sin. Death is the symptom, Sin the disease. For all of Nature's striving and Genius' bombast, the best they can hope to offer is symptomatic relief. Furthermore, Death cannot be conquered carnally—through the works of Nature—but only through the operations of grace; and, as we have seen, Lady Nature cannot comprehend the realm of grace—she can only applaud its advent. For someone living in the era of the Incarnation, the "claims of Nature" and man's "debt to Nature" are thus greatly modified. But Paul goes even farther than this: not only does he maintain that the works of carnal man cannot bring spiritual life; he also shows how they typically bring spiritual death. He associates sin with the "concupiscence of the flesh" and with what he calls the "law of the members." We have already identified Genius with man's *naturalis concupiscentia*, and the "law of the members" seems closely related to the strange legislation enjoining man's use of his "tools" which is so enthusiastically promulgated by Genius on behalf of Nature. Jean is toying with a bold paradox. Lady Nature's attempt to overcome Death only leads to Death. Chaucer, similarly reworking Pauline formulations about the Old Man and the inadequacies of carnal attitudes toward the spiritual realities of the revelation of grace, makes a similar poetic statement in the Pardoner's Tale. In Jean's poem Amis and, more overtly, La Vieille make appeals to "natural" sexual behavior unrestrained by law and *seigneurie*; but the *franchise* they glorify is in fact illusory, the "liberty" of the chains which bind Venus and Mars in the mythographic *exemplum*. For even the most "free" and "natural" behavior is dictated by law—the "law of the members" which wars against the law of the mind (Romans 7:23). It is this law which enforces sin, and the wages of sin is death. It is curious that scholars who have taken the carnal views of Nature and Genius as Jean's own should hold them up as modern, anticipating the naturalism of modern attitudes; for they are the attitudes of the Old Man, and they were already ancient at the time of the establishment of the Law under Moses. Medieval Christianity, it is true, recognized that such "natural" attitudes were both powerful and perennial, so that they were certainly morally topical in the thirteenth century, but they could hardly be regarded as avant-garde.

As modern readers we shall stand helpless before the *Roman* and a great deal else in medieval literature unless we are willing to assess the implications of the profound and essential differences between the foundations of medieval thought and those of our own—which is easy enough to say, but laborious to try to carry out. The exercise of the historical imagination requires both hard work and creative insight; it can promise at best only partial success, and it often fails totally. Yet the game is worth the candle. We can have Jean's poem, if we want it, on terms other than those of the *Ovide moralisé*, that is, its "meaning for our age." The central metaphor of the *Roman* is sexual, and the general attitude toward sex in the twentieth century is, by and large, very different from what it was in the thirteenth. Freudian psychology, widely accepted in diluted and popularized formulation, suggests that man's sexuality is his essential characteristic and the dynamo of most, if not all, his actions. Civilized restraints upon his natural sexual drives, both internal and external, are said to be at the roots of his prevailing mental illnesses. The medieval psychology to which Jean de Meun subscribed, on the other hand, taught that man's essential distinguishing characteristic was his reason. His sexuality, which he was said to share with brute beasts, was a constant embarrassment which needed careful, constant, rational control and the force of positive law to constrain. Man's nature was viewed not solely in terms of internal conflicts between opposing teleologies ("Life against Death"), but in moral categories based upon supernatural revelation. Man's principal "ends" were not natural—to reproduce himself before leaving behind a rotting corpse—but supernatural—the glorification of Almighty God and the salvation of his immortal soul. The crudely sketched outlines of "natural man," which is all that remains of the medieval picture when the supernatural is erased, can easily enough be made to serve as an *ébauche* for Freud's much richer painting. Lady Reason can be a *censor*, and Lady Nature the *id*. This ingenious exercise will not greatly illuminate the *Roman*, though it may mislead us to believe that Jean praises what he in fact condemns.

Nature's strange "confession" ends with an order to her confessor. Genius is to go to the camp of Amours and publish Nature's "pardon," which she then dictates. After granting absolution and imposing the somewhat unusual penitential counsel that Nature should continue to do exactly what she has been doing, Genius doffs his amice for mufti ("as if he were going carolling"), puts on his wings, and flies away. He greets the host, except for the false mendicants, who flee before him—suggesting not that they have been guilty of chastity, as Professor Gunn would have it, but that their vices include the *peccatum contra naturam*. The joy of Love's barons, when they hear Genius' glad tidings, is without measure. Cupid decks Genius out as a bishop, and Venus, unable to control her laughter, sticks a candle into his hand. Thus arrayed and armed, his grace climbs onto a high scaffold and begins reading from his bull of excommunication the "definitive sentence" about love. That it is possible to interpret this jaunty narrative sequence as anything other than burlesque, and rather broad burlesque at that, seems to me a most remarkable tribute to the "oldness" of literal analysis rather than the newness of Jean's ideas. Yet, with a methodical serious-mindedness which ruthlessly obfuscates Jean's comic achievement, critics from Jean Gerson to Alan Gunn have ransacked Genius' bull for passages which, when triumphantly produced, will prove that Jean is either a vicious fool or one of the great original minds of the Middle Ages, depending upon one's point of view. Here we shall find Jean's *significatio*, his "sensualism," his "naturalism," and the full flowering of his "anti-Christian spirit." It will, accordingly, be necessary to analyze in some detail this "definitive" statement, but not before first attempting to establish the literary mould in which it is cast. That is parody.

In the *Roman de la Rose* love is a religion. Its theology is not as rich nor its trappings as elaborate as the similar religion of love which in poems both anterior and posterior to the *Roman* can celebrate *bone amour* as well as *fol amour*, but it is a clearly developed strand in the metaphoric pattern of the poem. The religion of love has a god, a mother of god, a revealed law, a sacramental system, and so forth. The religion so established clearly parodies Christianity, but it is important to distinguish in what way the parody works. Very broadly speaking, literary parody is of two kinds. Chaucer in "Sir Thopas" seems to be drawing attention to certain stylistic and intellectual deficiencies in the form of the popular English romance. The "Gospel According to Marks of Silver," on the other hand, does not expose insufficiencies in the Gospel of St. Mark, but pokes fun at venal and simoniac ecclesiastics. The parody of religion in the *Roman* is of the latter sort. It does not discredit the religious system which it apes; it ridicules the idolatry of the Lover.

This distinction in kinds of parody is important, for from a critical point of view, it is as corrupting to mistake the kind of parody present in the *Roman* as to ignore its presence altogether. Such critical confusion totally sabotages, for example, Helmut Hatzfeld's article about Jean de Meun's "Mystique Naturiste." In this article Hatzfeld proposes to "confront Jean de Meung with one of the outstanding traditionalists of the 13th century, namely, with Saint Bonaventure, in order to prove the anti-Christian spirit in Jean de Meung by method of contrast."[23] Since he assumes that the parodic statements made by the Lover, Nature, Genius, and others all express the views of Jean himself, insuperable confusions become inevitable. By this same excellent method, after all, one could collate the speeches of Iago with selected texts from the Judicious Hooker in order to prove the anti-Christian spirit of Shakespeare "by method of contrast." Yet this critical blunder does not vitiate Hatzfeld's perception that in the *Roman* there is at work a "parodic revolt" evidenced by overt "attacks against Christian concepts."[24] It does not greatly matter that Hatzfeld thinks he exposes Jean de Meun when in fact he merely topples some, but not all, of Jean's straw men, for the process itself is an instructive one. It is possible to argue that, in Jean's own historical context and in the intellectual ambiance suggested by his poem, the choice of Bonaventure as the exemplar of thirteenth-century theological and moral traditionalism is eccentric; but this is a quibble, for that great saint will serve. The method itself, that is, the comparison of the sophistical and parodic arguments presented by various characters in the *Roman* with the cherished intellectual traditions of Catholic Christianity, is what Jean de Meun obviously invites.

[23] *Symposium*, II (1948), 145.

[24] "La mystique naturiste de Jean de Meung," p. 267. Religious parody, totally misunderstood, is also the subject of Marcel Françon's article "Jean de Meun et les origines du naturalisme de la Renaissance," *PMLA*, LIX (1944), 624-45.

What, then, are we to make of Nature's confession, her pardon, Genius' bull of excommunication, and his plenary indulgences? Jean's modest expectation is that his readers will bring to these parodic elements of his poem quite elementary theological principles, the distortion or denial of which gives the poem its comic impetus and adorns his old and profitable *sententiae* with new and delightful literary garments. Jean is a notable if traditional moralist, and his poem is an allegorical description of man's moral problems as they were traditionally conceived in the Middle Ages. It is unlikely that he regarded the sacrament of penance lightly, so that the curious business between Nature and Genius in the *Roman*, very significantly altered from its source in *De planctu*, can legitimately excite the reader's suspicions. Nature's lengthy interview with Genius displays neither the form nor the content of an auricular confession. It is chiefly taken up with a technical commentary on a wide variety of natural phenomena, and the closest Nature comes to confessing a real sin is to lament that she ever created man. Man's perversity has indeed rent Nature's garment, but this is man's fault not Nature's. Furthermore, Genius' role as a shrift-father is somewhat bizarre. He has no authority, other than Nature's, yet it is this same Nature whose non-sin he absolves. Once again the testimony of the iconography is striking. Both D. W. Robertson and Rosemond Tuve have drawn attention to the fact that the illustrators of the *Roman* commonly represent this confession in a way which makes it clear they regarded it as a hollow form.[25] The altars in Nature's cathedral are adorned not with the emblems of Christ's passion, promises of absolving grace, but with little pagan idols, the vain stone images of idolaters and those outside the realm of grace.

But why should Jean de Meun present a spectacle of Nature making a "confession" which is not a confession of a "sin" which is not a sin to a "confessor" who is not a confessor? The "confession" is neither an empty charade nor self-indulgent poetic cuteness. It strikingly brings home the theological truth that Nature, *per se*, is outside the realm of grace which the sacrament of penance pre-eminently represents in the Christian system. Nature is of the flesh, not the spirit; Genius can assign her no penance other

[25] Robertson, *Preface to Chaucer*, p. 200; Tuve, *Allegorical Imagery*, p. 268.

than her old accustomed tasks, just as *concupiscentia naturalis* can urge men only to the "old" works of the Old Man. The confession scene, with its obvious and comic burlesque elements, thus reinforces the point about the insufficiencies of "natural" behavior which Lady Nature has already clearly if obliquely stated herself.

The parody comes close to getting out of hand in the passage in which the god of Love dresses Genius up as a bishop. Genius is supposed to give the definitive statement to the god of Love and his men, but Fig. 37 makes it plain who is really in charge. *Cucullus non facit monachum*; neither can Cupid consecrate bishops. But Genius, like Faussemblant, is Protean. No wonder Venus laughs out loud—would that more of Jean's readers would join her! For the studied buffoonery of this scene there is a parallel in the ribaldries of the Feast of Fools, when a "boy bishop" or "fool bishop," often accompanied by a so-called "Prince d'Amour," was formally installed in the episcopal *cathedra*.[26] There is no general scholarly agreement as to what these parodic ceremonies were intended to accomplish, aside from providing a dramatic representation of misrule and thus obscurely promoting the development of the vernacular theater. In any case, Genius' claim to episcopal vestments and authority is about as great as that of the choir-boy chosen to be the boy bishop.

Genius' authority did not, apparently, seem definitive to many illustrators of the manuscripts. For example, the treatment of Genius in the lavish Harley MS 4425 in the British Museum is entirely comical; robed in splendid episcopal paraphernalia, he reads the definitive sentence from a scaffold made of wine barrels (Fig. 39). Miss Tuve aptly remarks: "The kegs on which his temporary platform is supported, and the character of his auditory, are enough to tell us whether this illustrator thought Genius' sermon and his pardon in the text was to be read as a serious revelation of the nature of love according to divine intentions."[27] The joke implied by such iconographic wit is the subject of a popular medieval proverb of classical origin—"Without Bacchus, Venus grows cold." In this specific instance, it is very probable that the illustrator found precise iconographic inspiration in

[26] P. L. Jacob, *Curiosités de l'histoire de France* (Paris, 1858), pp. 14-15, 25.
[27] *Allegorical Imagery*, p. 257n. and Fig. 94.

Horace (*Ars poetica*, ll. 208ff.), where the decadence of the custom of propitiating Genius with wine is lamented.[28]

One of the points made by Robertson needs to be stressed, and that is that Lady Nature does not exemplify "wrong" attitudes, merely inadequate and irrelevant ones. So far as man is concerned, the inadequacies of her views can be redeemed by his divine gift of Reason and by supernatural grace, so that as long as he behaves reasonably he can, so to speak, mend the tear he has made in Nature's garment. It is perfectly possible for Lady Nature to work together with a symphony of theological virtues, as in Alain, or walk in step with Reason and Pallas Athena as in the *Echecs Amoureux*. In Jean's poem, of course, Amant obstinately rejects Reason, who alone can correctly and authoritatively define his proper relation to Nature. She is, in effect, left alone at her forge, while Jean's poem satirically explores the frightening implications of a loveless slavery to *natura vitiata*. Yet while Jean could realize a modest comic potential in Lady Nature's prolix femininity, he does not cease to respect her greatly and to see in her, damaged as she is, the majesty of the divine Creator. He sees no such majesty in her chaplain, Genius, who is both a fraud and a buffoon.

Lest this last statement be misinterpreted, or seem to contradict what I have said earlier, it needs qualification. Genius in the *Roman de la Rose* represents *naturalis concupiscentia* or what the *Echecs* gloss calls *l'inclination general*. This natural concupiscence or inclination, as Lady Reason pointed out, is a post-lapsarian necessity; it urges man to perpetuate the race. In *De planctu naturae*, where Genius works hand in hand with a Nature informed by Reason, he stays strictly within the bounds of his modest authority, and can be said to "do good." But in himself he is neither good nor bad, but the motivating force of the neutral *amour naturelle* described by Lady Reason: the *primus motus* of sensuality considered generically. The most influential moral theologians of the Middle Ages, of course, tended to speak of man's sensuality as, at best, a frequent embarrassment, and many Augustinians associated sexual concupiscence with a "morbid quality." Genius is the badge of man's fallen stature, and even the sensual joys of sexual intercourse he promises are imperfect vestiges of the sexual delights man anciently enjoyed in Paradise

[28] See the *Scholia*, IV, ed. Botschuyver, 470-71.

when his sexual motivation was totally reasonable.[29] It is true that Lady Reason speaks of Genius as having the power of excommunication (as in *De planctu*), but this power has been misinterpreted. Genius excommunicates those guilty of the *peccatum contra naturam*, homosexuals chiefly, whose sexual concupiscence leads them to "unnatural" acts from which generation cannot possibly result; his pretensions to "excommunicate" anybody else must be looked upon with grave suspicion, and, indeed, all his operations need careful rational direction. It is precisely this direction which he lacks in the *Roman*. Genius becomes a buffoon when he is elevated to the seat of authority repeatedly denied to his proper mistress, Lady Reason, when man's lowest faculty supplants his highest. He becomes a fraud when, unguided by Reason, he makes promises in the name of Nature which can only be made on the authority of divine grace through the Passion of Jesus Christ.

The parodic context established, we may move on to Genius' sermon itself. Jean has prepared us for comedy and ironic inadequacy in Genius' pontifical pronouncements, not a serious, coherent, intellectually respectable system of theological schema; and his performance is equal to the promise. Professor Robertson has aptly characterized the sermon as "an elaboration of the counsel of Gen. 1. 28: 'Increase and multiply,' " in which "Genius sticks to the letter."[30] Genius, like Amis, La Vieille, and above all the Lover himself, is unregenerately carnal and literal, and his fantastic speech is Jean's most robust exemplification of the principle that the letter slayeth—a principle, incidentally, which should govern the scholarly search for Jean's *significatio* in the concluding major speeches of the *Roman*. The document which Genius reads from his little pulpit reveals an immediate confusion: it begins as a sweeping sentence of excommunication and becomes, within a sentence, an equally broad plenary pardon. On the "authority of Nature" Genius first excommunicates those who are

---

[29] Thus Ulrich of Strassburg: ". . . potius tanto maior fuisset illa delectatio quam nunc sit, quantum natura fuit perfectior; sed fuisset sine deformitate deordinationis hominis et suffactionis rationis, quam nunc habet, quia ratio totum quod fuit in homine, sub pleno dominio habuisset." See Wilhelm Breuning, *Erhebung und Fall des Menschen nach Ulrich von Strassburg* (Trier, 1959), p. 231.

[30] *Preface to Chaucer*, p. 201.

traitors to her works, then promises that all who loyally persevere in her works will wear floral chaplets in Paradise. The metaphors used here are ecclesiastical; they make reference to the institutional church. But, as we have just seen, Nature has small authority over the human race redeemed by grace—a grace of which the reader is forcibly reminded by the talk of pardons—and Genius has even less than Nature. For him to suddenly publish a broad excommunication is startling; but to promise Paradise, inhabited by a Church Triumphant dressed up to look like Oiseuse and Venus, is preposterous.

The confused viewpoint from which Genuis propounds his "theology" is immediately established. Those who do not properly use their sexual organs—here referred to, after Alain but with a new coarseness, as "plows" and "furrows" among other things—are traitors to Nature in her struggle against Death. If all mankind remained virgins for a mere sixty years, the race would die out. Genius is decorously terrified at such a prospect since, while he can pretend to distribute supernatural and eternal rewards, he in fact knows nothing outside the realm of nature: so far as he is concerned, God's greatest purpose for mankind is indefinite physical perpetuation. Any man who does not actively work toward this purpose is, in Genius' view, an outlaw. Now such a limited vision of man's place in God's plan can make no room for the operations of divine grace, and Jean immediately makes it his poetic strategy to probe this inadequacy. Genius states quite overtly that he cannot understand grace. If anyone were to say to him that chastity may be a gift of divine grace (ll. 19599ff.), he would simply not know how to respond. He must leave all that, he says, to the "masters of theology." There are, of course, no masters of theology among his little congregation, only the forces of carnal license who have installed him as a puppet bishop and who are only too happy to have the spurious authority he can lend their devious plot; so no one asks any questions. But the unanswered question of master Jean de Meun and his attentive readers remains to vitiate Genius' arguments and expose their damning theological insufficiencies. Chaucer may have had this comic passage in mind when, in a similar context, he described the Wife of Bath's complacent ignorance of the meaning of Christ's words to the Samaritan woman: "What that he mente therby I can nat seyn!" The Oldness of nature cannot understand the Newness of grace.

There is some witty play made of Pauline doctrines of grace in what follows. To condemn those who follow Orpheus, homosexuals or *peccatores contra naturam*, is one thing; to condemn those who abstain from the works of Nature for whatever reason is something else. But Genius lumps them all together under one bitter excommunication, announcing that such criminals against natural concupiscence should be brutally emasculated, their chaste members torn from their bodies. That is, Genius counsels the creation of a new caste of eunuchs; all those who, for one reason or another, refuse "naturally" to use their physical organs of generation deserve to lose them. Eunuchry is a moral category, the stigma of those who violate the commandment of "Increase and multiply." Likewise Christ speaks of eunuchry as a moral state, but of course he speaks figuratively rather than literally when he speaks of eunuchs "which have made themselves eunuchs for the kingdom of heaven's sake" (Matthew 19:12). Such eunuchs are, in Pauline terms, those who have put away "the works of the flesh" for the "works of the spirit," who have "crucified the Old Man." The passage in Matthew is frequently adduced by monastic writers of the Middle Ages, among others, to argue the superiority of the state of chastity, but the "spiritual eunuch" is really a poetic concept, a part of the rich vocabulary of metaphoric oldness and newness to which Christian writers from the time of St. Paul turned in their efforts to give account of the mysteries of grace. In the iconographic details of the portrait of his unspeakable pardoner, as well as in the spiritual themes of the Pardoner's Tale, Chaucer plays with the implications of such eunuchry in a most satisfying way, possibly taking his lead from Jean de Meun. As is typically true of scriptural imagery, the poetic potentialities of eunuchry arise from the distinction between letter and spirit. Genesis 1:28 ("Increase and multiply"), the Wife of Bath's favorite Biblical text, had a paramount spiritual, as opposed to literal, meaning for Christians living under grace. Spiritual increase could refer to the extension of the Church or the nurture of virtues in the individual. Those who make of themselves eunuchs for the sake of the kingdom of God are, by a superficial paradox, spiritually very fruitful. On the other hand,

slavish abandon to the works of the flesh, which can literally ful-
fill the injunction of Genesis 1:28, indicates a kind of spiritual
sterility or eunuchry. In the schematic theology of Genius' tidy
inversions, the poetic image of the spiritual eunuch is neatly
reversed as letter triumphs over spirit.

In evaluating the speeches of Lady Nature and Genius it must
be constantly remembered that their principles of natural sexual-
ity become troublesome only when applied to cases outside their
competence. Such cases are admittedly very numerous since, for
Christians, human sexuality was qualified by a supernatural reve-
lation. For Genius to excommunicate Sodomites is permissible and
decorous; for him to publish a manifesto by which Jesus Christ
and all the doctors of the Church for a thousand years merit brutal
emasculation and eternal damnation is fantastic beyond blasphemy.
The logic of *natura vitiata* can be so quickly reduced to absurdity
because its dynamic force is the obsolete principle which is the
next subject in Genius' sermon: the imperative to combat Death.
In accordance with the legislative *detritus* of the age between
Adam and Moses, when Death reigned, Genius exhorts his follow-
ers to sexual heroics; his exhortation is comically undercut by epic
agricultural metaphors taken from *De planctu naturae* and blown
up for parodic purposes. The comedy of this passage is very broad
indeed; it is that of the coarser fabliaux. Yet it will probably
escape us if we bring to it the high seriousness and solemnity about
the functional aspects of the sex act which are characteristic of
some influential modern novelists. The comparison of sexual inter-
course in its various minutiae with the labors of plowing a field is
not particularly "profound" or "reverent," but it is rather funny.
Jean, after all, while he may have believed that faith could move
mountains, probably did not know that copulation could make the
earth move. Love's barons must plow, says Genius, to battle
Death. "You have only one enemy, and you are attacked on only
one side." It is in such ludicrous *sententiae* as this that the enthusi-
astic explorers of medieval "naturalism" would find the meaning
of Jean's *Roman*. Poor Jean; can he really have been so simple,
or so ignorant that he had never heard of the world, the flesh,
and the devil? One must wonder what St. Paul, or the author of
the *Enchiridion*, would have made of the assertion that man's
only enemy is Death. Venus and Cupid, listening to this new

213

gospel with rapt attention, would of course be greatly relieved by such intelligence, since most medieval preachers seemed of the opinion that man had a number of enemies (usually reckoned at seven) among whom they themselves were included.

In the first part of Genius' sermon Jean de Meun's chief poetic technique is parodic inversion. Man's fallen nature reclaims the domains which, in Christian theology, it has yielded to grace, establishing a burlesque revealed religion whose topsy-turvy institutions reflect the logical absurdities of such an inversion. Probably the most extravagant parody in the entire poem is the passage in which Genius, man's *naturalis concupiscentia*, offers the key to the Christian Paradise to all those who follow his lead. That this fantastic hoax should seem convincing to the Lover and his friends, sworn enemies of Reason, is perhaps understandable; that it should also mislead a small army of modern scholars is a cruel exposure of the helplessness of academic philology before the elementary techniques of medieval allegory. There can be no doubt that, according to the letter of the text, Genius offers the free gift of Heaven to all those who energetically indulge in sexual intercourse and preach its energetic indulgence (ll. 19932ff.). Of course Genius has no authority to offer Heaven to anyone, though his proper and blameless function is to incite men to natural sexual intercourse. Presumably, then, the kind of elementary statement with which a literary critic can begin his analysis of this passage will be to the effect that Genius, a character in a dramatic poem, is pursuing his decorous office but comically attempting to exceed his authority. Instead, quite surprisingly, we read that the passage principally illustrates the influence of Averroism on Jean de Meun.

Jean's supposed Averroism is perhaps the most depressing of recent critical misapprehensions about the *Roman*, and I should have liked to avoid the subject altogether. However, since it has been the object of a good deal of serious-minded and historically oriented scholarship, particularly in the sadly misconceived books of Gérard Paré, and since it is now frequently featured in popular accounts of the *Roman* to provide an "historical background" for the most improbable opinions there ascribed to Jean, the question cannot be entirely ignored. The problem, or rather pseudo-problem, is this: in 1277, Etienne Tempier, Bishop of Paris, condemned a long list of heretical theological statements formulated as propositions for debate in the University. His letter of condemnation, preserved in the university *chartularium*, has long been regarded as among the most important documents for the history of medieval philosophy, since the extensiveness of the list —219 propositions, covering an enormous range of subject matter sublime and ridiculous—attests to the deep penetration of radical Aristotelian method into the arts faculty. The importance of the condemnations for the study of the *Roman de la Rose* is much less clear. Although there are absolutely no specific points of reference between the document in the *chartularium* and Jean's text, the condemnations have repeatedly been adduced to demonstrate the influence of Averroism on the poet. Furthermore, it has been maintained that in the condemnations Tempier was, in spirit if not in letter, censuring the *Roman*.[31] This very serious misconception provides no illuminating "historical background," merely another critical stumbling-block. It seems to grow out of the correct perception that a few of the condemned propositions, three or four out of two hundred odd, do vaguely correspond with ideas which can be extracted from Genius' sermon. Taken, in the accepted fashion, as Jean's own ideas, these few propositions have been produced to prove that the poet, if not an Averroist himself, is dangerously tarred with the Averroist brush. The most apparently relevant propositions are three: number 168 in Tempier's list ("Quod continentia non est essentialiter virtus"); number 169 ("Quod perfecta abstinentia ab actu carnis corrumpit virtutem et speciem"); and number 183 ("Quod simplex fornicatio utpote soluti cum soluta, non est peccatum"). The 183rd proposition in particular has been the subject of lively interest. No one in the *Roman* actually maintains such a position, of course, and the very term *fornicatio* is part of a moral vocabulary outside the ken of

---

[31] For example, see Peter Dronke, *Medieval Latin and the Rise of the European Love Lyric* (Oxford, 1965), I, 80-83. The passage from Lady Reason's speech (ll. 4403-4420) adduced by Dronke to illustrate the Aristotelian doctrine of the "eternity of the species" does not illustrate it, but offers an Augustinian explanation for the origin of concupiscence. The idea that Jean "ran the danger of ecclesiastical condemnation" (Dunn, p. xxvi) is perhaps suggested by analogy by A. J. Denomy, "The *De Amore* of Andreas Capellanus and the Condemnation of 1277," *Mediaeval Studies*, VIII (1946), 107-49. See further, *Romance Philology*, XVIII (1965), 430ff.

Lady Nature, who does not follow St. Paul in listing it among the vices of men. Nonetheless, Genius' pardon is based on the supposition that frequent and apparently indiscriminate use of the sexual organs for the purpose of generation is a universal duty; and the *vetula* says that Nature excuses adultery. There is at least a tenuous link between proposition 183 and the text of Jean's poem, and there may be similar connections with others. It is quite possible to believe that some of the Paris propositions provide analogues, or even sources, for ideas which Jean presents as parodies of Christian theology. But to deduce from this very unsurprising discovery that Jean de Meun is advancing Averroistic ideas in the *Roman*, or that the poem is one of the unspecified objects of Tempier's condemnations, is both sloppy history and sloppy criticism.

Students of the *Roman* have been asking the wrong questions about the condemnations of 1277. It is not astonishing, after all, that a thirteenth-century bishop should maintain that fornication is a sin. What is of considerable interest is that he should find it expedient to condemn the formal airing of a purely academic and theoretical proposition put forward by a number of the soundest theologians of the later Middle Ages. There can be absolutely no doubt that in the academic theology of the thirteenth and fourteenth centuries scholars were constantly maintaining the proposition that simple fornication is not a deadly sin—as a straw man for Catholic rebuttal. The *quaestio* "Utrum fornicatio simplex sit peccatum mortale" certainly was not new in 1277. It appears, for example, in William of Auxerre's early thirteenth-century *Summa aurea*, a pioneering Aristotelian commentary on the *Sentences*. William poses the question—Is simple fornication a deadly sin? —and supplies a number of negative arguments, the most modern of which is that in sexual intercourse for the sake of generation (*causa prolis*) no one is injured; indeed such intercourse *multiplicat et populum*, and is therefore no sin.[32] Of course William's refutation of his own Socratic arguments is massive and it turns out, probably not even to Bishop Tempier's surprise, that simple fornication is a deadly sin, that it is contrary to natural reason, that it turns what should be the temple of God into the temple of the devil, and that it injures God. Tempier's condemnations

---

[32] *Summa aurea* (Paris, 1500), fol. 287ʳ.

did not inhibit Simon Hinton from positing the arguments of both Genius and La Vieille before demolishing them. Fornication "is a natural act, and a natural act is not a sin"; furthermore, "coitus is necessary for the preservation of the race."[33] Hervé Nedellec also debates the *quaestio*;[34] but its most popular discussion in the fourteenth century must have been that in the Sapiential commentary of Holkot, one of the "bestsellers of the age."[35] These texts, chosen more or less at random for the sake of illustration, could be multiplied; proposition 183 was clearly something of a commonplace.

Why, then, did Tempier take alarm? This is a question which has occupied a number of scholars far more competent than I to deal with it, and I do not pretend that the following remarks are anything but superficial; still, some explanation must be attempted. Tempier was probably shocked by the academic tendency, encouraged by Averroism but by no means peculiar to it, to indulge in purely theoretical formulations seemingly "true according to philosophy" without reconciling them with the truths of faith. It is possible, though unlikely, that University men were arguing the proposition that fornication is not a sin totally without reference to those arguments which William of Auxerre and Holkot used to demolish it. If so, the bishop's wrath is understandable; the penitential handbooks of the later Middle Ages make it clear that it was considered a sin for a scholar knowingly to argue against the truth without ostentatiously losing the argument.[36] But it also seems likely that the vagaries of intellectual style were in play; Tempier probably found some ideas so abhorrent, or so dangerously misleading, that it was wrong to discuss them at all. Looking back on the rich blossoming of scholastic philosophy in the thirteenth century, when so many brilliant minds labored so earnestly and fruitfully to accommodate the exciting new intellectual possibilities of Aristotelianism with the cherished

[33] "The 'Exceptiones' from the 'Summa' of Simon Hinton," *Angelicum*, XIII (1936), 312.

[34] *Quodlibet* vii, 23; see P. Glorieux, *La littérature quodlibétique de 1260 à 1320* (Kain, 1925), I, p. 206.

[35] *Lectio* xxi; Holkot's discussion arises in the context of an explanation of the iconological significance of roses. See Robertson, *Preface to Chaucer*, p. 306.

[36] St. Antonius of Florence, *Summa confessionum seu interrogatorium pro simplicibus confessoribus* (Monte Regali, 1472), cap. c.xxxv.

faith of their fathers, we rightly regard the period as one of the most glorious in the intellectual history of the West. It is possible, however, to maintain another view; and many thinkers, from William of Saint-Amour to Erasmus have found the episode a dull one when "all true Diuinitie yeelded to Sophistrie, and *Paul* to *Aristotle.*" The condemnations of 1277 seem to me to reflect that medieval anti-intellectualism impatient with the techniques of *scientia,* which can avoid and sometimes contradict *sapientia.*

Jean de Meun nowhere exhibits the intellectual tendencies to which Bishop Tempier probably objected; nor do the theologians from whom he takes his controlling ideas and themes in the *Roman*—St. Paul, St. Augustine, and the Blessed Alain de Lille. The arguments of La Vieille, Genius, and others in Amours' camp are not presented by Jean as being "true according to philosophy." Rather they are presented by him, in varying degrees of transparency, as sophistical in technique and comic in content, ruthlessly exposed by doctrines clearly enunciated in the poem by Lady Reason, whom both Jean and Guillaume de Lorris before him associated with Divine Sapience. This is not Averroism: it is comic poetry. To search for Jean's Averroism is to chase a ghost; the searchers have found nothing substantial, but they have raised enough dust to obscure the real importance of the condemnations of 1277, and of the wider context of Scholasticism generally, for the *Roman.* In Jean's poem there are those who argue *quod sic,* others *quod non.* All arguments are not of equal weight, and their adjudication is not confined to a solipsistic world of unadorned intellect.

Genius' pardon neither formally confronts nor contradicts any principle of Christian theology; it merely formulates, in a self-mocking parody, a number of "laws" which ignore the Christian revelation. It is true, of course, that the formulation of Averroist arguments which appear "true according to philosophy" reveals accidental similarities to Jean's poetic method—and this no doubt bears looking into—but as a literary device Jean's method long antedates any localized philosophical episode of the thirteenth century. Jean was not even the first major poet to write a satire against the folly and evil of men's disingenuous appeal to the law of Genius; Bernard of Cluny is as close to Jean as is the Paris *chartularium*:

218

Nam meretricia nosse cubilia gens putat aequum;
Lex genii jubet, inquit, ut hic cubet, illaque secum.
Cur etenim data foemina vel sata, ni patiatur?
Sexus id imperat, inquit, ut haec ferat, ille feratur.
Quomodo prandia sic meretricia proba licere
Gens putat ebria, scilicet inscia se cohibere.[37]

Critics who have sought to find the central meaning of Jean's poem in a paraphrase of the literal claims of Genius' pardon, the claims of the "text itself," have indeed "reinterpreted" the *Roman*; and the critical enormity of which they stand convicted is compounded rather than mitigated by a pseudo-historical appeal to the supposed sexual mysteries of Chartrian Platonism or Parisian Aristotelianism. Jean de Meun had at his disposal neither the ideas nor the vocabulary of his latter-day, *soi-disant* defenders and admirers. Chancellor Jean Gerson and Professor Norman Cohn share, apparently, a similar view of Jean's attitude toward the authority of Genius' pardon; but what Professor Cohn calls the "world-view of a thirteenth-century Parisian intellectual" Chancellor Gerson calls the "dream of the Old Man." Gerson has at any rate the virtue of speaking a language which Jean de Meun would have understood. Our thirteenth-century intellectual displays a rigorous mind, and his poem invites a rigorous and logical analysis. If Jean de Meun really thought that the *lex genii*, or "law of the members," was the supreme, authoritative, and definitive divine teaching on love, this belief would mean nothing else than that he considered the claims of nature greater than those of grace, that the Incarnation of God and His death on the Cross, as also the teachings and the sacraments of the Church to which Jean offered up his book, are of less authority as guides to human conduct than the natural inclination observable in any Duroc hog. Although there are a great many people today who believe in the superior authority of nature, in thirteenth-century Christendom there were not very many. That Jean was among whatever few, if any, there may have been I strenuously doubt; but if I am mistaken, I maintain a final request. It surely is wrong to applaud Jean de Meun with the self-flattering accolade of mod-

[37] *De contemptu mundi*, ed. Thomas Wright in *The Anglo-Latin Satirical Poets and Epigrammatists of the Twelfth Century* (London, 1872), II, 55.

ernity if the ideas which he advances are those which Christian writers for more than a thousand years had considered old, archaic, and reactionary.

Genius peddles shoddy goods, not divine dispensations, but his sermon does offer some serious and literally accurate statements about Amant's condition. Specifically, he offers a clear explication of the significance of the Golden Age, a theme which has haunted Jean's poem, and he offers a valuable iconographic analysis of the garden, considered *in bono* and *in malo*; that is, he delineates "the hell of the wicked and the heaven of the just." There is nothing surprising or artistically disturbing in the fact that Genius, the fake pardoner, can offer valuable commentary to profound Christian truths. In the *Canterbury Tales*, at the end of the Pardoner's prologue, Chaucer's most notable *in malo*, spiritual eunuch opines that Christ's pardon is best, even as, with excited cupidity, he urges his fellow pilgrims to come up and kiss his fraudulent relics. One may know what crown jewels look like without being a king. Genius cannot be expected to be responsive to the spiritual implications of such concepts as original justice, but he is sound enough on the literal details of the Golden Age or the Park of Paradise—that is, the literary integuments which clothe such a concept.

Genius offers Paradise to all who follow him. That it is Christian heaven there can be no doubt; the imagery is uncomfortably moist, as in some of the friars' lyrics, but the elaborate metaphors of sheep-life develop unmistakably the idea of Christ as the Agnus Dei and the souls of the blessed as God's flock. This paradise, this park of the Good Shepherd, is illuminated, says Genius, by light even more pure than that of the Golden Age, before Jupiter cut off Saturn's genitals. He then proceeds to gloss the story of the violent end of the Golden Age in a disturbingly literal way, using it as an illustration of the evils of castration and as a pretext to make some unflattering remarks about eunuchs. It is presumably this passage which suggested to Alan Gunn that Jean must have used the example of the castration of Saturn as a kind of fertility myth. "This is a parable of the doctrine that the loss of the organs of reproduction, the means by which the race is replenished and the bounty of God poured out over the world, is the greatest calamity that can befall man, whether considered individually or collectively."[38] This is not only strange doctrine, one must remark, but it is strangely illustrated by the castration of Saturn, the fruitful result of which was the birth of Venus (Fig. 33) and, with her, all the throbbing sexuality which Gunn associates with the "bounty of God." The New Testament makes it reasonably clear that it is not less calamitous for a man to go to hell with all his members intact than to heaven with a few lopped off; and the general calamities of the expulsion from Eden and the Flood, brought about because of lechery, are presumably as great as any the race could fear.

There is, furthermore, excellent evidence earlier in the poem to suggest that a literal interpretation of the myth may be foolish, for it was over the very word *coilles* in this same story that Lady Reason and the Lover quarreled. Lady Reason maintained that the word, like the myth, was meant to be understood in "another sense." Amant's complacent ignorance of the meaning of "metaphors," his inability to see that the carnal text can yield a moral sense, is shown to be as fatuous as his squeamishness and hypocritical clean speech. Genius, unlike Amant, is not a morally responsible, reasonable agent. He is rather a personification of a natural inclination which is old, carnal, and literal. It is therefore merely simple poetic decorum that his sermon should be a literal development of a sacred text and that his interpretation of classical myth should similarly be literal. Yet just below the literal cortex of Genius' talk of feminine habits and eunuchs lie those spiritual concepts made new by St. Paul. As Robertson puts it, "Genius is not grace; he is merely the inclination of created things to act naturally. . . . ideas like the mortification of the flesh, the crucifixion of the Old Man, or the value of the sacraments are completely beyond his ken."[39] That they remain beyond the ken of the Lover as well, that the spirit beyond the letter remains undeciphered, is what gives the *Roman de la Rose* the elevated stature of tragedy which complements the rich comedy of a boisterous satire.

After his digression on the subject of castration, Genius returns to the formal explication of the meaning of the Golden Age. Jupiter, taking no heed of the unspeakable cruelty of his enormous

[38] *Mirror of Love*, p. 258.
[39] *Preface to Chaucer*, p. 200.

crime, destroyed man's innocence with his rapacious blade. The Golden Age was over, and man's sad progress through the Age of Iron had begun. The controlling irony of Genius' explanation, taken as a whole, is that he himself is the first-fruit of Jupiter's unnatural act. He is the natural inclination with which man was burdened at the Fall—that is, at the end of the Golden Age, "as the poets feign." It is accordingly not very surprising that the iconographic characteristics of Jupiter's brave new world make it seem strikingly similar to the Garden of Deduit. Jupiter's first law for his New Order was that all men should live in idleness and follow pleasure (ll. 20095ff.), which is the same as to say that they should join in the merry dance with Oiseuse and Deduit. Genius then lists the sad sophistications introduced by Jupiter, closely following Vergil in the first book of the *Georgics*: Jupiter is responsible for the introduction of plowing, for poisonous snakes and ravening wolves, for numbering and naming the stars, and for the complicated paraphernalia of the chase. "In short," says Genius, "Jupiter changed what was good to bad, and what was bad to worse."

The Valencia artist conceives of the world under Jupiter's rule as an elaborate hunting scene (Fig. 38). The game here is not the rabbit of the text, but other *fugaces*: at the left a stag, already torn by the hounds, and at the right waterfowl. This is also, of course, an accurate iconographic *paysage* from Amant's world, the world of the cony catcher; likewise the technique of plowing invented by Jupiter ironically qualifies the enthusiastic "plowing" which Genius urges on the animal world of Nature. Love's barons who attend with strict attention the homily of Genius in Fig. 39 are in effect the progeny of those happy ancients in Fig. 38 who listen with equal pleasure to the ban proclaiming indiscriminate delight. But while Genius himself is totally amoral he knows (rather than understands) that the path of mythography leads very quickly to Christian morality, so he also knows that the likely consequence of following the dispensation of Jupiter is eternal damnation in a hell which is the negation of the Good Shepherd's Paradise. Jean's eschatology commands but a few brief lines in an enormous poem, but it captured the imaginations of his earliest readers. The illustrators seize upon it (as in Fig. 7), and his commentators would seem to have regarded it as intimately connected

222

with his *sententia*. Laurent de Premierfait compared the *Roman* to the *Divine Comedy* in its treatment of heaven and hell, and the *Echecs* gloss links Jean's poem to the great mainstream of medieval moral allegory flowing from the *Somnium Scipionis* on account of its exploration of the last things. However imbalanced such judgments may seem to us, they reflect an important truth about the *Roman*: to wit, that the "life of love" there analyzed is not a psychological or emotional phenomenon exempt from the scrutiny of schematic theology by reason of its subtlety, mystery, or this-worldly values, but a moral operation subject to moral analysis and moral judgment.

As Jean approaches the end of his great work, he presents a tidy collation of its principal icons considered, in the manner of St. Paul, *in bono* and *in malo*. Genius schematically contrasts the Garden of Deduit, its landscape and its pleasures, with the heavenly garden to which it stands "as a fable does to truth." Here, if not in the poem's earlier contrasts of the well of life and its carbuncle with Narcissus' well of death and its deceptive crystals, Jean lays bare the neatly welded seams which join his own work so snugly with Guillaume's that, iconographically, it seems *tout un*. Jean promised to gloss the Lover's dream, and make clear what had been dark; and in this passage he probably thought he had done so by returning with Amant to retrace the steps which first took him to the wicker *guichet*, the bright carol, and the perilous fountain. Amant was hardly into his dream before he came to a painted river for a stage setting, a praeternatural stream, "cold as any welle," in which he refreshed himself. Twenty thousand lines later the reader learns what the illustrators already knew (Figs. 3, 40), that the source of this stream is Narcissus' well, and that it offers no refreshment. What Ovid said of Narcissus, Guillaume obliquely said of Amant: "Dumque sitim sedare cupit, sitis altera crevit." For the authors of the *Roman* and for their audience, for all who mined the Egyptian gold of the *Metamorphoses*, this statement was rich ore; the "divine Ovid" adumbrates in his characterization of the pool of Narcissus the spiritual qualities of Jacob's well, where Christ encountered the woman of Samaria—"Whosoever drinketh of this water shall thirst again" (John 4:13)—and where Chaucer, in another way, encountered the Wife of Bath. Here, late in the *Roman*, Genius once again

223

picks up Guillaume's Ovidian imagery to coax Christian *sententia* from it. The fountain in Deduit's garden is but a vain and illusory imitation of the *fons aquae vitae* in the heavenly garden of the Trinity in the Canticles and the Apocalypse. The first fountain makes live men dead, the other dead men live: "Cele les vis de mort enivre, / Mais cete fait les morz revivre." Those who drink from the well of the carbuncle "shall never thirst again."

The scholarly explanations for Genius' ruthless exposure of the Garden of Deduit have been peculiarly ingenious and unconvincing. C. S. Lewis claims that Jean's abrupt appeal to ultimate reality is a way of fobbing off the "courtly love" which Guillaume de Lorris had set out to explore; Gérard Paré, who considers Jean an "anti-Guillaume" in all respects, plays a variation on this theme. In fact, Genius does no more than subject Guillaume's garden to the kind of iconographic analysis it invites. The schematic contrasts of *terrenus* and *caelestis* which emerge provide a useful recapitulation of the chief Pauline themes of Genius' sermon taken as a whole. Genius, like Chaucer's fraudulent pardoner after him, is in effect saying that Christ's pardon is best. This does not mean that he ceases to be a fake or gives up the attempt to dole out his pardons. As a matter of fact, in the immediately succeeding lines he repeats his preposterous offer in slightly altered terms. But Genius remains—insofar as he "is" anywhere—smack in the middle of Deduit's garden, preaching to the god of Love and his mother, together with the whole army of Love's barons whose business is the prosecution of the "love affair" which began when Amant gazed with fascination into the *miroir périlleux*.

The principal characteristic of the world in which Amant moves is not courtliness but disorder. The claims of passion rank higher than those of reason, and the elaborate stage set prepared by Guillaume de Lorris lies littered with the smashed fragments of the hierarchical structures of marriage, grace and nature, and the spiritual and the literal, which provided the ordering principles for Jean's world. With specific reference to Genius' episcopacy, his sermon, and his pardons, it must be remembered that his authority comes from Nature, not from the Christian Church; and, in the context of Jean's poem, even Nature's authority has been appropriated by Venus and Amours for private and eccentric purposes. Genius is a "bishop of their opinion," and his congregation cares not a feather for the views of all the saints and councils for a thousand years: they are little disposed to abandon the chase with the quarry in sight and the hounds frantically baying. They seek a literal and carnal pardon, a scrap of paper, not spiritual understanding. Hence, they have absolutely no interest in adjudicating the enormous contradictions implicit in his sermon. If Genius' purpose in the divine order is to furnish a *carte blanche* for irrational passion, then it is quite likely that loyal subjection to the laws of the Iron Age promises a rebirth of the Age of Gold, or that to drink of the well of death is a foretaste of the *fons aquae vitae*; for this is precisely what it means for Genius to promise heaven to his followers.

It may be that Jean's method is here too bold; certainly the most serious misunderstandings of his poem, from the time of Gerson up to our own, spring from the intricacies of his handling of Nature and Genius. But if Jean is at fault, he is generously at fault, for he has assumed that his audience will have the learning and the literary sensitivity, not to mention the sense of humor, to follow his text with both laughter and logic. His poem makes the reader do some hard thinking about difficult Christian concepts such as love, nature, and grace. Since the principal theoretical works on Christian allegory, such as *De doctrina christiana,* the Introduction to the *Anticlaudianus,* and Boccaccio's *Genealogia* agree that a chief purpose of allegorical indirection is to conceal sacred truths from swinish dullards and to offer difficult labors of cerebration to make more pleasurable the discovery of sweet truths, Jean's apparent obscurity may be considered a virtue. Jean presumably hoped there would be few among his audience like Amant, who thought poetic metaphors mere foolishness.

William of Conches says of Genius or natural concupiscence that "whatever he judges to be good, whether it is or no, he desires." Genius' opinions are strong, but his judgment erratic. This is not, as we have seen, his fault; "he is merely the inclination of created things to act naturally." Love's barons, of whom Amant is one, have no such extenuation, for they have available to them channels of supernatural grace and the importunate faculty of Reason. But they, too, greatly desire what they judge to be good, whether it be or no. The pontifical sermon done, Jean's little religious parody comes to an end with one of his finest shots:

Genius throws down his "candle," the breaking of which betokens the severance of excommunication. The perfumed smoke spreads through his whole congregation, leaving its odor in the "bodies, hearts, and thoughts" of the ladies. The bishop's candle, its fire lit from Venus' lantern, thus generates a good deal of heat, if not much light. "Amen, Amen," shout Love's barons with enthusiasm not unlike that with which the Norman knights are said to have greeted the preaching of the Crusade, "Fiat! Fiat!" *Deus (naturae) vult.*

Love's carnal crusaders, spiritually armed for their battle and fired by Venus' candle, rush to the siege. The hot goddess herself stands at the castle gates, a harridan, screaming imprecations at its defenders. The revolution has come: Bel Accueil will be freed, and everyone, cleric or lay, will pick roses. Venus' description of the Utopian new day, when the old morality will be turned upside down, defines the Misrule which logically results from Genius' episcopacy (ll. 20746ff.). The particular objects of her wrath are Reason's daughters, Fear and Shame, since, as Venus points out, anyone who listens to them will never follow *amour par amours.*[40]

The ancient rites of martial boasting duly performed, Venus sets about her work in earnest, draws her bow, and takes careful aim at the little arrow-slot below the torso of the graven image on the castle wall. The sudden appearance in the text of this image, not previously mentioned in the letter, is only superficially surprising. Amant's *passio* began with the contemplation of an image, that of a rosebud reflected in the pool of Narcissus; and the description of his behavior throughout the poem is the iconographic delineation of sexual idolatry. Here, in the advanced stages of "heroic love," the object of his attention becomes a literal idol. The essential stages of the psychological processes here described, as they were known to medieval theology, have been very convincingly dealt with by Professor Robertson;[41] so we may turn our attention immediately to the artistic devices which draw atten-

---

[40] The qualities represented by Fear and Shame, whose chief duties it is to arouse sluggish Danger, are not merely psychological characteristics peculiar to the lady in the "love story," but generalized tropological categories. Henry of Lancaster uses them, quite rightly, as the fear of hell and the shame of sin, *Livre de seyntz medicines,* pp. 60-61.

[41] *Preface to Chaucer,* pp. 100ff.

tion to the idolatrous implications of the literal fable. The image
is a somewhat unusual one, as Fig. 41, where the literal details of
the text are scrupulously honored, will attest. Jean's description
of the statue begins at the bottom, so to speak, and works up,
reversing the order of anatomical description favored by the
School of Chartres and recommended by medieval rhetoricians.
Amant begins with the "arrow-slot," which, whether he call it
rose or *relique*, is the single-minded object of his long pilgrimage.
This hole in the wall-tower is placed between two pillars or col-
umns of silver—obviously the idol's legs. Now I suspect that
what we have here is a kind of collage of imagery from the Canti-
cles where, in the passage in the fifth chapter which led Gerson
to contrast the dream of the Old Man with the dream of the New
Man, the Church announces to the "daughters of Jerusalem" that
she is "sick of love" (5:8). Her lover (Christ) "misit manum
suam per foramen, et venter meus intremuit ad tactum ejus"
(5:4). She goes on to describe her lover (from top to bottom,
incidentally), figuring his graces beneath the integuments of
sensuous detail. His legs, she says (5:15), are "columnae mar-
moreae, quae fundatae sunt super bases aureas"; and the image of
the pillars echoes that in 3:10 describing Solomon's chariot:
"Columnas ejus fecit argenteas." While these echoes and hints
do not constitute the kind of developed parody of the Canticles
documented elsewhere in vernacular literature, they are the
appropriate literary adornments of a description of the idol which,
for Amant, is both his god and his "sanctuary," both *sponsus* and
sponsa. The illustrators, who indifferently produced sometimes
silver pillars and sometimes stone ones, probably picked up the
reference. In any case, astride the pillars, and above the little
hole, is a graven image in silver; and since the Lover's pilgrimage
is not to Jerusalem but to Babylon, one may suspect that in its
consummate beauty it is similar to those images of silver which
the Scriptures compare with a menstruous rag (Isaiah 30:22). The
actual idol is then described by Amant in terms which closely
parallel his earlier description of Lady Reason (ll. 2978ff.),
which perforce reflects the description of Reason's iconographic
mother, Lady Philosophy; and, indeed, Amant tells us that there
is not a sanctuary more costly or precious this side of Constanti-
nople where, as some of his readers may have known, there was a

splendid sanctuary dedicated to Divine Sapience. It is this savorous shrine—not a "lady," not "love," and not an "entelechy"—which has for Amant displaced Christ, Lady Reason, and the Blessed Virgin. The battle for Jealousy's castle is another war of the *cunnus*.

The Ovidian story of the artist Pygmalion (*Metamorphoses*, X, 243ff.), which Jean de Meun uses as a kind of classical analogue and commentary to Amant's own iconophilia, is probably quite well known by most readers; yet the familiarity may be dangerous, so far as understanding its implications for the *Roman* is concerned. Jean had, no doubt, his Ovid "moralized," but he could not have had it moralized by Rousseau. While the mythographic interpretations of the story of Pygmalion in the Middle Ages show a marked variety, none shows any awareness that Ovid is concerned with the mysterious capacities of art or the unique aspirations and torments of the artist. As we shall see, there are a number of indications, textual, contextual, and iconographic, which suggest that Jean viewed the matter very much in the spirit of Arnulf of Orléans, the most important Ovidian mythographer whose work he could have known; but this is a conclusion dictated by the evidence of the poem, not an *a priori* assumption. It is quite possible to discern Jean's artistic purpose in the Pygmalion episode by seeing what he does to it "as a story." While he follows Ovid quite closely, he adds what Langlois called a number of "jolis développements" (indicated in the following summary by italics), which have not been sufficiently noticed.

Pygmalion was a famous carver who, to test his art and *to win great praise*, made an extraordinarily life-like and beautiful ivory statue of a woman. *Helen and Lavinia were not so good looking.* Pygmalion was so ecstatic when he looked at it *that he was unaware that Cupid had so enslaved him that he did not know what he was doing.* Pygmalion then delivers a long soliloquy which is entirely Jean's work:

I have never fallen in love with one of my images before. . . . I am the greatest fool in the world. This love does not come from Nature, who dishonored herself in creating me. But it isn't her fault; if I choose to love insanely, it is only my business. Still, even madder cases are on record, such as that of

228

Narcissus. I am less of a fool than he, for at least I am able to kiss my statue while he had only a shadow in the fountain.

Jean, but not Ovid, remarks on the peculiar symptoms of Pygmalion's mania: his disposition changes at each instant; he loves, he hates; he laughs, he cries; he is happy, then sad; elated, then depressed. Jean returns to his Ovidian text to recount the history of Pygmalion's actual courtship of his graven image. This fascinating story is itself worthy of our close attention, unfolding as it does like one of the lesser marvels of Krafft-Ebing, but I should first like to draw attention to the general tenor of the "jolis développements" which Jean added to the Ovidian fable. They are themselves mythographic in nature—they constitute, that is, a kind of running moral commentary on the myth by which the reader is helped to see its relevance to Jean's own fable and the intellectual issues it raises. We have come to expect allegorical sophistication on Jean's part, and he does not disappoint us here; his moral insinuations have none of the ham-handedness of the *Gesta Romanorum*, and he does not underrate his readers with notations of "Id est Christus" or "Diabolus significatur." The general drift of his artistic interpolation is nonetheless clear. Pygmalion's vainglorious motive in making the statue, the comparison of the image with the object of the most extravagant lust of antiquity, the imputation of Pygmalion's madness to subjection to Cupid—all this, and more, brings the myth within the moral orbit of Jean's poem and thus within range of the reader's moral judgment. Pygmalion is not a remote antique pagan, but someone whose "sex life" may be the proper subject of the *planctus Naturae*. The symptoms of his "love" are not merely Ovidian, but Christian and clerical, the symptoms of cupidity, or *fol amour*, as diagnosed at length by Lady Reason. It is, accordingly, not the collation of external mythographic tradition, but the literary response to Jean's own mythographic interpolation, which offers the first and most valuable indications of the use to which he puts this "fable of the poets." Returning to Pygmalion, it must be said that his behavior really is rather extreme, even for an artist or a lover, as the chief episodes in his courtship, brilliantly captured in synoptic illustration by the Valencia artist in Fig. 22, may suggest. First he kneels before the image, weeping, offering his glove;

then he fondles it. Next, he adorns it richly with fine robes, ear-rings, and a crown of gold, not omitting a flower chaplet. Pyg-malion then presents his hunk of ivory with a gold ring and so "marries" it, calling on Hymen and Juno, the true deities of marriage, rather than a priest or prelate. Joyfully, he sings a mass the parts of which are love songs, and serenades the statue with the splendid symphony of instruments which is captured in such meticulously archeological detail in the central panel of Fig. 22. Next, he takes the statue to bed and makes love to it, without conspicuous success it must be said, since "pleasure which is not shared is not entirely attractive." Jean's further comment needs no commentary: "Ainsinc s'ocit, ainsinc s'afole" (l. 21065).

It is at this point that Pygmalion, like not a few other literary lovers of the Middle Ages, goes to pray at the temple of Venus. "Holy Venus," he prays, "forgive the sin of chastity which I have committed." If Venus will grant that his image become his ani-mated *amie*, Pygmalion agrees to be damned in hell if he does not renounce chastity. Venus, says the poet, "was delighted to see him abandon chastity, and offer her his services in the spirit of a penitent," and so she made the statue come alive. Pygmalion rushed home, for though he did not yet know of the miracle, he had great confidence in Venus (cf. Luke 7:1ff.). There, to his inexpressible joy, he found a living, pulsating *tendre amie*: "Am I awake, or do I dream?" After prayers of thanks to Venus, Pygmalion hopped into bed with his cooperative *amie* to make good his vow; and Jean concludes the episode, less "far from the matter" than he himself playfully confesses, by reporting from Ovid the tragic posterity of this blissful union.

The Pygmalion episode in the *Roman* was very frequently illustrated, and a good deal has already been written about its iconography.[42] Before discussing iconographic implications, how-ever, it may be well to recall the specific point of congruence between the Pygmalion story and the history of Amant's love affair, which, at the simplest literal level, makes the Ovidian fable an appropriate analogue to the broader action of the *Roman*. Jean introduces the Pygmalion story as a long aside. The image

[42] Robertson, *loc.cit.*; Tuve, *Allegorical Imagery*, pp. 262ff. I shall also refer to the illuminating article of Virginia Egbert, "Pygmalion as Sculptor," *Prince-ton University Library Chronicle*, xxviii (1966), 20-23 and Plates 1-6.

on the ramparts of the castle, the object of Amant's pilgrimage and the target for Venus' flaming arrow, is said to be more beautiful, as a lion is to a mouse, than the image which became the object of Pygmalion's passion; and it is this comparison which introduces, as well as concludes, the "retelling" of the tale in Jean's text. Both Pygmalion and Amant are iconophiles whose passion reflects a submission to Cupid and whose hope for solace lies in the supplication of Venus. To use the word which best answers the moral insinuations of Jean's poem, they are both idolaters.

This charge may require amplification in the face of some recent discussions of Jean's poem, but I believe it will hold true. Alan Gunn maintains that the *exemplum* is a fitting poetic statement of mature love, indicating that "a lover may stand to his beloved in the relation of a teacher or initiator into the courteous rites of an enduring devotion." Textual support for such an interpretation is claimed from the fact that Pygmalion contrasts "the wild and self-directed love of Narcissus . . . unfavorably with his own."[43] This will not hold water, however, or even the smaller pieces of ice. What Pygmalion says is that he "is less of a fool" than Narcissus—which is in itself, considering the dimensions of Narcissus' foolishness, hardly more meaningful than saying he is younger than Methuselah; and the specific evidence adduced makes it possible to doubt that even such modest self-congratulation is warranted. He is less a fool, he says, since he at least "can walk up to his image, take it in his arms, and kiss its lips," thus obtaining some stony solace, however slight; Narcissus could not do as much. That Pygmalion's behavior or pronouncements suggest mature love, insofar as this expression has any specific conceptual content with which Jean de Meun could have been familiar, seems to me absurdly mistaken. Is it not possible to leave a trace of humor in his poem?

In fact, Pygmalion's *passio* exhibits the same essential characteristics as that of Narcissus. They are both, in different ways, lovers of their own images. The differences between the two episodes are not chiefly iconographic, or having to do with content, but stylistic. Ovid was not a twelfth-century Christian, he merely

[43] *Mirror of Love*, pp. 287.

wrote surprisingly like one; and the potentialities of the Pygmalion story, for a mythographically-minded Christian poet, are rather richer in some respects than those of the Narcissus story. Furthermore, as we have already seen, Jean's Gothic style is more exemplary and schematic than Guillaume's, and he is altogether more imaginative and original in the handling of his materials. If it had been he who introduced the Narcissus story early in the poem, we would have expected him to handle Ovid's text with the liberty he demonstrates elsewhere, decorating it with a Gothic façade of specifically Christian iconographic reference. As it is, the specific comparison Pygmalion draws between himself and Narcissus, whether one chooses to admit or deny an ironic dimension, is a comparison between varying degrees of madness (*folie*), characterized elsewhere in the *Roman* and other popular medieval moral writings as *passio*, *fol amour*, or *amour par amours*. It is, furthermore, an elementary critical perception that the love exemplified in these two Ovidian fables is also that pursued by Amant. The image with which he fell in love when he looked at himself in the well of Narcissus (Fig. 23 with its rubric), now altered in form but still the object of his fervent worship twenty thousand lines later, is different from the image with which Pygmalion fell in love only in its superior beauty.

The vices which the story of Pygmalion exemplifies, in the hands of Jean de Meun, are lechery and idolatry; the *exemplum* is thus at the heart of Jean's matter, rather than at its distant frontiers. As we know, these two vices are closely related emblematically in the theological vocabulary of medieval Christianity. Idolatry, or "fornication of the heart," is the broader implication of fornication of the flesh. Indeed, it is the commonplace nature of this conception which makes possible the enjoyment of love stories for their moral meanings, as the *Echecs* gloss says, and the appropriate use of a love affair as the central metaphor of a philosophical poem like the *Roman*, which deals with the most elementary problems of man's nature and God's grace. In Jean's treatment of the Pygmalion story both the lechery and the idolatry are literal, but the spiritual implications of the text are pleasingly suggested by scriptural echo and ironic parody and are made visible to the eye in the clever figurative language of the manuscript illustrations.

The chief episodes in the story which are the subject of textual illustrations are five: Pygmalion's carving of the statue, his abuse of it, his dancing before it, his marrying it, his supplications before Venus, and his final love-making. Since a number of these vignettes are conveniently and delightfully captured in the continuous narration of Fig. 22, it is possible to use this single illustration to discuss a wide variety of iconographic indicators found in a large number of manuscripts, from many different schools of illumination, in the fourteenth and fifteenth centuries. As a point of departure, we may consider the observation that not a single one of the seventy-seven miniatures dealing with the Pygmalion sequence which I have examined actually follows the letter of the text regarding the material from which the statue was made. Jean, following Ovid, says it was ivory; but the illuminators show Pygmalion working in stone or, more rarely, brass. Just as Pygmalion's *sententia* was made contemporary by medieval artists, so was his craftsmanship; ivory was used in the Middle Ages only for miniature carvings.[44] Pygmalion, for various reasons, needed a life-size figure; and the illustrators were not squeamish in suggesting what those reasons were. For example, the obscence implications of Pygmalion's use of his tools in one of the woodcuts in an early printed edition have been pointed out by Miss Tuve.[45] Pygmalion also frequently fondles the breast or *mons Veneris* of the statue in the process of carving it, or hacks at it with a phallic chisel in a thinly disguised suggestion of the sex act like those found in illustrations of Venus' firing at Amant's image, and Amant's worship at the "sanctuary." In the very act of its creation, Pygmalion's graven image becomes the object of an obscene and disordered passion. But there is something even more bizarre, and emblematically suggestive, in the kind of sculpture which the illustrators imagined Pygmalion to be carving. Mrs. Egbert has drawn attention to the fact that many illustrations show "a recumbent figure reminiscent of contemporary tomb sculptures." Sometimes the tomb itself is actually included in the illustration, as in British Museum Add. MS 42133; and a number of illustrations show Pygmalion at work on what is unmistakably a sepulchral

[44] "Pygmalion as Sculptor," p. 21.
[45] *Allegorical Imagery*, p. 263, Fig. 97.

brass.[46] In Figure 22, the deadness of Pygmalion's image is clearly suggested by its crossed wrists, the posture of the recumbent corpse in monumental effigies of the fourteenth and fifteenth centuries. Such iconographic insinuations do not reflect a misunderstanding of the text, but its spiritual understanding. Arnulf of Orléans, commenting on the Pygmalion story, suggests that the animation of the statue is simply the projection of the carver's fetid imagination upon a lifeless form; Jean himself says that Pygmalion did not know whether his image was alive or dead, and this ambiguity is echoed in poems derived from Jean's such as the *Echecs Amoureux* and Froissart's "Paradys d'Amours."[47]

That Pygmalion attempted sexual intercourse with a graven image neither Jean's text nor the illustrations in such manuscripts as Douce 364 or Douce 195 in the Bodleian leave in any doubt.[48] What may be doubted is that, even in the misty Middle Ages, such a performance constituted a tutorial in "the courteous rites of an enduring devotion." It was probably called, instead, "fornication of the heart." Jean indeed makes Pygmalion go so far as to marry the statue in the peculiar ceremony illustrated in the top left-hand scene of Fig. 22, where Pygmalion genuflects to the image as he reaches toward it with a wedding ring. Most of the readers of Jean's poem in his own day would probably have known that the ring, in the liturgy of Christian marriage, was the token of an investiture, and that in such a ceremony it was the vassal who knelt before the lord. Pygmalion is here shown "giving his power over to the woman" (Ecclesiastes 9:3), that is, not simply quashing but precisely inverting that hierarchy of *seigneurie* which cannot exist, as Amis has long since pointed out, in conjunction with the kind of *amour* which Pygmalion and Amant pursue. The words with which Pygmalion pronounces his union with a dead piece of ivory mimic those in the Canticles (5:2) which announce the union of Christ and His Church, though, as

---

[46] "Pygmalion as Sculptor," p. 22; Fig. 6; Figs. 4 and 5.

[47] Jean's immediate scriptural source is probably Wisdom 15:5, and fourteenth-century illustrations may well have been influenced by the extremely popular Wisdom commentary of Robert Holkot. "Et talis insensatus *diligit mortuae*: id est, non viventis imaginis *effigiem sine anima*, sicut fecit Pigmalion: de quo Metam. 10 narrat Ovidius," *In Librum Sapientiae* (1586 ed.), p. 562.

[48] Robertson, *Preface to Chaucer*, Figs. 18 and 19.

is proper in this parodic context, the words he echoes are those of the *sponsa*.

The entire episode of Pygmalion's musical entertainments is, as we have noted, Jean's own creation; what has not been pointed out, to my knowledge, is that its basis is scriptural. According to Jean, Pygmalion played so well and noisily that one would not have been able "to hear God thunder"; and the music which thus drowns out the voice of God is made from a mighty orchestra of instruments: *cimbales, fretaus, refretele, chalumeaus, tabour, fleute, timbre, citole, trompe, chevrie, psalterion, vielle* (ll. 21042ff.). The great musician of the Old Testament is, of course, David, who on one notable occasion honored the ark of God rather as Pygmalion venerated his shrine: "David autem, et omnis Israel ludebant coram Domino in omnibus lignis fabrefactis, et citharis et lyris et tympanis et sistris et cymbalis" (II Kings 6:5). Similarly Pygmalion dances and leaps before his *ymage* (ll. 21054ff.) even as King David cavorted before the ark (II Kings 6:16). David's curious behavior, which his uncomprehending wife thought so degrading and disgusting, betokened a profound spiritual joy for God's mighty aid against the Philistines and a humility before Him: charitable joy and humility are very fitting for the author of the New Song. Pygmalion, of course, is not interested in the New Song but the *olde daunce*, as his offer of the glove in the lower left-hand scene of Fig. 22 demonstrates. Idolatrous passion frequently leads medieval literary lovers to comical excesses, but seldom to the hilarious absurdity of the central scene of Fig. 22 where Pygmalion—the illustrator having picked up the textual *double entendre*—hops about the room, organ in hand, in an attempt to excite his *ymage*.

The idolatry is literal rather than figurative in the lines in which Pygmalion prays to Venus and makes his noble vow of lechery. Venus, however, is merely one of his idols; in Douce 364 both the goddess and the *ymage* are on little pagan pedestals.[49] The Valencia artist executed the idolatry scene with a certain amount of ambitious architectural detail: the Venus whom Pygmalion worships here is installed in a proper shrine or chapel atop an altar decorated with a fleur-de-lys cross frontal. She stands with bow in hand, lifting her skirt in an iconographic gesture

---

[49] Robertson, *Preface to Chaucer*, p. 101 and Fig. 20.

indicating lasciviousness as does the scene's scriptural source, Isaiah 47:2-3: "Uncover thy locks, make bare the leg, uncover the thigh. . . . Thy nakedness shall be uncovered, yea, thy shame shall be seen."[50] The iconographic detail of the lifted skirt appears regularly in fourteenth-century illustrations of Oiseuse, La Vieille, and Pygmalion's *ymage* itself, before degenerating into a more or less formal cliché in the fifteenth.

The literary techniques which Jean de Meun employs in the *exemplum* of Pygmalion, no less than the pictorial techniques of the artists who illustrated it, can properly be called "iconographic." Jean narrates a more or less verisimilar fable with an allegorical, or extra-literal, significance; several elements of the story make specific reference to discursive concepts outside the text of his poem and independent of it. The process of artistic creation as it operates in this episode and in the *Roman* as a whole displays neither the invention of an original literal fable of compelling interest nor the formulation of private intellectual propositions, but rather the pleasing and disciplined ordering of familiar elements in such a way as to lead an initiated reader to a fresh confrontation with a generally accepted truth. Though such poetry may exhibit surface ambiguities, it is characterized by specific discursive content. Multivalent and unresolved suggestion sparkles on the literal surface, engaging the reader's interest and teasing his intellect, but the poem communicates clear and unambiguous ideas. The claims of iconographic analysis—that is, the analysis of significant content—accordingly precede those of aesthetic intuition.

The specific content of the Pygmalion episode is a concept of idolatry. A sexual *passio* whose object is an image is satirically explored as a kind of humbug religion. The moral implications of the episode, as indicated by the iconography of the poetry, are broader than statements about the sexual love of the literal fable. To put this another way, a story about Pygmalion, his image, and Venus makes a specific and intelligible statement about the psychology of sexual passion as understood in the thirteenth century,

---

[50] See the *Postilla super Isaiam* by Albertus Magnus, *Opera Omnia*, XIX, 474: "*Revela crura* [47:2], quod meretricum est, quae revelatione crurium ad libidinem provocant. Propter hoc etiam Venus pingebatur, quod veste aliquantulum elevata crus revelavit, ut ad libidinem provocat."

which is at the same time a specific statement about a concept much broader than sexual passion—idolatry. The episode conveys specific meanings or kinds or levels of meaning not exhausted by its literal sense. The application of statements made about Pygmalion is not limited to him, or to the general category of sculptors who attempt sexual intercourse with their graven images, or even to the yet more general category of young men who develop *passiones* for young women. And what is true of the Pygmalion *exemplum* is also true of the much larger action of the *Roman*, for which it is such an apt analogue.

The history of Pygmalion's *passio* introduces the final scene of the *Roman*, one which raises a number of vexing critical problems and presents special difficulties of analysis. The ending of the poem is, as everyone knows, a thinly veiled allegory of sexual intercourse, considered in specific functional detail and described at one remove in the coarse and loveless language of a fabliau. It is deeply obscene, and its implications can rightly be called revolting. Yet the critics who have written about its obscenity, like Christine de Pisan, have mistaken its nature. Though obscene, it is charged with considerable moral seriousness—but again, not of the peculiarly modern kind which can identify sexual intercourse as the chief manifestation of divine grace. At least three serious artistic purposes are advanced by means of the final section of the poem. The extravagance of the religious imagery—the shrine, the relics, the pilgrim's gear—drives home the concept of idolatry. At the same time, the absurd hyperbole of Amant's sexual bravado clearly suggests his lunacy: these are, after all, the ravings of a man far advanced in a *malladie de pensée*. But the principal function of this obscenity—which, like most obscenity, is filthy not because it refers to sexual matters in an "open" and "healthy" manner, but because it does not—surely must be to reveal, in the most transparent terms, the venality, the unworthiness, and eventually the lovelessness of Amant's passion. In the coarseness and violence of his language are reflected the coarse and violent attitudes of the Old Man; these reflections totally sever Amant from any claim to "courteous" behavior even as he follows to its logical conclusion the code of false courtesy to which he has sworn himself, and which "denatures" him in his slavish obedience to ancient "laws of nature" long since amended by God's grace.

237

From a purely technical point of view it may be said that while the *allegoria* of this section is unusually rigorous for Jean's part of the *Roman*, where the details of the love affair are seldom schematically worked out, the *littera* is splendidly and delightfully confused as—in what may well be the most enormous mixed metaphor in Western literature—the Lover's sexual paraphernalia and their object become staves, rods, hammers, shrines, ditches, moats, and so on. Furthermore, there is a marked tonal shift toward the end of the passage when Amant pauses in his tawdry dirty story to give formal, and unedifying, instruction in love; he himself becomes the last of the *doctores amoris*. Nonetheless, close analysis of this concluding section of the poem reveals the same kind of iconographic and rhetorical techniques which Jean has used elsewhere in the poem: *ironia*, scriptural and learned wit, dramatic bombast, mock-epic comedy.

Venus, having held her bow drawn during all the lengthy recitation of the history of Pygmalion, tarries no longer: she shoots her torch right through the little slot between the pillars (Fig. 41), the castle immediately bursts into flames, and all its defenders flee. The physical suggestion here requires, presumably, no comment; but the emblematic meaning may be missed. Luxuria has scorched with the fires of concupiscence the sexual members of Amant's image so badly that rational will, fear, and shame are powerless. Critics have frequently written of Amant's "winning" his rose, but this is not accurate. The effective agent is not Amant but Venus; the effective means is not the worthiness, maturity, or even mere indefatigability of his love, but blazing Citherean concupiscence. Iconographically, the action here described repeats, in a more exuberant style, that of the episode of Venus' first appearance in Guillaume's part of the poem; but this time, of course, Venus' victory is final, enabling "courtesy" to claim the booty won by lust. In fact Courtoisie herself immediately appears amid the rubble of the castle to rescue her boy, Bel Accueil, and to give him some maternal advice to the effect that he should grant the rose to the Lover who has suffered for so long on his account: "Recevez lui e quanqu'il a; / Veire l'ameneis vous offre" (ll. 21320-21). This statement is curious since Amant, who shows so many signs of being a clerk that he is often tonsured in the illustrations, is a poor fellow whose parsimony outrages Richesse and whose conquest is made despite her. There is here an echo of La Vieille's mercenary sexology, and hence of Christ's advice to the young man that he should sell all that he had. Amant, figuratively, stands ready to do so; that he is prepared to give over his *ame* as well, not for the hope of "treasures in heaven" but for the love which inspires him to the carnal delights constantly contrasted with which those "treasures," points toward the spiritual rewards of fornication of the heart.

Bel Accueil, who is after all *bel accueil*, finds his mother's advice convincing, especially as it is buttressed with the wise *sententia* from the *Bucolics* which served as the somewhat ambiguous motto of Chaucer's Prioress: "Omnia vincit Amor." In fact he has long been convinced of Amant's worthiness, so that the Lover at long last can get on with the final step of love, *factum*—not, however, without first boring the reader with a tedious encomium of his penis and scrotum (ll. 21353ff.). The only delights in the surface allegory here are those of calling *coilles reliques* and *reliques coilles*; and the fatuity of that sport was long since exposed by Lady Reason. However, there is a comic element more satisfying than the surface obscenity in the scriptural wit which flickers behind it.

The most persistent metaphor which Amant uses to betoken his genitalia is that of the scrip and the staff, the *escharpe* and the *bourdon*. Langlois, in his notes, reports with the solemnity of scientific philology that the *escharpe* and the *bourdon* are the conventional paraphernalia of a medieval pilgrim, but that they here carry a "double meaning." They are, however, somewhat dubious arms for a Christian pilgrim even in their primary sense. When Christ sent his twelve disciples into the world to preach the kingdom of God and to heal the sick, His first commandment to them was "Nihil tuleritis in via, neque virgam, neque peram" (Luke 9:3). Since one of the synoptic texts, Mark 6:8, reads "*nisi virgam*," the comparative suitability of scrips and staves for "apostles" became the subject of one of the more tedious squabbles in the debate about the apostolic life and the interpretation of the Rule of St. Francis which began in earnest in the second half of the thirteenth century; the details in Jean's poem may be further evidence of his documented interest in antifraternal polemic. In any case, the familiarity of the text in question and

239

its most common exegetical commentaries—the scrip and staff are taken as types of various carnal impedimenta to spiritual perfection[51]—impregnates the imagery with an amusing nucleus of clerical wisdom. Amant thus boasts for a few lines about his testicles, the two little hammers which he keeps in his scrip to shoe horses along the way; these hammers, he says, he values more than he does his *citole* or his *harpe* (1. 21376).

It is doubtful that Jean expected his readers, at this point, to titter with naughty delight at this latest audacity of his bourgeois realism; nor did he ever dream that, Christian phallicists to a man, they would gaze with religious wonder on the awfulness of God's plenitude as revealed in these extraordinary testicles, valued in excess of £50,000,000 (1. 21392) or, alternatively, in excess of the value of Amant's *citole* and *harpe*. A more appropriate response from any reader who had been following Jean's text with anything more than vapid literalism would be "What *citole*? What *harpe*?" And the cleverer and more thoughtful among them would doubtless have been able to provide the witty and satisfying answer. The angelic instruments which so startlingly appear in Jean's text unannounced do not indicate that Amant has been concealing from us a musical virtuosity to compare with his green thumb in the garden; these details too, like the *escharpe* and the *bourdon*, are scriptural and they too carry a "double meaning." The *citole* and the *harpe* correspond to the stringed instruments of the New Song of the psalms, the ten-stringed *psalterium* and the *cithara* (Psalms 32:2). These instruments, conventionally identified with those made by David to praise the Lord (I Paralipomenon 23:5), appear repeatedly in the psalms, and they provided the greatest exegete of the entire Middle Ages with one of his happiest meditations, one to which he said he found it valuable to return time and again. In the *Ennarationes in Psalmos*, St. Augustine several times makes a complex distinction between the spiritual meanings of the *psalterium* and the *cithara* on the basis of the positions of their sounding boards; and it was copied by so many other exegetes, and incorporated into so many reference works, that it was presumably widely known. In essence, Augustine took the *psalterium* to represent the spirit and

[51] For example, see St. Ambrose, *Expositio evangelii Lucae*, CSEL, xxxiii, 258-59.

the *cithara* the flesh, so that their music in the New Song was the symphony of spiritual and corporal good works.[52] Thus it is that in this passage in the *Roman*, the clever bawdy jest of Amant's preferring one set of *organa* to another, prepared for by Jean in the Pygmalion episode, gives way to a more profound and satisfying statement clothed in borrowed scriptural imagery. Amant prizes the discord of his unruly members more highly than he does the charitable melodies of the New Song. In this particular instance, the scriptural iconography, by which Jean makes the most carnal chaff of his *littera* bring forth spiritual fruit for the initiated reader, was probably especially appreciated by the monks in his audience, of whom there were no doubt substantial numbers.[53] It was their chief work to sing the New Song, literally in the offices of the choir which endlessly repeated the praises of the psalter, and spiritually in the inner works of those who (incomprehensibly to Genius) "have made themselves eunuchs for the kingdom of heaven's sake."

The concluding lines of the poem need not be analyzed in detail, though they offer further vivid commentary on Amant's brutal *amour*. The passsage, taken as a whole, is chiefly a poetic icon of "glorying in the flesh." In his Priapean obsession and his tedious promiscuity (ll. 21393ff.), Amant is as far removed from "the courteous rites of an enduring devotion" as he is from a pious meditation on his place in the great chain of being. The idea here exemplified, by means of iconographic principles which have little to do with literary realism of whatever social class, is *lechery*. Amant thinks like a lecher, talks like a lecher, and acts like a lecher. When he pauses briefly in the midst of the exuberant cele-

---

[52] St. Augustine, *Ennarationes in Psalmos*, in ps. 70, sermo 2, cap. 2: "Sed quid est psalterium? Organum ligneum cum chordis. Quid significat? Interest aliquid inter ipsum et citharam; interesse dicunt qui norunt, eo quod concavum illud lignum cui chordae supertenduntur ut resonent, in superiore parte habet psalterium, cithara in inferiore. Et quia spiritus desuper, psalterium spiritus, per citharam caro. Et quia duas dixerat reductiones nostras spiritum in spe, alteram secundum corpus in re." *Corpus Christianorum*, xxxix, 970. See also ps. 32:2, in *CC*, xxxviii, 250-51; and ps. 42:5, xxxviii, 477-78.

[53] Among the fourteenth-century writers who thought highly of Jean's work were Gilles li Muisis and Honoré Bovet (OSB), Peter Ceffons of Clairvaux and Guillaume de Deguilleville (O. Cist.), and Philippe de Mézières, who died a Célestin.

bration of his lechery to offer in his own voice some formal teaching on love, he shows no indication whatsoever that he has enjoyed a comprehensive education in *tout l'art d'amours* and graduated with a diploma issued on the authority of love's divine and definitive teachings. He speaks with a meretricious cynicism, which is comical rather than profound, about the pros and cons of sexual congress with *vetulae*. Our youthful Old Man is an authority only on the love of old women.

I suspect that the kind of poetic statement Jean intends in his description of Amant's difficult copulation with a virgin is simply no longer available to readers today; but we shall do well to remember that, however strange and modern the teachings on love and nature which gush forth from his fountain of medieval naturalism may be, Jean had had no opportunity to study the lesser novels of D. H. Lawrence or to hear it proved in the Queen's court that extended descriptions of sexual intercourse in which vivid technical detail is combined with rustic phallic euphemism are profoundly puritanical, spiritual, reverent, and above all serious-minded. Jean had no dark gods in his blood, only some of the Old Adam. When he compares Amant's difficult passage with the labors of Hercules, he may be writing carnal-minded verse like the *dits* repented for in the *Testament*, or he may be making Christian comedy which it is no abuse to gloss *moult favorablement*; but he is not being a stuffy sex mystic. In fact, the reference introduces a fairly obvious mythographic joke which enriches the ludicrousness of the literal comparison of Hercules' assault against the gate of Cacus with Amant's against a maidenhead. As we have already seen, there are sound iconographic grounds for making some comparisons between Hercules and Amant, though they are all rather unflattering for the Lover. Hercules was, in medieval poetic tradition, the hero of the "two ways" par excellence. It was he who had stood at the crossroads of the Pythagorean Y, faced the alternatives of a life of easy pleasure on one hand and a life of arduous discipline on the other, and chosen the latter. In the moral tradition which Christian poets inherited from stoic and cynic philosophy he was, therefore, the type of virile virtue. The two paths which he considered—whether regarded as Virtue and Vice, Reason and Sensuality, the spiritual and the carnal, *caritas* and *cupiditas*, or whatever—were easily enough identified with the straight and narrow path and the "wide gate" and "broad way" of Matthew 7:13-14. Since Amant's choice in the *Roman* is precisely between the "way" counseled by Reason and that counseled by the forces who have installed *naturalis concupiscentia* as their prelate, the careers of the two heroes are, up to a point, markedly similar. A few lines before the point at which Amant makes his Herculean simile, however, he has formally declared himself one of those who follow the *deduisanz sentiers* (l. 21430) and *jolies senteletes* (l. 21432). But now, in the final consummation of the sin in deed, Amant, following Hercules, discovers an *estreite veie* and a *sentele . . . estreite e petite* of a maiden's vagina (ll. 21637-38).[54]

There is one final point about this description of the sex act which needs to be considered, and that is Amant's casual claim that he has impregnated the rose. By ignoring the context of the passage, as well as its actual words, critics have been able to construct more or less elaborate fantasies about its central importance for the interpretation of the poem. The school of Cosmic Generation is, understandably, very big on the passage; and the lines in question have recently been adduced as though in themselves a sufficient refutation of D. W. Robertson's analysis of the *Roman*.[55] "Thus the rose becomes," in the words of Charles Dunn, "the first important pregnant heroine in European literature."

It is, of course, impossible to confront absurd judgments on their own terms without being absurd oneself. To meet this one head on would involve us in enumerating the important pregnant heroines of Western literature, evaluating their importance, measuring their pregnantness, and then adjudicating the claims of priority of an extremely long list headed by the mother of

---

[54] The virginity of Amant's idol has given rise to the unconvincing theory that the *Roman* teaches a proper "initiation in love." In fact, this detail, part of the fabliau fabric of the concluding lines of the poem, underscores the enormity of Amant's *factum*. As Chaucer's Parson puts it, "Another sinne of Lecherie is to bireve a mayden of hir maydenhede; for he that so dooth, certes, he casteth a mayden out of the hyeste degree that is in this present lyf, and bireveth hir thilke precious fruit that the book clepeth 'the hundred fruit.' " (The reference is to Matthew 13:8, allegorically interpreted.) The "fruit" of virginity is the subject of some satirical marginal *obscoena* in Bibliothèque nationale fr. 25526; see Robertson, *Preface to Chaucer*, p. 328n.

[55] F. Parmisano, in *Medium Ævum*, xxxv (1966), 279.

mankind and including the Mother of God. This would all be rather amusing, but too far removed from the subject of this book to warrant its inclusion. If, instead, we turn to the text, we may note the comic and qualifying context of the passage in question. Bel Accueil is being ridiculed for a peculiarly feminine weakness, or hypocrisy, well documented in the fabliaux and other courtly literature: the lady threatens that she will scream (but does so in a barely audible whisper) if the lover does not stop. What Bel Accueil has said, specifically, is that he wants no *outrage* committed, and the Lover has answered, with the wisdom of the serpent, that he will do nothing which they do not both want to do. Since the abstract quality of Bel Accueil is precisely that which wants to do what Amant wants to do—which is why he has to be carefully watched by Reason's lackeys—Amant's reassurances may be regarded as disingenuous. It is in this setting that Amant mentions, casually and in the bawdy euphemism of a fabliau, the mingling of "seeds" which results in the "swelling" of the bud. And he speaks of this feat not as a mighty triumph of generation but as "tout quanque j'i forfis!" Such is Amant's only moral scruple after twenty thousand lines of an idolatrous *passio* which led him to swear total allegiance to the god of *fol amour*, abjure Reason, offer his soul to an idol, and fornicate with a carved grotesque (Fig. 42). But all's well that ends well; God bad us for to wexe and multiplye.

So Amant ends his carnal pilgrimage very much as he had begun it, renewing his allegiance to his false gods (ll. 21753ff.) and spurning Divine Sapience (ll. 21760ff.). His labors have been mighty, but his reward sufficient, for he has the *grant joliete* of picking the rose (l. 21777). The dream, or rather the nightmare, is over: "Atant fu jourz, et je m'esveille."

In Reason's long dialogue with the Lover, with which Jean de Meun began his part of the *Roman*, one of the moral *exempla* she uses to illustrate the operations of Fortune in the world concerns an ambiguous dream: the tyrant Croesus dreamed that two gods ministered to him in a tree; Jupiter washed him, and Phoebus dried him. The dream flattered him greatly, but his daughter Phanie maintained that it was an ironic dream; it meant, she claimed, that Croesus would be hanged on a gibbet, and that his corpse would be washed by the rain and dried out by the sun. But

Croesus, blinded by his *folie* and pride, could not see "sense or reason," so that he stubbornly insisted on the truth of the dream's literal significance. He scolded his daughter for presuming to teach him *courtesie*, and for her stupid allegory:

> Car sachiez que cist nobles songes
> Ou fausse glose voulez metre,
> Deit estre entenduz a la letre. . . . (6608ff.)

The "nobles songes" of the *Roman* may be similarly ambiguous. What we make of the dream depends largely on the ideas of *courtesie* we bring to it, and the manner in which we arbitrate the conflicting claims of its letter and its spirit. Croesus, at any rate, was wrong: *puis refu pris, et puis penduz* (l. 6503).

This book has been largely concerned with the analysis of literary and pictorial iconography, with an attempt to demonstrate what the Lover's dream means, as opposed to what it actually says. My aim has been no more ambitious than to describe what the *Roman* is about, and to provide some guideposts for its study which are not a *fausse glose*. The account of the poem which iconographic analysis has yielded is, accordingly, a foundation rather than an edifice. Yet one or two questions must at least be raised. If all of Jean's ideas are unoriginal, his poetic vocabulary largely conventional, and his dramatic configurations more or less commonplace, how are we to account for the brilliant success of his poem in his own time? An answer to this question would have to begin with a more thorough and informed analysis of Jean's style than has ever been made in order to attempt to discover exactly what features of it made readers think that what had so oft been thought was ne'er so well expressed. I suspect that his sporadic surface verisimilitude, which as "bourgeois realism" has been properly praised by literary critics, would emerge from a close analysis as less important than the intellectual techniques of his allegory, his kinds of *ironia*, the sophistication of his iconographic constructions, the qualifications and the control of his exemplary narrative elements. Yet a stylistic analysis would provide only another kind of foundation. That such a book as the *Roman* could have been written, let alone that it could have so totally engaged the imagination of the literate classes for over a century that the history of late medieval poetry is largely the history of its influence and its inspiration, makes as forceful an argument about Jean's audience as about his art.

So far as I know the first reader of the *Roman* who devoted so much as a sentence to talking about Jean's "art" outside the context of his moral teachings was Jean Gerson; and he did so with disastrous results. For the most part Jean's audience seems to have been made up of tropological readers; readers, that is, who considered the *Roman* chiefly in terms of its moral significance and application to individual situations often far removed from the immediate suggestions of its plot. To be sure, Jean's early readers probably thought that his description of "falling in love" had a kind of surface reality about it which we may not see. When Froissart, in his "true history," came to write about the actual sudden and fatuous passion which Edward III developed for the Countess of Salisbury, his psychological description uses the same iconographic language as the *Roman*. But to be able to say that the content of the *Roman* provided the direct inspiration for the *Divine Comedy* requires a kind of allegorical understanding of the poem which has little to do with its apparent literal subject. A first step towards such understanding is no doubt the realization, apparent in the anonymous *explicit* of Bibliothèque nationale MS fr. 1566, that the love analyzed in the *Roman* is one possible attitude not merely toward a sexual object but toward all kinds of *bona temporalia*; another step is to apply the implications of this attitude to all the confrontations with *bona temporalia*, and all the moral decisions they involve, which make up a man's life on earth and determine ultimate disposition of his immortal part. Thus, the *Roman* is a "vite humane speculum."[56] To attempt to account for this process, that is to describe the relationship which existed between Jean's allegory and his audience and to determine to what extent and in what ways that relationship can properly be said to be within the orbit of artistic creation and artistic control, is to undertake a task vastly more difficult than the analysis of literary style. It will be shunned by all those for whom the "text itself" is sufficient as well as those who maintain that "The whole idea that the 'intention' of the author is the proper subject of literary history seems, however, quite mistaken."[57] Such a task nonetheless remains, in my view, the labor next awaiting us.

[56] Jean de Montreuil, *Epistolario* in *Opera*, I, ed. Ornato, 221.
[57] Wellek and Warren, *Theory of Literature*, p. 42.

Finally, a word must be said about Jean's attitude toward the Lover; for surely, it will be objected, it is a strange and harsh Christian charity which Jean displays in pillorying, mocking, and condemning his "hero," mercilessly and without sympathy, through thousands of lines of mordant verse. Such an objection seems to me to miss an essential point, and to fail to make a vital connection. Since the major action of the *Roman* is an iconographic re-enactment of the Fall, and an extended description of the typical operation of sin of whatever kind as it was conventionally analyzed in the thirteenth century, that action may be considered tragic. In abjuring his reason Amant sins against God, not against Jean; and it is no more fitting for Jean to be merciful and sympathetic in his attitude toward Amant's sin than it would be to demonstrate such attitudes toward Adam's—or his own. But the tragedy need not be final and irreparable, since there operates in the world a supernaturally effectual mercy. Curiously enough, it is Jean Gerson who inadvertently brings this point home. Gerson formulated sound critical principles, but unfortunately did not always practice them; and, so far as one can tell, he read the *Roman* as largely autobiographical and thought that Jean de Meun *was* Amant. The formal moral judgment he makes on Jean (Amant) is therefore most revealing. Gerson would find it impossible to pray for Jean, he says, if he did not know that he had subsequently repented.[58]

Gerson was able to apply to the moral action of the *Roman*—however grossly he mistook its artistic design—the category of grace which the poem constantly invites, and which alone offers the definitive answers to the urgent problems of the "human condition" discussed therein. Even Jean de Meun (Amant), Gerson is effectively saying, reprobate son of Adam that he is, and blackest devil who ever trod the rue Saint-Jacques, is not beyond the range of God's love and mercy and the divine grace of penance. When the *Roman* ruthlessly exposes the insufficiencies of a nature wounded by man's sin, and ridicules the works of the Old Man, it inevitably invites contemplation of the bountiful sufficiencies of grace, and the freshness of the works of the New Man. Pierre Col says the poem is full of "teachings to flee all vices and pursue all virtues."[59] For Jean the chief manifestation of divine

[58] *Opera*, ed. Ellies du Pin, III, col. 931.
[59] Ward, *The Epistles on the Romance*, p. 67.

grace was not, I believe, sexual intercourse, but the Incarnation of God, that great mystery, with its extensions in the Sixth Age in the sacraments of the Church, before which Lady Nature stands in uncomprehending reverence. Divine grace may, of course, be pushed out of Deduit's garden like the "pious pelican" in Fig. 4 which is a common emblem for Christ's Passion; but that Passion was sufficient for the Middle Ages, and that grace importunate— it waited patiently for the quickening of the rational will. Amant's "problem," like mankind's, is sin; and sin has a specific remedy in the dispensation of grace: repentance. It is toward the concept of repentance that the repeated and varied "confession" scenes in Jean's poem point. The Lover parodically confesses to Cupid the sin of listening to Divine Wisdom; Antichrist's man uses the confessional as an ambush for homicide; Lady Nature confesses a sin which is not her own to a priest who cannot absolve it. Yet the means are there, ready and sufficient, for all *amatores mundi* to do penance which is not a carnal charade but the promise of spiritual life.

Geoffrey Chaucer ended the *Canterbury Tales*, a poem which owes as much to the spirit of the *Roman* as to its letter, with a sermon on penance. While Jean did not do as much, he seems to have brought his poem to an end with one final ambiguous scriptural echo which could have directed his readers' thoughts toward the idea of penance. The last line of the *Roman de la Rose* is "Atant fu jourz, et je m'esveille." The dawn has come, and the dreamer wakes: his dream is done. Yet as Petrarch's comment on the narrator of the poem suggests, Amant's "waking" is only literal; there is no difference between the way he talks when awake and when asleep: "sopitoque nihil vigilans distare videtur." This line is not easy, but I take it that Petrarch means that the narrator himself makes no remark in the poem, narrated when "awake," to indicate that he is aware of the true meaning of his "sleeping" vision; he knows that dreams can be true, but does not show that he knows the truth of his own. The text is, in effect, as ambiguous as Fig. 4, in which the recumbent clerk seems to be awake and asleep simultaneously. But what can it mean to be figuratively awake, and what does waking have to do with the *art d'amours*? In the letter which provides the principal ideas for Jean's poem, St. Paul says that "Love is the fulfilling of the law"

248

(Romans 13:10); and he continues with an exhortation to "waking" made famous by St. Augustine, in the greatest history of Christian conversion from sin to penance, and lovingly explicated in a thousand medieval sermons for the first Sunday in Advent.

We know the time, that it is the hour for us to awake from
sleep. Our salvation is now nearer than we had believed.
The night is far spent, and the day approaches. Let us
therefore put off the works of darkness and put on the
armor of light. Let us walk honestly, as in the day,
not in rioting and drunkenness, not in lechery
and wantonness, not in strife and envying. But
put on the Lord Jesus Christ, and make no
provision for the flesh, to fulfill its lusts.

INDEX

virgin birth, 201
vita contemplativa, 78
Vollert, C., 147n
Waleys, Thomas, 193n
Ward, C. F., 47n, 62n, 104n, 135n, 247n
Weitzmann, K., 13-14, 27, 40n
Wellek, R., 4n, 246n
wheat and chaff, 168-69
William of Auvergne, 58-59, 60n
William of Chartres, 58

William of Conches, 121n, 134n-35n, 193, 225
William of Saint-Amour, vi, 25, 61, 162ff
William of Shyreswood, 182n
Wilmart, A., 102
Wit, J. de, 21n
Wright, T., 219n
Wyclif, John, 165
Ziegler, J. G., 153n